SECOND
EDITION

HC&SCo PUUNENE MEAT MARKET 1926

OPERATIONS AND SUPPLY CHAIN
MANAGEMENT

SUPPLY CHAIN LEADERSHIP CENTER

Kendall Hunt
publishing company

Cover images provided by the author.

Kendall Hunt
publishing company

www.kendallhunt.com
Send all inquiries to:
4050 Westmark Drive
Dubuque, IA 52004-1840

Copyright © 2014, 2018 by Supply Chain Leadership Center

ISBN: 978-1-5249-3865-9

Published in the United States of America

Contents

Introduction: The Operations Management Chain

The goal of this text is to present operations and supply chain management for nonbusiness majors from a practitioner's approach rather than the standard academic approach to a study of operations and supply chain management. Carl von Clausewitz wrote a book in the early 1800s on military strategy based on the observations of the Napoleonic Wars. In his book, *On War*, Clausewitz stated that all things change when you go from the abstract to the concrete. This is as true for the study of operations and supply chain management as it is for the study of military strategy. This text is designed to give the nonbusiness student at the undergraduate and graduate levels an understanding of the principles of the operations chain and supply chain management. The goal of the book is to show the students the concrete or real-world applications rather than just the academic or abstract view of operations.

This text is designed to provide a foundation in the principles of operations using real-world examples and then provide the student with a working knowledge of supply chain management to enable the student to grasp the concepts and apply them in the ultimate laboratory—the global business world. Operations and supply chain management are part of the biggest team sport in the world—commercial business. It is imperative that students of all majors understand business principles in order to succeed in whatever business that they end up in.

A very special thank-you to the students at the University of Kansas for allowing me the honor of spending time with them as they pursue their education and to the School of Business for giving me the opportunity to share information and experiences with the students.

HC&SCo PUUNENE MEAT MARKET 1926

An Introduction to Operations Management

Why is it important to study operations management and the operations management chain as part of a business education? Regardless of what business activity you may find yourself associated with in the future, there will be an operations management chain supporting it in some fashion. Not only is it important to study operations management as part of your business studies, it is equally important to study current operations management practices to remain in tune with the latest development and identify positive and negative trends in business operations to ensure that your business remains current and competitive in today's changing business environments. For example, the Hawaiian sugar industry continued to perform operations the same way for decades and found themselves to be outdated and no longer competitive, resulting in the closure of the Maui Sugar Company operations in 2016.

What is operations management? *Operations management* is the core of almost every business. Operations management includes all of the planning, design, production, sourcing, supply chain operations, customer service, and even the return of products that do not meet the needs of the customers.

It may be easier to ask, what is not operations management? From a purely academic perspective, almost anything can be classified as part of the operations management chain. From a strictly manufacturing and distribution perspective, everything could be considered part of operations management. And from a services perspective, everything fits under the operations management umbrella. Operations management terms, principles, and techniques are consistent across all spectrums of business—regardless of whether the business is a for-profit business, a not-for-profit business, or a service industry. This look at operations management will deal with the principles of operations from the manufacturing and services perspectives. Inherent to the study of operations management are the basics of supply chain management. Without supply chain management, no operation can be successful as some of the "dot.com" companies discovered in the late 1990s were not. Some of these companies designed great Web sites, but overlooked the need to have an excellent supply chain to deliver the products advertised on the Web sites. This contributed to the "dot.com bust."

Why is the approach of this book different from the traditional academic textbooks? How is this book different from the traditional textbooks on operations management? The goal of this book is to present operations management from the perspective of a practitioner and not from the traditional academic approach to operations management.

Why is operations management important to you as a student? Operations management is the foundation of all business operations. Without operations management and the tactics, techniques, and procedures associated with it, a company cannot be successful. The foundation established by this study on operations management will assist you in your study of business, and the principles of operations management are transferable to other areas of studies even outside the study of business. Some of the techniques covered in this book can be applied to work, study, and your personal life.

Why is operations management important in business? All businesses need operations management or at least most of the topics covered in this text to be successful. Organizations exist to meet the needs of societies that people working by themselves cannot produce. For this, the companies must master the tactics, techniques, and procedures of operations management discussed in detail in this book. The tactics, techniques, and procedures of operations management do not appear similar to a menu in a restaurant or as an optional list of topics that owners of companies can choose from and ignore the others. Failure to apply the concepts of operations management could result in having to close operations like the Maui Sugar Company (shown in Figure 1.1) did in 2017. All of

Figure 1.1: Maui Sugar Company Operations, May 2016, Shortly Before Closing Down All Operations

the topics discussed in this book as part of the operations management chain work together to create the synergy necessary to meet the needs of society and make a profit, if the company is a for-profit organization. Most businesses operate for two reasons: (1) The primary reason is to make a profit; and (2) the secondary reason for many companies is to put the competitors out of business. Some companies will state in their brochures that they are in business to provide a certain good or service, but the real reason people go into business is to make a profit. Few individuals go into business to lose money unless they are already rich and need a tax shelter to compensate for other income streams. Some professional sports teams appear to fit into this category; the owners are not really concerned with winning or making a profit, but just seem to want to show losses to counter other income. Most companies are into business to make money and hope to put the competitor out of business. Any for-profit company that claims to be in business for any other reason is not being honest with the customer or with themselves.

Companies provide goods and services for a reason—they are in business to make a profit. The only way that a company can make a profit is to focus on the basics of operations management. Some companies are successful even without focusing on the basics of operations management, but those are exceptions to the rules.

A systems approach to operations management looks at the entire system from the beginning to the end. Supply chain management now looks at the supply chain as extending from the supplier's supplier to the customer's customer. Here, it is important to introduce a new concept: an operations management chain. An operations management chain connects the inputs such as raw materials that go through transformation processes at various levels to finally provide a good or service to a customer. It further continues through the life cycle of the product or service. This includes the life cycle management of the product, the design of the product or service, the manufacture of the product, the delivery of the service and, if necessary, the return or reverse supply chain, and the ultimate disposal of the product if need be. As you can see, the operations management chain is similar to the supply chain, and the two concepts are intertwined and will be addressed in this text.

This look at operations management will be based on a systems approach. Dr. W. Edwards Deming once stated, "If you cannot describe what you are doing as a system, you do not know what you are doing." The economic meltdown of 2008 to 2009 showed the world that a lot of companies did not know what they were doing. Some of the problems that surfaced during that economic crisis were the results of decisions made decades earlier, some were the result of the focus on the short-term bottom line with no regard for the long term, and some were an example of Darrow's Survival of the Fittest. Businesses operate in a cycle—failure to plan for survival during the next business cycle may very well result in severe problems when the cycle appears. The operations management chain requires a total systems approach and a long-term focus in order to be successful. The goal of this study of the operations management chain is to assist the student in being able to describe what they are doing as a system and look at operations management from a systems approach.

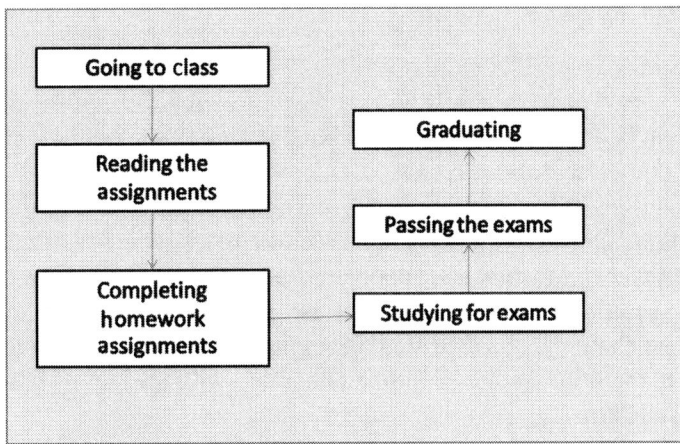

Figure 1.2: Example of a System of Interrelated Events

A system can be defined as a group of interrelated items, events, or actions. Here are some examples of systems:

- Going to class—reading assignments—doing the homework problems—studying for exams—passing exams—passing classes—graduating. Figure 1.2 shows these actions as a system.
- Practice—analyzing practice—watching game films—adjusting the plan—practicing the plan—winning games.
- Taking steroids—getting a bigger head—setting new records—lying to the grand jury—falling from grace—going to jail.

INPUTS TO THE OPERATIONS MANAGEMENT CHAIN SYSTEM

Regardless of the industry that you are working in, operations management is the core process that determines the effectiveness of the business and the profitability of the company. Operations management can be described as a system that includes the inputs, a transformation process, and outputs, usually in the form of a good or service. Figure 1.3 shows the operations management chain as a system. Critical to this system are the feedback loops between each of the three components of the system.

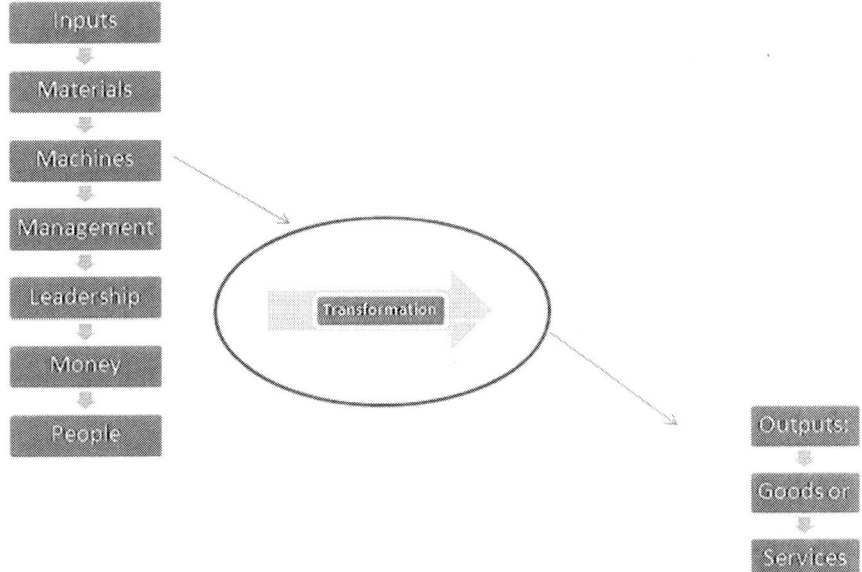

Figure 1.3: The Operations Management System

The inputs to the operations system include:

- **Materials**—The materials inputted into the operations management chain are raw materials, components, assemblies, or other parts. These materials will be transformed into final products, other assemblies, or components, which will be further transformed, in another link of the operations management chain, into a completed product or used to provide a service.
- **Machines**—Although the machines are the products of a transformation process that converted raw materials, parts, and components, machines are, in turn, inputs for the transformation of other materials, assemblies, or components into products. Machines as inputs to the operations management transformation process is an example of the operations management chain. No product or service is produced in a vacuum. The operations management chain may be extended through several links from materials to machines to components to machines to the final product and then integrated with the supply chain to provide the product or service to the final customer.

  There is a link between the machines and the materials. No matter how good a machine is, the machine cannot produce a quality product without quality materials.
- **People**—Unlike materials and machines and other inputs to the operations management chain, labor is not a commodity that can be moved and managed. People must be led, not managed (we will discuss this in greater detail in subsequent chapters). People are a major link in the operations management chain. People are necessary to run machines, procure products and materials, maintain machines and systems, move materials, and move final products through the supply chain to the ultimate customer—which is another link of people in the operations management chain. The move to automate systems and remove people from the manufacturing chain at General Motors in the 1980s led to serious problems and placed General Motors on the *Supply Chain Digest* list of the worst supply chain disasters of all time.

  There is a link in the operations management chains between people and machines. The best machine in the world will have trouble producing a quality product if the operators of the machine do not know how to operate it. Furthermore, even the most talented people in an organization need quality managers and leaders to reach new levels of excellence in the production of goods or providing quality services.
- **Management**—Someone has to manage the system. Without management, systems can get out of control easily. With management systems also in place, they may turn uncontrollable and produce poor-quality products. A manager may very well make the difference between a good operation and a mediocre operation. Moving from a line worker to a manager is a big step in a career and does not happen without education and training on how to be a manager. We will look at the Theory of Constraints throughout this study of operations management and the operations management chain. Too often, the constraints of an operations management chain are the level of training and experience of the manager or management and their policies. One of the goals of this study of operations management is to assist the student in identifying systems and operations management chain constraints and how to improve the systems by removing the constraints—even if the constraint is the management.

  Every transformation link in the operations management chain needs managers to ensure that operations work properly. This is the link that exists between people, machines, and product quality. The next input in the operations management chain is leadership.
- **Leadership**—All too often used interchangeably with management, there is a distinct difference. The simple dichotomy was explained by a Reserve Officer Training Corps (ROTC) instructor at North Carolina State University early in my college days. He explained to us, "You manage things and you lead people." All too often, leaders believe that they lead organizations. In fact, leaders lead the people that make up the organization. Just as a good manager can make a difference in an operation, a good leader will be the difference between a good and a great organization. A mediocre organization will not attract talented people; without skillful people to work on the machines, there will be no good-quality products produced, no matter how well the managers try to manage the system. Without good-quality products, companies will not be able to remain in business for too long.

  Just as moving from the line to management is a big step, so is the move from management to leadership. Just being a good worker on the line does not ensure that without additional skills training that very person will be a good manager. The same is true for leadership. Not everyone can be a leader; also, not everyone wants to be a leader. A good manager does not automatically become a good leader. There are skills necessary for leaders that are not inherent in every manager. These skills can be taught, but all too often, companies assume that a good manager equals a good leader. Business schools teach business management and crank out business majors with no exposure to leadership.

In order to be a good-quality company, the company has to have a leadership development program that helps develop leaders who can lead the people and managers of the organization.

■ **Money**—Without money as an input to the operations management chain, there is no chain. Why, because if nobody is buying anything, then no one is selling anything. If no one is buying or selling, there are no materials, components, or parts to make the products or provide the service. If no one is buying or selling, there is no money to hire quality managers, leaders, or workers. With no workers, nothing is produced. And if there is no money, no one is purchasing services from the operations management chain.

OPERATIONS MANAGEMENT CHAIN TRANSFORMATION PROCESSES

What types of transformations take place in the operations management chain? Figure 1.4 provides examples of the transformation processes that take place in the operations management chain.

■ **Physical**—A physical transformation is seen in manufacturing where the raw material input is transformed into a finished product. This form of transformation is the most commonly discussed transformation process in the operations management chain. Another example of a physical transformation can be seen in building a house as the materials are transformed from a collection of inputs to a finished house. When Dell was in the assembly business, they conducted a physical transformation from subassemblies to a finished computer.

■ **Movement/storage**—In the distribution link of the operations management chain, the inputs are the goods provided by the manufacturer (as can be seen in the operations management chain, there may be multiple transformations in the chain) to the distributor for the movement or storage of the goods. If the goods are moved, the transformation process is the movement and distribution of the goods; if the goods are moved and then stored, the transformation process is the storage of the goods until another move transformation takes place.

■ **An actual exchange of goods**—In retail operations, there is a transformation that includes the input of a customer with cash or credit and the input of a retailer with a good or service. The transformation is the exchange of the good or service for the cash or credit. The output of the process is the customer with the new product or service and a retailer with the capability to procure more goods to sell to another customer. This, in turn, stimulates the physical processes of the manufacturing transformations. This same exchange process may take place between a wholesaler and a retailer or the distributor and the retailer.

Transformation Processes

• Physical
• Movement and Storage
• Exchange of goods or services
• Health Care
• Entertainment
• Communications

Figure 1.4: Examples of Transformation Processes

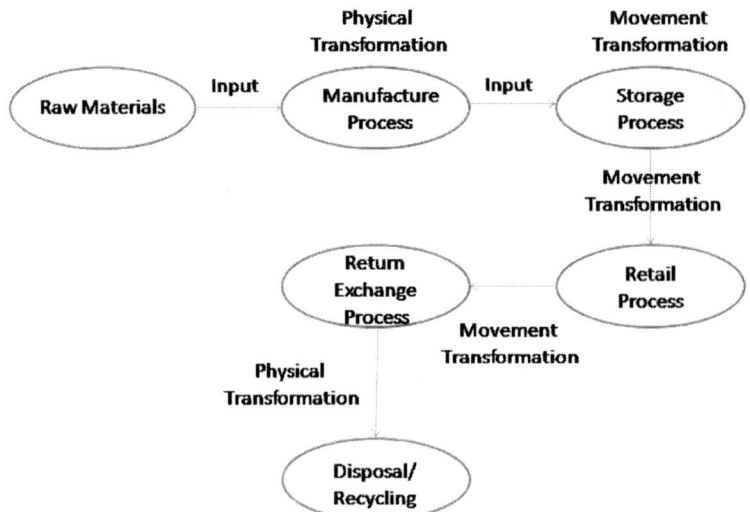

Figure 1.5: Example of Multiple Transformations in the Operations Management Chain

- **Physiological**—A physiological transformation has as its input a sick patient; a transformation process that includes the appointment with a health care provider and perhaps the use of a medication and advice from the doctor. The output of this system hopefully is a patient who has regained good health.
- **Entertainment as a transformation**—Assuming that entertainment may be a transformation in an operations management, the inputs would be customers needing some form of entertainment and the payment for that entertainment; the transformation is the entertainment (good or bad); and the outputs of this transformation would be customers who are either happy with the process or unhappy with the transformation. The output is dependent on the quality of the transformation process.
- **Communications transformation**—Effective communications require a very good transformation process to be effective. The inputs are the messages or words from one source; the transformation is the understanding of the message; and the output may very well be the actions taken as a result of the transformation and understanding.
- There may be more than one transformation process in the operations management chain as shown in Figure 1.5.

TOPICS IN OPERATIONS MANAGEMENT

Decision Making. Operations management involves decision making, which will be discussed in greater detail in Chapter 3. Decision making can provide a competitive advantage. Is decision making a core competency of a company, should it be, or could it be?

Customer Service. Is customer service important to the operations management chain? Should customer service be a part of the study of operations management? Is customer service a product/an output/an input/a transformation process? An argument could be made for each—we will take a detailed look at each from an operations management chain perspective.

During our look at operations management, we will look at the differences between products and services as we look at the product/service design processes. This discussion will look at forecasting and why forecasting for services is a little more difficult than forecasting for products.

The quality of a product is determined by the customer. The quality of a service is very similar. Strength, durability, and performance are examples of attributes of services—this includes the length of repair time, the quality of repairs, and the ease of repairs. These attributes are just some of the factors that separate services operations management from manufacturing operations.

The study of operations management will look at the design of a product or service, and the need to incorporate quality into the product or service being designed instead of trying to inspect it later. Management and leadership of the company should not only be part of the design process, but must be involved to such an extent that the launch of the product or service will be successful. A company's strategy should drive the product development, the service development, and the competitiveness of the company or country. We will look at strategy and competitiveness in the next chapter.

All operations add cost to a product or service, but not all operations add value to a product or service. Operations managers are responsible for determining which processes or operations add value and which ones are nonvalue adding. If a process does not add value to the bottom-line profits, the experience of the customer, or the quality of the product, then there is no value added. Our look at process and product design will discuss the methods for identifying value adding and nonvalue-adding processes and how to improve the operations management chain by eliminating nonvalue-adding processes.

Impacts on Operations Management. In order to fully understand the basics of the operations management chain, it is necessary to look at the impacts on operations management from history.

- In middle school and high school, most of us studied about the **Industrial Revolution**. In junior high school, we looked at the impact of the Industrial Revolution on the manufacturing of goods and the start of the transformation from an agrarian society to a manufacturing society. The impact on manufacturing, in turn, influenced the views on operations management even though the concept of operations management was not yet conceived. The impacts on operations management from this period of time included:
  - □ James Watt and the invention of the steam engine in 1769. As every school kid learns in grade school, this had an extreme impact on the building of products and how products were produced.
  - □ In 1776, while the colonies that later became the United States were discussing a break from England and were drafting the Declaration of Independence, Adam Smith was studying the concept of the **division of labor** in manufacturing. His research and theories are still taught in business schools today.
  - □ School children in the Southern United States, especially, learned about the impact on the growing, processing, and sorting of the seeds of the cotton plant from cotton following the invention of the cotton gin by Eli Whitney. What is not taught is the fact that Eli Whitney is also the father of the use of interchangeable parts in manufacturing. In 1790, Eli Whitney received a US government contract to manufacture muskets for the Army. He was later called in to meet President Jefferson to explain why he was lagging in delivering the weapons to the Army. Whitney took with him a weapon to the meeting with the president. Whitney explained to the president that he was developing a system where the parts of the muskets could be interchanged between weapons. Prior to this, if a musket part broke, the weapon was useless and worthless. With the advent of the interchangeable parts as designed by Whitney, the muskets he was making could be repaired without loss of the weapon completely. In modern-day analogy, without **interchangeable parts**, if the light bulb in your lamp blew out, you would have to get a new lamp rather than replacing the bulb.
- **Scientific management** focused on the way items were made and the people that made the products. The impacts on operations management by scientific management include:
  - □ Frederick W. Taylor came up with the principles of scientific management and the analysis of workflows in the later part of the nineteenth century and became popular in the early twentieth century. These same principles are still in use today. In fact, the works of Taylor focused on gaining efficiency and reducing waste—not unlike the lean and Six Sigma movements of the late twentieth century.
  - □ In 1912, Henry Gantt invented the activity scheduling chart that bears his name and is still in use in program and project management today as will be discussed in more detail while dealing with program and project management. Gantt charts, which are simple-to-use bar charts for program management, were used in projects such as in the building of the Hoover Dam and can be seen on episodes of the television program *Extreme Makeover: Home Edition* for tracking project progress.
  - □ In 1913, Henry Ford designed the moving assembly line at his Rouge River Plant. The basics of the assembly line can be seen in today's automobile and motorcycle assembly plants. Henry Ford gets the

credit for designing the assembly that is not different from the lines used by automobile manufacturers today. In addition to the assembly line, Ford is also the father of the modern-day reduce, reuse, and recycle concepts. He was "green" long before political leaders started pushing the "green" movement and long before being green was politically correct. Ford had his suppliers deliver parts to the plant in wooden boxes that were specially designed with holes in specific places. The suppliers could not figure out why the holes were in specific places. Ford was apparently using the sides of the wooden boxes as the floor boards of the cars. In addition, Ford was known for saying "you can have it in any color you want as long as it is black." It was not that he was that fond of black paint; it was because through research he knew that the black paint cured faster than other colors, thus prompting his demands that the Model A stay black even when other colors were available.

- **Human relations** or the lack thereof. Human relations/human resources should be the office and activities that allow companies to find the right personnel—however, somewhere along the line, the human part of the human relations equation changed. Instead of trying to fill the right person in the right slot, somewhere along the line, in a lot of companies, the concept became "let's fill the slot with the right resume" regardless of the real qualifications. If an applicant does not have the right "buzz words" in the resume, the applicant does not even become a candidate regardless of how qualified that person may be. The advent of the computer age and the Internet has allowed companies to depersonalize the human aspect of human relations/human resources. The human resources concept has encouraged human resources managers to use management theories and practices to manage people like any other commodity.

The US Army moved away from local personnel offices at every installation to regional hiring offices in the name of efficiency and cost savings. The result was a decline in the human aspect of human resources and a loss of local advisors for hiring officials. This led to a lack of confidence in the human resources process.

Another example of the loss of the human factor in operations management came a couple of years ago when a company advertised for a supply chain manager and then after a plethora of resumes were received, the company called and asked what skills should they look out for in a supply chain manager. This was a question that probably should have been asked prior to the advertisement of the job opening.

Another example came when I was talking in a human resources conference. I was informed by the vice president of the human resources of a major company that they "did not have time to focus on the people as they were focused on profits." This was in response to a comment that a focus on hiring, training, and retaining the right people is critical for the successful operation and is a measure of the leadership of the company. Later, in the discussion, it came out that this particular company was having trouble retaining people because the company was in bankruptcy. My suggestion was that since the company was focusing on profits rather than on people and was in bankruptcy, perhaps, the time was now to start focusing on people as the current focus was not working.

A part of the human resources focus on operations management includes looking at how employees are treated and compensated. This includes answering or at least looking at the question: Does employee ownership impact operations? Southwest is a good example of employee ownership. In the Kansas City area, Hy-Vee is an employee-owned grocery store that prides itself in the ownership and the service provided by the employees. The Publix grocery store chain has survived and thrived for the same reason—the employees are also the owners and care about customer satisfaction.

The Home Depot has always had employee ownership through its stock options and profit-sharing programs. This employee-ownership pride took a hit when the founders, Bernie Marcus and Arthur Blanks, retired and were replaced by Bob Nardelli from General Electric.

The new leadership moved toward a more part-time workforce as a cost-savings move. This move led to fewer employee owners and a drain of employees to other companies accompanied by a low level of employee morale. The pride of ownership and the accompanying lack of concern led to a significant loss of market capitalization and employee owner stock value. It also led to a multimillion dollar buyout and severance package for Bob Nardelli. However, the removal of Nardelli helped to restore employee pride and has resulted in record profits in recent quarters.

Many books, written a few years ago, point out to the success of the Chrysler-Daimler–Benz merger as a successful merger that improved operations. However, the appearance of CEO, Bob Nardelli, in front of the US Congress asking for assistance for Chrysler after the split with Daimler Benz would suggest that the merger was not a successful one and had serious impacts on the operations management of the company.

Human resources management includes not only which employees are hired and how the employees are trained, but also how the employees are treated while being employed by the company. Furthermore, how the employee is treated impacts customer service and how the employee treats the customer. In his autobiography, *Made in America,* Sam Walton states that it takes about 2 weeks for the attitude shown to the employees to reflect in the attitude that employees show to the customer. Does human resources management impact operations management? Absolutely! If the right people are not hired or retained, the operations suffer. If the employees are not properly trained, the quality of the product or service is impacted as demonstrated by the concerns of Jim Koch (founder of Samuel Adams Brewery) when asked about his concerns about spending money on training employees and having them leave. Jim Koch responded that he would be more concerned about not training employees the right way to do processes and then having them stay with the company.

Some of the human resources impacts on operations management include:

- From 1927 to 1932, Elton Mayo conducted his famous Hawthorne studies at the Western Electric Hawthorne Works. During this series of motivational studies, lights at the Hawthorne plant were turned up and production went up—assumed to be linked to the increase in lighting; then the lights were turned down and productivity went up. As it turns out, the improvements in productivity and motivation were tied to the employees feeling that someone was concerned about them and had nothing to do with the brightness of the lights.
- Abraham Maslow developed his motivation theories in the 1940s, and published his findings in a paper titled "A Theory of Human Motivation" in 1943. Maslow's hierarchy of needs is still taught in business schools over seventy years later and is considered in hiring actions in major companies. One company that I interviewed with was so focused on meeting basic needs that they overlooked the need for self-esteem and self-actualization.
- In the 1950s and 1960s, Frederick Herzberg and Douglas McGregor developed their motivational theories. Herzberg looked at the factors that caused satisfaction and dissatisfaction at work. McGregor published his book, *The Human Side of Enterprise*, in 1960. His Theory X and Theory Y views of motivation were detailed in this publication. McGregor's theories assumed that workers are inherently lazy and need to be motivated or were inherently motivated and did not need a lot of external motivation to get them to work. Dr. William Ouchi later came along with his Theory Z approach stating that workers fit into both categories and therefore the one-size-fits-all approach may not be the answer and that job satisfaction is tied up with employee retention and loyalty.
- The study of management as a science (**management science**) has allowed companies to focus their efforts on improving the management of resources and operations. Some of the impacts on the management of operations from management science include:
  □ Linear programming was developed, in 1947, by George Dantzig. Linear programming, now automated, is still in use to maximize production of products and product mixes to increase customer satisfaction and/or profitability.
  □ The development of the first digital computer by Remington Rand in 1951 led to a whole new way of managing and later a new way of communicating and sourcing. What an impact this had on the management of the operations management chain, especially after the advent of the Internet!
  □ Operations research/systems analysis paved way for the advent of simulation. With the use of simulations to determine the impacts of systems and decisions before implementation, cost avoidance and systems miscues can be minimized. DuPont and the US Navy developed the techniques of the **critical path method** (CPM) and the **program evaluation and review technique** (PERT) that will be discussed in greater detail while dealing with program and project management.

- □ Joseph Orlicky working for Oliver Wight developed a simple technique for material planning and time-phased ordering known as **material requirements planning** (MRP) in the 1960s. When originally designed, the MRP system was simple because most companies were manufacturing only a few products. As companies implemented automation and increased their product lines, the MRP programs became more complicated and now MRP is seen as the precursor to modern-day enterprise resource planning programs that are being widely used .

- ■ The **quality emphasis** movement has had great impacts on the management of the operations management chain. This will be discussed in greater detail in a separate chapter. The focus on quality adds a whole new perspective to the management of operations. The focus and emphasis on quality have forced companies to transform from producing products to producing quality products. Some of the impacts of the quality emphasis movement, which will be discussed in greater detail, include:

  - □ **Just-In-Time (JIT)**. The JIT movement was originally thought to be another great Japanese import in the 1970s. Taiichi Ohno developed the Toyota production system based on lessons learned from Dr. W. Edwards Deming. This misunderstood concept will be discussed in a separate chapter. Of note about this concept is that when it first came over from Japan, the American Production and Inventory Control Society[1] created a series of concept papers titled the APICS Zero Inventory Papers contributing to the confusion on the concept of JIT.

  - □ **Total Quality Management** arrived in corporate America in the 1980s. Just as he had done in Japan, Dr. W. Edwards Deming helped to shift the focus on quality in the United States. Dr. Deming continued to preach his 14 steps to quality until his death. In the chapter on quality, we will look at the impacts of Dr. Deming and his peer, Joseph Juran, on the quality movement.

  - □ **Reengineering** emerged in the 1990s as a result of the books by Hammer and Champy. Their series of books prompted companies to look at reengineering the company and management. Unfortunately, most of the companies that undertook reengineering (approximately 70% of all reengineering projects) failed. Most of these programs failed due to a lack of leader involvement. Hammer and Champy recently admitted that they missed out an important aspect of management and operations. What was not considered in the original books was the human aspect of reengineering. In fact, when Xerox implemented a reengineering project using the guidelines put forth by the books, the result was a large number of employees having to reapply for their jobs.

  - □ **Information Age/Internet Revolution**—Once Al Gore "invented the Internet," the availability of information and the ability to pass this information to almost anybody have impacted the management of operations, while at the same time, it has created a new set of problems for information security. Globalization and the Internet age coupled with the information revolution provided a number of impacts on operations management, the biggest impact being the advent of electronic commerce or e-commerce.

    E-commerce provided operations management with new forms of businesses. These include business to business (B2B), business to consumer (B2C) such as consumers buying directly from a company from their website, thus eliminating the need for a bricks and mortar operation or in conjunction with the bricks and mortar operation, consumer to business (C2B) as in a reverse auction site like Priceline. com, and consumer to consumer (C2C). E-bay was originally designed to be a C2C business, but has morphed over time to be both a C2C and a B2C, as more companies began using E-bay to sell overstock and refurbished items.

- ■ **Globalization of Supply Chains.** Just as the advent of the Internet impacted operations management, it also impacted the management of supply chains. With the Internet, companies can source from Asia, build in the States, and sell to customers in Europe without ever speaking face to face with the supplier or the customer. Just as the information age added the problem of information security, the globalization of supply

---

[1]The American Production and Inventory Control Society is now APICS—the Society for Operations Management and is the largest international operations management and supply chain organization. For more on APICS go to http://www.apics.org.

chains has added a whole new problem in the area of supply chain security. The problems associated with supply chain security will be discussed in a separate chapter.

THE OPERATIONS MANAGEMENT CHAIN

The operations management chain includes the product design process, which will be discussed in detail in another chapter. A good design process includes not only the product design, but also the process design. While the process design describes how a product will be made, the product design includes:

- Designing a product or service for a specific purpose—although sometimes the design for a specific purpose does not always end up with the product and purpose originally intended. Viagra was originally designed to be a product for high blood pressure, but has obviously been more successful for other purposes. The post-it note was a by-product of an attempt to develop new glue. Obviously, that mistake was a very profitable one for 3M. The product Minoxidil was not originally designed to help grow hair, but a world-class powerlifter and amateur chemist named Tony Fitton noticed the side effect of the drug and used the product to help balding males to grow hair.

  The design process sometimes includes the planned obsolescence of the product. Not a popular technique, but it is still used by computer designers and many other electronics product designers. The design process within the operations management chain has to include answering the question—"What should the product look like?"

  The design process has to also answer the question—"What should this product do?" The answer to this question should come from the needs of the customer and from the first step of Six Sigma according to Motorola. In an introductory course on Six Sigma at Motorola University, students are taught that the first step of Six Sigma has to focus on the customer and should answer three basic questions:

  Who is the customer? (Define who the customer is.)
  What does the customer want/need? (Define what the customer wants.)
  How can we do it better than the competitor? (Define what we need to do to provide this product or service better than the competitor.)

  What additional options and features should the product have? This is another question that the design process should answer. While deciding what new products to design and produce, companies also have to decide what products need to be improved and what products need to be phased out of production based on the product life cycle.

  Sometimes, some companies discover that some products are better off not being altered. Companies such as Waffle House[2] and In-N-Out Burger[3] have opted to keep the simple products simple. In-N-Out pride themselves on their simple menu. Keeping operations and options simple is not always a bad decision, as the success of these companies as can be seen in Figure 1.6.

  Where do we get product ideas? What impact does the generation of ideas have on the production process and operations? This will be discussed in the product design chapter.

---

[2]The simplicity of Waffle House can be seen in their visible food preparation operations that are on display for all customers to see while waiting for their food.

[3]The In-N-Out Burger chain was formed in 1948 in California. In-N-Out was the first drive in hamburger store and the first restaurant to use two-way communications to order food at the drive in. The menu of In-N-Out has not changed since its inception and the process of fresh ground beef, fresh cut potatoes, and fresh bread and vegetables has not changed since the first restaurant was opened by the Snyder family in 1948. Because of the link with the growth of the freeway system and the fresh products has contributed to contributing to the In-N-Out chain becoming almost a cult-like following and customer loyalty. In-N-Out will only expand into areas that can be supported from their corporate-owned and -operated meat-processing plants.

Figure 1.6: Simplistic Restaurant's Food Preparation Area

OPERATIONS MANAGEMENT AND FREE TRADE

Do free trade agreements really help promote more trade? This was the promise of the North American Free Trade Agreement (NAFTA) (go to http://www.ustr.gov/trade-agreements/free-trade-agreements/north-american-free-trade-agreement-nafta to learn more about the North American Free Trade Agreement). This promise has not been as successful as promised as evident by the lack of "free" movement across the US–Mexico border for Mexican-based truckers.

The Free Trade Agreement created by the formation of the European Union has been much more successful. The free trade zones (FTZs) within the United States have provided a form of improvement in the operations management chain by allowing products to come into the US FTZs, be assembled into products, and then shipped out without paying tariffs.

GLOBALIZATION AND COMPETITIVE COMPANIES

> *With the storehouse of skills and knowledge contained in it millions of unemployed, and with the even more appalling underuse, misuse, and abuse of skills and knowledge in the army of employed people in all ranks of industries, the United States may be today the most underdeveloped nation in the world.*

—W. Edwards Deming, *Out of the Crisis*, 1982

The globalization of corporations has impacted operations management while lengthening the operations management chain. Corporations have expanded globally in order to compete with other corporations globally. (Each of the companies listed below have hyperlinks to their corporate websites. Use the hyperlinks for additional information on these international companies.)

Some corporations have been forced to expand globally in order to cut costs. At least, the stated objective of offshoring operations and expanding globally was to cut costs and control more of the operations management chain and the supply chain from sourcing to manufacturing and to manufacture in a lower cost country. This has not always been the result. In some cases, the expansion has actually cost the companies more in transportation and supply chain inventory costs, so that the expansion goals for cost cutting were not met.

Some companies have expanded globally in order to enter new markets. As we will see in the next chapter, this has to be part of the overall corporate strategy and researched carefully. Wal-Mart (see www.walmart.com) used this technique to expand into Germany. Germany had a discount chain that somewhat resembled a Wal-Mart supercenter known as Wertkauf. Wertkauf carried out almost all of the aspects you would find at a Wal-Mart supercenter do by including clothes, food, household goods, and recreational equipment. During my tour in Germany, this was one of my favorite local stores for shopping. Wal-Mart wanted to expand into Germany and saw Wertkauf as a logical expansion opportunity. The Wal-Mart culture and the German mindset did not mix, leaving Wal-Mart with a failed expansion attempt and leaving Germany without Wertkauf.

In order to compete with local companies, it may be necessary to expand globally as Wal-Mart attempted to do in Germany and as Wal-Mart has done successfully in Mexico and China. In other cases, the only way to get into a market is to establish a "local" operation. In other cases, it may become necessary to compete globally to expand out of a corporation's home country. The Home Depot announced in 2012 the closing of their stores in China as a result of not fully understanding the market and the culture.

Look at this list of companies that do the preponderance of their business outside of their home country:

Nestle (www.nestle.com)—Switzerland—There is no way Nestle can be a global corporate power if it tried to sell its chocolate products only in Switzerland. To be competitive, Nestle had to expand outside of Switzerland. We will look at some of the actions taken by Nestle in the area of food safety to remain competitive when we look at supply chain security.

Nokia (www.nokia.com)—Finland—One of the wireless powerhouses and cell phone innovators had to look outside the borders of Finland to be competitive globally. Obviously, there are not enough people in Finland to purchase all of the cell phones that Nokia must sell to be competitive globally. An expansion out of Finland was necessary to remain competitive.

SAP (http://www.sap.com/index.epx)—Germany—Systems, Applications, and Programs (SAP) started as a small German company. The company was started by engineers at IBM, who thought that the concept of enterprise resource planning software was the wave of the future for corporations. These engineers went to their bosses at IBM and laid out the concept only to be told that the concept was not a good one. Now, SAP is the largest producer of enterprise resource planning systems and the majority of the sales of SAP are outside the borders of Germany.

Almost 80% of the total sales of **Exxon Mobil** (www.exxon.com) are outside the United States. Americans get riled every quarter and each year that Exxon Mobil reports record profits and are quick to blame gas prices and oil price speculations. Reality may include those reasons, but are mostly tied to the global sales of Exxon Mobil.

Even the American standard **McDonald's** (www.mcdonalds.com) receives almost 60% of its sales dollars from overseas sales. Even with the boost that McDonald's has received in the United States as a result of the 2008 to 2009 recession and the changes in American eating habits, the preponderance of sales remains overseas.

In the 2007 best seller, *The World Is Flat,* Milton Friedman looked at the globalization of companies and their supply and operations management chains that have become flattened by the globalization of operations. Friedman also discussed the outsourcing and offshoring of operations to other countries for taking advantage of the resources of the countries. Friedman's book is a detailed discussion of the globalization of companies, their operations, and their supply chains.

OPERATIONS MANAGEMENT AND ETHICS

A comprehensive look at operations management would not be complete without looking at ethics and operations management. Recent headlines have placed several states and their leaders in the spotlight for violating ethics. Almost every company has an Ethics Department and Ethics Statements. Just because a company has an Ethics Statement or Ethics Advisor does not mean that they are following ethical behavior. Ethics is usually defined as doing the right thing. There is no right way to do the wrong things. Most people are born with an ethical compass that points true north. However, somehow, some folks have their ethical compasses demagnetized. Have you ever seen a compass that has been demagnetized? It will spin and never point to north again. The same thing happens to some people in business. Greed takes over and "situational ethics[4]" take over. We will look in detail at ethics in supply chains when we discuss supply chain leadership.

---

[4]Situational ethics is a term invented to insinuate that ethics can change based on the situation. The reality is that what is right does not change because of being in a different country or location. Situational ethics may be the impetus to the saying "What happens in Vegas, stays in Vegas." What is right in business does not simply change because a business partner has a different view point.

One of the latest views of ethics concerns corporate responsibility and ethics. The Green Movement in businesses is an outcropping of that view. This view states that companies are responsible for the environment as part of their ethics. The Trinchero Family Wineries[5] (http://tfewines.com/tfe-green) took this concept to the next level. This company plants a tree for every bottle of wine that they sell. To date, they have planted over one million trees. Hopefully, this new ethical movement will not prove to be a fad, but a true focus on ethical stewardship of the environment.

SUMMARY

Operations management is a complex subject that has impacts on every aspect of a business. A systemic approach to operations management looks at the inputs, the transformation processes, and the outputs of an operations management chain. Operations management does not operate in a blind way or a vacuum. Operations management is a system of interrelated processes that include sourcing, manufacturing, distributing, and consuming products and services. This study of operations management will look at the processes and links that make up the operations management chain.

Discussion Questions

1. How does the Department of Labor define services and products? http://www.dol.gov

2. What are the differences between the outputs of goods and services?

3. What are the inputs to the operations management chain?

4. Why does the author introduce the term *operations management chain* as a concept, and what is the operations management chain?

5. Discuss the operations management chain from the systems perspective?

6. Is labor a commodity input to the operations management chain?

7. How did the Industrial Revolution impact operations management?

8. Is there a difference between a purely academic approach to operations management and a practitioner's approach?

9. What is the product design process, and why is it important to the study of the operations management chain?

10. Dr. W. Edwards Deming once said, "If you cannot describe what you are doing as a system, you do not know what you are doing." Describe operations management as a system.

---

[5]Go to http://tfewines.com/tfe-green to see how Trinchero is working to improve the environment through ethical practices.

2 Strategies: Developing Strategy and Converting Strategy to Actions

Operations describes the sequence and interaction of processes directly involved in the production of a product or the delivery of a service.[1]   Kendall, 2004

In Chapter 1, we looked at the foundations and history of operations management. In this chapter, we will look at the link between the operations management chain and strategy and decision making. In order to lead the processes that are involved in the production of a product or delivery of a service, a company has to have a long-term strategy and must make the right decisions. A company's strategy may define its competitive advantage.

What is strategy? Why does a company need a strategy? What is competitive advantage and how does a company develop a strategy and competitive advantage? Does competitive advantage differ from core competency? What is core competency and why is that important to operations management?

Let us start by looking at some definitions to lay the foundation for our discussion of strategies and decision making.

- Strategy: according to dictionary.com, "a plan, method, or series of maneuvers or stratagems for obtaining a specific goal or result."[2] The Merriam-Webster Dictionary defines strategy as: "the art of devising or employing plans or stratagems toward a goal."[3] For our discussion of strategies in operations management, this definition provides a good starting point.
- Decision making: "the cognitive process of reaching a decision."[4] A company's leadership needs to have a cognitive process to guide them to making decisions. In this chapter, we will look at decision making under uncertainty—when we really have no idea of what will happen in the future; and we will look at decision making under certainty—where we have some idea of what may happen in the future.
- Core competency: "a defined level of expertise that is essential or fundamental to a particular job; the primary area of expertise; specialty; the expertise that allows an organization or individual to beat its competitors."[5] For our discussions, a core competency is that area in which a company excels at and does better than the competition. The latter part of the definition: "the expertise that allows an organization or individual to beat it competitors," best fits our discussions.
- Vision: The best definition I could find for a business vision comes from a former professor of mine, Gene McCoy. Gene defined business vision as where the company wants to be in the future. With this as a definition, Gene also viewed strategy as the leader's bridge between the as is situation, where the company is today, and the destination situation, where the company will be in the future (the vision).

---

[1]Viable Vision, p. 52.

[2]Strategy. Dictionary.com. Dictionary.com Unabridged (v 1.1). Random House, Inc. http://dictionary.reference.com/browse/strategy (accessed: September 21, 2009).

[3]Strategy. http://www.merriam-webster.com/dictionary/strategy (accessed October 12, 2012).

[4]Decision Making. (n.d.). *WordNet® 3.0*. Retrieved September 21, 2009, from Dictionary.com website: http://dictionary.reference.com/browse/Decision Making

[5]Core competency. (n.d.). *Dictionary.com's 21st Century Lexicon*. Retrieved September 21, 2009, from Dictionary.com website: http://dictionary.reference.com/browse/Core competency

In the first chapter of the *Art of War*, Sun Tzu states, "The Way is what causes the people to have the same thinking as their superiors."[6] The vision and the corresponding strategy of the company is "the Way" that Sun Tzu speaks about that allows all of the members of the company to understand the thinking of the leadership.

A company's strategy is the road map that guides the direction of a company. Just as a road map and plan are needed to make a family vacation or a trip to the beach successful, a company needs this same road map to get the company to its destination. Without a map or plan, you will not get to where you are going or know you are there when you actually get there. Without a strategy to guide the company, the company will not reach its goals or destination. If you get lost or do not reach your destination, you can stop and ask for directions to get back on track. If a company does not have a map to lead them to excellence and profitability, they cannot simply stop and ask for directions and there is no Garmin or GPS to guide the company as there is for the boat or family car.

Long enough without a viable strategy may very well result in the collapse of the company. In the military, the lack of a strategy leads to defeat; in business, the lack of a strategy leads to corporate defeat. A good corporate strategy is as important to the success of the corporation as a good military strategy is to the battlefield commander.

A company's strategy and core competency may focus on short delivery times, speed to market, quality products, or simply cost. A company's core competency and strategy determine how the company will position itself. In order to properly position the company, another key aspect is necessary—what does the customer want? The first step of the Motorola approach to Six Sigma is Define. Define who the customer is; define what the customer wants; and define how we can service the customer better than the competition. Another way of determining our strategy and meeting the customers' requirements is through a SWOT analysis. What is a SWOT analysis? SWOT is an acronym that stands for strengths, weaknesses, opportunities, and threats. This analysis will assist the company in a variety of ways.

The strengths part of the SWOT analysis will help the company to truly identify what their strengths are. Obviously, the strengths of the company better include those areas that the leadership of the company has previously identified as their core competencies. If the company has not already identified their core competencies, an accurate and detailed strength analysis will identify those areas of the company that are the core competencies. The preferred methodology is to identify the core competencies prior to the SWOT analysis. A simplified format for a SWOT Analysis is shown in Figure 2.1.

Strengths identified by the SWOT analysis may include brand awareness or company reputation. In the 1980s and 1990s, the brand reputation of IBM resulted in a situation where regardless how much was spent on computers, if they were from IBM, no one complained. Apple enjoys the same brand reputation today in many companies. Another strength that should be discovered in the SWOT analysis must be the company's real estate value. K-Mart discovered this a few years ago, thus giving the company a new advantage in the marketplace allowing them to buy Sears. A company's products and/or patents should be a strength identified in the SWOT analysis. Although as A.H. Robins learned with the Dalkon Shield, sometimes the patent or product is a weakness.[7]

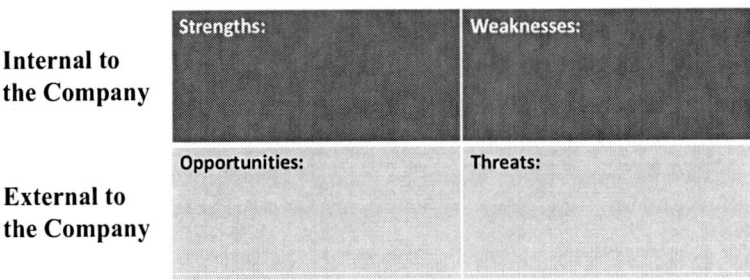

Figure 2.1: SWOT Analysis

---

[6]Sonshi. (2012). https://www.sonshi.com/sun-tzu-art-of-war-translation-not-giles.html

[7]A.H. Robbins purchased Dalkon, the developer of an Inter-Uterine Device (IUD) and continued the development, testing, and eventual sale of the Dalkon Shield IUD. The tests showed that the IUD caused uterine and cervical cancer in the test animals but was discounted as an anomaly. In fact, the Dalkon Shield was later proven to have a causation effect in the development of uterine cancer in humans, and the result was very large class action suit and settlement charges as a result of the numbers of uterine cancer caused by the Dalkon Shield. This should have surfaced during the SWOT analysis prior to buying the company and could have preserved one of the oldest pharmaceutical companies in the United States.

The weaknesses analysis should identify those areas that are not core competencies. A thorough SWOT analysis may very well identify an area that the leadership thought was a core competency that in actuality is not a core competency at all and may be a candidate for a process improvement program or contracting out (we will discuss this concept in greater detail in another chapter). The purpose of the weakness portion of the SWOT analysis is to identify those areas within the business or corporation that is not a strength and that may need additional focus and attention in order to convert that particular area into a strength. Not every weakness needs to be outsourced or contracted out. Some weaknesses may be the result of a lack of emphasis by the management or leadership of the company. We all know that we only do well the things that are either on the annual performance appraisal or that the boss checks on. A weakness may just need attention in order to turn it into a strength. Because of this, the SWOT analysis, contrary to some textbooks, is not a one-time analysis; the SWOT is another form of continuous process improvement.

Weaknesses identified in the SWOT analysis may identify the weakness of the brand. A potential weakness may be the ability to get products to the market or access to distribution systems. Recent experiences off the coast of Somalia may indicate a weakness in the routes used to get products to the market. This form of weakness—supply chain security—will be addressed in detail in another chapter.

Where the strengths and weaknesses portion of the SWOT are internal-looking analyses, the rest of the SWOT—opportunities and threats—are external views at the company.

The opportunities portion of the SWOT analysis is conducted to identify those areas or products/services that we have the capability to produce or provide to improve the company. These may fall into one of three categories—they may be weaknesses of the competition and thus a way to expand market share or introduce new products or services; the opportunities may be areas that we have fallen behind the competition but have the strengths identified earlier in the SWOT analysis to compete in that market; or the opportunity identified by an unmet customer need.

The threats analysis is a wider area than the first three phases of the SWOT analysis. In this phase of the SWOT, the company needs to identify those areas where the competition is stronger and, therefore, may identify an area of weakness that may impact the profitability of the company. An area of threats that is important, especially if conducting this analysis on supply chains, is the concept of security threats and risk analysis. We will cover both of these topics in the chapter on supply chain security. During the threats analysis, a company needs to look at the entire operations management chain for weak links and threats to the strength of the operations management chain. One threat that may be revealed by a detailed SWOT analysis is a change in customer preferences for the company's products.

The SWOT is useful in helping the company leadership prepare for the development of the corporate strategy. The strategy is where the leadership sees the company in the future. The strengths, weaknesses, opportunities, and threats identified will assist in shaping the future of the company.

The SWOT analysis is also a valuable tool for personal analysis. Everyone, especially those moving to the workforce, should conduct an honest and thorough personal SWOT analysis to identify personal strengths and weaknesses and those opportunities and threats that should be considered in the workplace and job search.

STEEPLE ANALYSIS

Another popular tool to assist companies in analyzing the external environment and developing strategy is known as the STEEPLE Analysis. STEEPLE is an acronym for:

Social—What is the societal view of our products or services? How does society view the company?

Technological—What is out there for technology? What do we have? What should we add to our company to be competitive with our competitors?

Environmental—What impacts does our company and products have on the environment? What can we do better to be a better steward of the environment? What is the competition doing that impacts the environment?

Economic—Where are we in the business cycle and how is the economic picture affecting our company?

Political—What are potential political actions that may impact our operations? Is the competition supporting some political action?

Legal—Are there any legal implications that may arise from our actions (refer to the previous discussion of the Dalkon Shield)? Are there laws in the areas that we want to expand to, which may impact our operations? Wal-Mart discovered that local laws in China required them to buy a certain percentage of their products from the local merchants.

Ethical—This should always be part of any strategy and decision making. Are the actions we are planning ethical and will the public perceive them as ethical actions?

What exactly is strategy? Dictionary.com defines strategy as, "a plan, method, or series of maneuvers or stratagems for obtaining a specific goal or result."[8] For a company, this plan or method leads to the goals of the leadership, which is the direction that they want the company to take for the future. Strategy should include goals and plans for expansion or retrenchment for the company, growth for the company's products, what future products by the company will be, and the focus of the company. Does every company need a strategy? Absolutely! Without a strategy, the company will be much like a rudderless ship moving in whatever direction the wind or current pushes it.

Once the leadership of the company sets the strategy and direction for the company, it has to be communicated to the workforce and shareholders. This is accomplished through the vision of the leadership. The vision is the method of communicating where the company is (as is situation), where the company is going (destination situation), and what will the strategy be that the company will use to get there.

Often companies confuse vision and mission. The vision is where the company will be in the future. The corporate mission states the reason for the existence of the organization. This statement provides the customers, the employees, and the shareholders a clear statement of that purpose. The corporate mission coupled with the strategy to accomplish the mission serve as guides for decision making. We will look at decision making models later in this chapter.

Here are a couple of examples of company mission statements:

- Google: to organize the world's information and make it universally accessible and useful
- Apple: to bring the best personal computing experience to consumers around the world through its innovative hardware, software, and Internet offerings

The vision and the guidance of how to accomplish the mission and goals of the company have to be clearly stated, communicated, and understood by the workforce that has to implement the strategy and vision. This is similar to one of Covey's "7 Habits of Highly Effective People"—seek first to understand and then to be understood. Just because it makes sense to you does not mean that it will make sense to your workers.

Why is a clearly stated vision necessary? Look at the guidance of Yogi Berra—"When you come to a fork, take it." I am sure that was clear to Yogi when he said it, but could be somewhat confusing. Outside Raleigh, North Carolina, when I was growing up, was a small crossroads village known as Six Forks. As the name would imply, at Six Forks you could go in six different directions. At that time, you could go to Raleigh, Durham, Creedmore, Wake Forest, Oxford, or the middle of nowhere. Choosing the wrong fork could put you miles into the middle of nowhere before you realized that you chose the wrong fork. The crossroads still exists within the Raleigh city limits; and you can still go in six different directions. Although none of them no longer leads into the middle of nowhere, using Yogi's guidance, which fork do you take?

In 1962, President John Kennedy made his famous proclamation, "We endeavor to go to the moon and return safely by the end of this decade." This vision seemed quite clear to the president; however it was seen as ridiculous by many because of the problems with getting a man into space at all while being perceived as quite clear and achievable by the folks at McDonnell, Douglas (later McDonnell–Douglas), and Rockwell.

In *The Art of War*, Sun Tzu states, "one who is confused in purpose cannot respond to his enemy." The vision is the way corporate leaders ensure that their employees know what their purpose is. Although the customer is not the enemy, if the employee does not understand the vision of the company, there is no way they can respond to the needs of the customer.

---

[8]strategy. (n.d.). *Dictionary.com Unabridged*. Retrieved October 02, 2009, from Dictionary.com website: http://dictionary.reference.com/browse/strategy

Compare Yogi Berra's guidance with the analysis of General US Grant by one of his aides after the American Civil War. General Grant had pretty much been a failure at everything he attempted, except for being a drunk, prior to being called back to active duty in the US Army at the start of the American Civil War. After the war, one of his aides was questioned about how General Grant went from failure to becoming the greatest battlefield commander in the US Army. General Grant's aide said what made the General so successful was that he made sure that his subordinates knew "exactly what he wanted, why he wanted it and when he wanted it."

The key with the vision is that not only must the vision be vital to the organization and the direction that the company needs to take; it also needs to be perceived as achievable by the people that have to implement it. Some years ago, the US Army established goals and a vision of where the leadership wanted to take the supply chain operations. The goals were imperative to prevent outside intervention in attempting to improving operations.[9] Unfortunately, for the first 2 years of this program, the goals for the US Army comprised one set of goals for the entire Army. At the time, the Army was divided into two major components—the Active Army (those soldiers that were full-time soldiers and worked every day in the Army's supply chain operations) and the US Army Reserves/Army National Guard (those soldiers that had other full-time jobs and only worked as soldiers 2 days a month and 14 days in the summer). One set of goals for both components did not work. The Active Army perceived the goals as achievable, but the Reserves and National Guard did not perceive the goals as achievable and went in the wrong direction with processing times. It was not until 2 years later that a separate set of goals were established, which everyone perceived as achievable, and started making progress in the right direction.

This is the second part of a successful vision; not only is it clearly stated, articulated, and understood; it has to be perceived as achievable if the vision and strategy are to be successful.

How does your strategy tie to a competitive advantage for your company and how does that tie to the operations management? A company's strategy also looks at how a company is going to be positioned. This positioning may very well determine if the company is going to be competitive. This competitiveness goes back to the first step of Six Sigma—defining who the customer is, what the company can do to meet what the customer wants, and how to do it better than the competition. Creating a competitive advantage for the company includes:

- Flexibility. If a company is competing on flexibility, it has to possess the ability to change rapidly between products, has to offer the customer various options, has to be adaptable to change, and must offer the customer a wide variety of products, options, and models. In order to do this, a company competing on flexibility has to possess the capability to crosstrain their personnel to accomplish various missions and make the wide variety of models and options to meet the customers' demands.
- Productivity. How do you create a competitive advantage through productivity? The productivity calculation is a simple calculation. Productivity is the output or amount of output divided by the inputs or the amount of inputs. Therefore, an increase in output from the same or less input increases productivity. Easy to write, but how do you do that?

Equation 1: Productivity Calculation

$$\text{Productivity} = \frac{\text{Output}}{\text{Input}}$$

- ☐ Decrease the amount of waste, thereby increasing the usable output from the same inputs.
- ☐ Produce the same amount of output with a more efficient system thus using less input.
- ☐ Produce a better quality with less input.
- ☐ Train the workers to be more efficient and effective.
- ☐ Adjust the production to make only what is needed and reduce quotas for production. (We will discuss this concept in greater detail when we talk about just in time and quality in other chapters).

---

[9]Just like most companies, the US Army has a board of directors. In the case of the US Army, the board of directors number 535—100 US Senators and 435 members of the House of Representatives. As most taxpayers know, it is better to keep this board of directors out of any business.

- Quality. In order to compete on quality, the entire organization must focus on quality—this will be discussed in greater detail in the chapter on quality. In order to compete on quality or use quality as the way to position the company, the company has to know what the customer wants and how the customer defines quality. Competing on quality—real or perceived—has its roots in the works of Dr. W. Edwards Deming and the quality revolution based on the techniques that the Japanese learned from Dr. Deming. Certain brand names such as Mercedes–Benz, Cadillac, IBM, Rolex, and Dell are considered quality products based on the brand reputation. Ritz Carlton hotels compete on the quality of customer care coupled with luxury. Depending on where you are in the Ritz Carlton management chain, an employee is authorized to spend up to $1,500 to make a customer happy during their stay.

  I had the opportunity to do a couple of seminars at the Ritz Carlton in Pasadena, California. The first year that I did the seminar, there were no problems. I drove my Ford Escort to the front door—not exactly the standard car at a Ritz Carlton. I did notice that when I went for my evening run that my car was parked on the lowest level of the parking deck out of sight of the road or front door.

  The second year I was there, I was greeted by the front desk by name, welcomed back to the hotel, and made to feel very welcome. I did encounter a small problem and this was not because I drove my little Escort again. When I returned from the evening session and dinner, I found my key card did not work. My first thought was that after a glass or three of wine that I was at the wrong room. A quick check showed I was at the right room, but the key card did not work. Suspecting that the card may have been demagnetized, I went to the front desk and got a new card. The new card did not work either. I called the front desk from the hall phone and an Assistant Manager came up only to discover that his master key card did not work either—seems when the battery in the door goes out, no matter how hard to yank on the door or kick the door, it will not open or how high you are in the management, if the battery is dead, your access card still will not work. Having had a similar experience in Florida a few years earlier, I was aware that the door will not budge when the battery in the lock is dead. (A few of my former students had the same problem at a hotel in Panama the semester after having heard this story and had a similar experience getting the battery changed).

  After finding a maintenance man to fix the door, I finally got into the room an hour later. Because of the inconvenience, I was given a free breakfast (about $25, which was part of the contract for my seminar anyway) and a bottle of wine (worth about $35). It seems that the Ritz Carlton chain has a policy to do whatever it takes to make the customer happy and employees can spend up to $1,500 to make the guest's experience a good one. There are reports of opening the kitchen after hours to make food for late-arriving guests. This is one way that the Ritz Carlton chain strives for quality and positions themselves apart from their competition. Had I known at the time that the manager could have spent up to $1,500 to make me happy, I would have had a round of golf, a massage at the Spa, and my free breakfast and bottle of wine.

- Time. Competing on time is critical in supply chains. FedEx,[10] UPS,[11] DHL, and the US Postal Service have determined that competing on speed is critical to the positioning of their companies. In order to compete on speed, a company has to walk their processes, identify nonvalue-adding processes, and measure the time for every process in the supply chain or manufacturing chain. Streamlining the process and reducing wasted movement, wasted waiting time, and wasted production quantities are necessary in order to compete on speed. Speed and time are relative terms, and FedEx and UPS have defined time spans to meet the time requirements of the customer.

- Price/Cost. To compete on cost or price, a company must reduce waste in the processes. Just like the competition on time, you cannot compete on cost, if there are inefficiencies and waste in your system. Every process adds cost, but not every process adds value. To identify these nonvalue-adding processes requires walking the process and identifying nonvalue-adding processes—a good process map is necessary to accomplish this (we will discuss process mapping and value chain mapping in greater detail in another chapter). It is also important to point out that after walking the process and identifying these nonvalue-added processes,

---

[10]Go to Fedex.com to see how they compete on speed and time.
[11]To compare UPS to FedEx, go to UPS.com

improvements must be put in place and not just changes for the sake of change. The difference here is that every improvement is a change, but not every change is an improvement. Some managers come in and have to change everything that their predecessor did just to make a mark on the operations. This usually impacts the entire operations management chain.

Southwest Airlines competes on cost successfully against the other major airlines. One of the ways Southwest is able to compete on cost is by flying one type of airplane for the entire fleet. This facilitates easy and rapid crew changes because of the familiarity of the equipment; one type of aircraft eases the record-keeping by having only one format of books; simplifies the maintenance operations because only one set of mechanics is necessary; and inventory costs are reduced because prior to buying AirTran Airways in 2011, Southwest only had to maintain repair and service parts for the Boeing 737 rather than the wide variety of parts required to maintain multiple model fleets.

Southwest also reduces costs by having more direct flights. Fewer transfers of passengers mean fewer baggage transfers, thus baggage-handling costs and personnel. One other way that Southwest has cut costs is by changing the way reservations are made. Southwest saves $30 million annually in travel agent commissions by requiring customers to use the Southwest Web site to make reservations rather than paying the monies to other sites such as Expedia, Orbitz, and Travelocity.

However, Southwest has experienced some hiccups since the purchase of AirTran, resulting in higher airfares in many markets and reduced service quality as measured by on-time departures and arrivals. A recent flight from Orlando to Kansas City was delayed over an hour and a half as Southwest tried to solve issues with two bags coming through customs from a newly implemented international flight. In this particular case, the pilots were as frustrated as the customers were, and the flight attendants became rude and short with customers.

- Are there other competitive opportunities in today's society and business world? What about electronic business and the Internet? Can this assist a company in developing a competitive advantage? Every brick and mortar business has to make a strategic decision on how to posture the company on the Internet and what aspects of electronic business the company should be part of. In today's business world, if you are not doing business electronically, you will not be in business very long. The question is not a matter of if, but how much of the company should be involved in electronic business and how much of the company should be involved in the brick and mortar portion of the company or should the company be totally electronic.

All of the other aspects of competitiveness and posturing discussed earlier also contribute to the competitiveness of an electronic company. A company can have the sexiest Web site possible and still not be competitive on price, cost, speed, flexibility, or quality. In brick and mortar businesses, these competitive aspects may be mutually exclusive, but in the electronic world, they are not necessarily exclusive aspects of competition.

What about e-business? What advantages does that do for you? The biggest advantage is that it opens your product to a whole new market. Teaching a class provides the ideas to a class of students, but putting the ideas in a book opens the doors to a new market. The Internet does the same for companies. Polo has eight Rugby stores located near college campuses. These stores only allow those students close to these stores to purchase the products, but putting the products online opens the market to everyone.

What are the theoretical and actual impacts of e-business and can you survive today without a Web presence?

Theoretically, doing business on the Web should enable companies to:

Provide better customer service—in actuality, fewer companies are providing quality customer service as a result of doing business on the Web. Some companies are content to sell products via e-commerce and never follow up with the customers. One prominent computer company has sold my company five computers over the past 7 years and has bothered to follow up only once to see if I got what I ordered and was satisfied with the purchase. However, they are very good at letting me know when my extended warranty was expiring.

Lower costs of materials—some companies do pass on the reduced costs of materials to their customers. These lower costs of materials are possible for several key reasons. The first reason that e-commerce provides the opportunity for lower costs is that companies can now find materials on the

Web without having to travel to the source. Another reason for the possible lower costs of materials is that the Internet now provides online marketplaces and exchanges, which allow companies to have alternatives and options to compare and bid on materials.

One concrete advantage of e-commerce and the Internet is the availability of information that provides potentially better decision making. Prior to the advent of e-commerce and the Internet, the only available information was in the catalogs or store. Gathering all the necessary information not in the catalogs required going to all the stores or sources of supply to see the products and compare them.

Examples of e-commerce success and lack of success are Toys-R-Us, Borders, and Barnes and Noble.com. Borders jumped into the e-business world with big fanfare, while the competition, Barnes and Noble, took their time in developing the supply chain to support the e-business storefront. Today, all of the Borders electronic business is handled by Amazon. Amazon started out to be a storefront with no assets, but quickly discovered that owning the entire supply chain produced a competitive advantage. Wal-mart.com is another good example of capitalizing on the electronic business. The successful e-business companies are the ones with a successful supply chain to support their operations.

- Can your supply chain produce a competitive advantage for your company? We will discuss supply chain operations in a later chapter. However, the earlier discussion on electronic businesses shows that a good supply chain is necessary in order to be competitive. Lowe's believes that the competitive advantage that they have over The Home Depot is their supply chain operations.

This may be true as Home Depot recently completely revamped their supply chain to compete more effectively against Lowe's and other home improvement companies. Lowe's did several things to improve their competitive advantage above and beyond the supply chain and improved their total operations management chain. Lowe's surveyed customers and determined that the majority of home improvement projects are designed or approved by the females in the household. To meet the needs of these customers, Lowe's added more pastel colors and more small appliances. Then, they added more consumer electronics and moved to be the number three retailer position for appliances in the United States.

Circuit City did not alter operations when Lowe's and Best Buy moved into the electronics and appliances business and now are no longer in business. Wal-Mart has perfected the supply chain operations and believes that their supply chain efficiency and effectiveness are what enables them to be the leader in business.

- Part of developing a competitive advantage is customer relationship management. What is it and why is it important? Customer relationship management is not a new concept. My uncle was a highly successful high-end furniture salesman. He maintained a deck of cards with all of the store salesmen that he called on, a card deck with the sales managers, a card deck with the store owners' information. He used these cards to refresh his memory before calling on a store. The information enabled him to call the customers by name, remind him of their interests, and their birthdays. The goal and the results were a very successful career and loyal customers.

Customer relationship management has the goal of creating relationships with customers, knowing what the buying habits of the customer are and using that data to create "customized" offers to the customers.

Casinos have been doing that with their slot club cards for decades. The goal of these cards is to develop trends to provide individual programs tailored to customers. Casinos use slot club cards as a way to capture customer data. Grocery stores do the same thing with their loyalty cards and credit cards. Cabela's went into the credit card business to gather data on where their customers were shopping and what the customers were buying that maybe should be stocked in Cabela's stores.

SUMMARY

The strategy of the company is communicated to the company through the vision of the company's leaders. The direction of the company should be based on the missions of the company, the vision of the leadership, the core competencies of the company, and the results of the strengths, weaknesses, opportunities, and threats analysis. This analysis will help the company identify those areas internally that are strengths and weaknesses and the external opportunities and threats. These areas will help shape the strategy of the company and how the company will position itself to be competitive in the marketplace.

Discussion Questions

1. Organizations exist
   a. To provide employment opportunities
   b. To meet the needs of society that people working alone cannot
   c. To produce goods in limited quantities
   d. To access the equipment and technology in order to produce goods and services.
   e. All of the above
   f. b and d

2. Operations involves:
   a. The distribution of company products.
   b. The production of goods and services.
   c. Obtaining people, capital, and materials.
   d. Accounting, marketing, finance, and engineering
   e. All of the above
   f. a, b, and c

3. Production and operations management is:
   a. Managing a company's level of inventory
   b. Managing the inputs to a production process.
   c. Managing the people who work in manufacturing companies.
   d. Managing the transformation process that produces goods and services.
   e. All of the above
   f. a. and d. only

4. Operations managers apply ideas and knowledge in order to
   a. Cut production time to speed new products to market.
   b. Improve flexibility to meet rapidly changing customer needs.
   c. Enhance product quality and customer services.
   d. All of the above
   e. None of the above
   f. Only a. and b.

5. Inputs to the transformation process of operations include:
   a. Goods and services.
   b. Accounting, finance, engineering, and marketing.
   c. Production planning, inventory control, and quality management.
   d. People, capital, and material.
   e. All of the above

6. The outputs of the transformation process of operations are:
   a. Accounting, finance, engineering, and marketing
   b. Production planning, inventory control, and quality management.
   c. Goods and services.
   d. People, capital, and material.
   e. All of the above

7. An important difference between goods and services is:
   a. Only goods are tangible
   b. Only goods are produced using materials and equipment.
   c. Only services are produced according to customer needs.
   d. all of the above
   e. None of the above

8. Ethics are set of standards that are generally:
    a. Lower than what is legal.
    b. Higher than what is legal.
    c. Equal to what is legal.
    d. Not considered in product safety.
    e. a. and d.
    f. None of the above.

9. Productivity is the ratio of inputs consumed divided by the outputs achieved.
    a. True
    b. False

10. An important step in developing a strategic plan is:
    a. Short-range forecasting.
    b. Measuring productivity.
    c. Working with suppliers on product design.
    d. Assessing the organization's strengths and weaknesses.

3 Decision Making and the Operations Management Chain

Decision making? What does decision making have to do with operations management? Everything! Every aspect of the operations management chain requires decisions. Decisions in operations management include:

- What products should the company make, buy, stock, or sell?
- What services should the company provide to the customers?
- What processes should be used in the manufacture or delivery of a product or service?
- What capacity should the company have and how that capacity should be expanded and if it should be expanded?
- What type of personnel and how many personnel should be hired?
- What level of quality should the company aim for and how will the quality be measured?
- What type of facilities the company should have?
- How should the company source parts, products, and materials? Where should these parts, components, and materials be sourced from?

The answers to these questions will be discussed in detail in the subsequent chapters. Decision making is inherent in all operations. This chapter will cover decision making and decision-making techniques.

ETHICS AND DECISION MAKING

In business and in our personal lives, we are faced with decisions. We can make the decision with the understanding that there are consequences for some of our decisions or we can avoid making a decision and let someone else make the decision for us. Not making a decision is actually making a decision. Allowing someone else to make the decision for you may not work in your favor. If someone else is making the decision, they will most likely make a decision that is favorable to them.

Missing from most definitions of decision making is the mention of ethics. Ethics is defined by Dictionary.com as: "the rules of conduct recognized in respect to a particular class of human actions or a particular group, culture, etc.: *medical ethics; Christian ethics;* moral principles, as of an individual: *His ethics forbade betrayal of a confidence.*"[1] Another definition of ethics is: "The rules or standards governing the conduct of a person or the conduct of the members of a profession."[2]

Just as we all face decisions that must be made, we also all face ethical decisions. What is ethical decision making? The process of applying ethics to decision-making models will enable the decision maker to look at the impacts and the consequences of the decision. Business is filled with decisions wherein it appears that the decision maker did not consider ethics while deciding or perhaps considered ethics, but chose to ignore ethics. There is no situational ethics. Ethics, as a benchmark of business leaders, is a simple yes or no; ethics do not change as situations change or conditions change. Ethics is a matter of right or wrong according to society.

---

[1]"ethics." *Online Etymology Dictionary*. Douglas Harper, Historian. Accessed April 04, 2010. Dictionary.com. http://dictionary.reference.com/browse/ethics

[2]"ethics." *The American Heritage® Stedman's Medical Dictionary*. Houghton Mifflin Company. Accessed April 04, 2010. Dictionary.com. http://dictionary.reference.com/browse/ethics

```
┌─────────────────────────────────────────┐
│                  Examples                 │
│                                           │
│   • Enron – 2001                          │
│   • Arthur Anderson – consultants for Enron│
│   • WorldCom – bankruptcy                 │
│   • Tyco – key officers convicted         │
│   • Rite Aid                              │
│   • Morgan Stanley                        │
│   • Citigroup                             │
│   • NYSE                                  │
│   • Martha Stewart – insider trading      │
└─────────────────────────────────────────┘
```

Figure 3.1: Examples of Unethical Decisions in Business

A business leader that compromises his or her ethics in the name of making a profit or personal gain compromises his or her ability to be a competent leader. There is no right way to do something that is ethically wrong. Unethical decisions usually lead to corporate scandals, which, in turn, lead to corporate ruin. The collapse of Enron in 2001 is a classic example of this sequence of events. In addition to Enron, Figure 3.1 shows other recent ethics issues in business.

Let us take a look at some of the business decisions over the past decade that have not gone well—even though the decisions appear to be the result of a cognitive process:

In the Enron case, the investors lost one billion dollars in stock value as the company collapsed under the strain of the scandal and unethical decisions. The unethical decision making that led to the Enron scandal and collapse also led to the passing of the Sarbanes–Oxley Law that was designed to protect the individual investor. By doing this, it also added a new level of bureaucracy to corporations.

The corporate officers for Enron focused on personal profitability and lost focus on the principles that the company was founded on. When corporate officers become so concerned about their own well-being at the expense of shareholders and employees, there will be serious consequences. In the case of Enron, they were assisted in this operation by their accounting firm —Arthur Anderson—once one of the premier accounting firms in the world. The association of Arthur Anderson with Enron and the ethical debacle resulted in the collapse of both firms.

WorldCom, Tyco, and Morgan Stanley all suffered from the unethical practices of their management. Martha Stewart participated in insider trading information and ended up serving prison time. Even the New York Stock Exchange had problems with ethical practices by their officers. Ethics are standards that are higher than what is legal. It is, therefore, possible to be legal without being ethical. For example, the US Supreme Court ruled in 2012 that the Stolen Valor Law was not legal. The ruling stated that falsifying accounts of military valor is not illegal although lying is unethical. As a result, the House of Representatives passed a new Stolen Valor Act in September 2012 that will at least prevent those that lie about their military records and awards from profiting from their lies.

Consequences result from decision making. Some of the consequences are good; sometimes, the consequences are not so good. Decisions may result in the downgrade of a company's credit or the company's bond ratings; still other decisions may result even in the collapse of the company. Ethics should help guide the company in making decisions and establishing corporate strategies.

STRATEGY DEVELOPMENT AND DECISION MAKING

Included in the decision-making process is knowing if a decision is necessary, when a decision is necessary, and what needs to be decided. This concept is similar to the Theory of Constraints premise that a decision maker needs to know what to change, when to change, and how to make the change. Decision making also includes knowing that there are consequences for decisions made. Here is an example of the consequences of decisions:

- When the decision is to drive after drinking, there is a definite consequence. I made this example in one class only to have a student tell me the next week that he was picked up for suspected driving under the influence. I was surprised when he told me that after the arrest, he immediately thought about the comment made in class about consequences.

■ A decision to use performance-enhancing drugs has the unwanted consequence of failed drug tests and the shame and disgrace suffered by athletes that make this decision. Recent headlines involving baseball players, Olympic athletes, cyclists, and American football players confirm these consequences. The decision to use performance-enhancing drugs falls under the ethics umbrella, but now it also falls under legal ramifications.

Included in decision making is the risk inherent in the making or not making a decision and the follow-up on the results of the decision—did we make the right decision and did we implement the right process or product? This includes using the After Action Review process to look at:

1. What was the plan or decision? What did we do or what did we decide?
2. What actually happened? What was the outcome? Did it match the expectations from the decision?
3. What went right that needs to be sustained in future decisions or plans?
4. What went wrong and why? It is important to point out that this step looks at what went wrong, not fixing blame on anyone. The goal is to fix the problem not the blame.
5. How can we prevent this from happening again in the future?
6. Who is responsible for the fix? This is the only "who" question in the process. The only reason a "who" is looked at here is that we all know that nothing gets done if someone is not checking on it. So, the purpose is to assign someone to ensure that the fix takes place.

DECISION-MAKING MODELS

The first model we will look at is known as the Military Decision-Making Model. Do not get hung up on the title; it is just the process. The Military Decision-Making Model is very similar to the Scientific Decision-Making Model and the Supply Chain Problem-Solving Model designed by Tompkins and Associates, a very successful operations and supply chain consulting company.

The goals of the Military Decision-Making Model are:

■ Analyze and compare multiple courses of action (alternative actions) to identify the best possible action
■ Produce integration, coordination, and synchronization for any action or decision
■ Minimize overlooking critical aspects—did we consider everything?
■ Produce a detailed plan

The steps of the Military Decision-Making Model are:

1. What is the mission or plan or decision that needs to be made? This mission/plan/decision may come from the boss or the headquarters staff. To illustrate this process, we will use the mission of expanding/building a new distribution center.
2. Mission analysis. Exactly what is the boss/headquarters asking us to do? What are the requirements from us to make this happen? What are the specified tasks? Specified tasks are those tasks that are specifically laid out in the guidance or directive from the boss/headquarters. What are the implied tasks? Implied tasks in this analysis are those steps that are not specifically dictated by the boss or headquarters, but from your experience or the experience of your staff or coworkers and are tasks that must be completed in order to accomplish the specified tasks.

   If the mission is to build a new distribution center, the specified task is to get a new distribution center built. The implied tasks include finding a suitable location, designing the new facility, and acquire all of the necessary permits. It may just mean expanding the current facility.

   For our example, we will use the alternatives of expanding the current facility, moving to an existing facility, building a new facility, or doing nothing.
3. Course of action/alternative development. Once the mission analysis is complete, it is time to start developing courses of action or alternatives to solve the problem or guide the decision maker to making a better decision. Obviously, one course of action is to do nothing—this is not always a good alternative. I had an instructor who used to emphasize on that a person can make a decision or not make a decision and let someone make the decision for you. Doing nothing may fit into this category. In some instances, doing nothing may be a viable alternative.

Each alternative or course of action has to be distinctive from the other alternatives. Otherwise, if the alternatives are not distinctive from the other alternatives, they are basically the same.

4. Once a set of alternatives or courses of action have been developed, it is time to analyze the courses of actions or alternatives.

COURSE OF ACTION QUALITIES
Suitability   Does it accomplish the company's mission and comply with the boss' guidance?

Feasibility
    Does the company have the capability to accomplish the mission in terms of time, space, and
        resources?

Acceptability   Does the cost justify the gain?
Distinguishability   Does it significantly differ from other COAs
Completeness   Who, What, When, Where, How, and Why

5. After analyzing the courses or action, it is time to compare the alternatives. In order to compare the alternatives, it is necessary to establish the success criteria or decision criteria that are important for the desired outcomes. Using a grid and the success criteria of expanding operations, posturing the organization for the future, and minimizing long-term costs, the comparison and analysis will look something like this:

ALTERNATIVE COMPARISON AND ANALYSIS			
Course of Action/Analysis	**Expand Operations**	**Posture for the Future**	**Minimize Life Cycle Costs**
Do Nothing	−	−	−
Expand Current Facility	+	+	−
Build New Facility	+	+	+
Move into Existing Facility	+	−	+

For this example we will weight the expand operations and posture for the future criteria. Using these criteria and options, the choices are expand current facility or build a new facility. The tie breaker is the life cycle costs.

6. The next step in the process is to brief the boss on the analysis and recommend a solution to him/her to accomplish the mission. This is one model for decision making; in the next section, we will look at some other decision-making models.

Our courses of action appear to fit the criteria. They will accomplish the mission of providing more distribution space. We will assume at this point that they all are feasible, given the current economic and business situations. They are distinguishable and seem to be acceptable given the mission.

DECISION MAKING UNDER UNCERTAINTY

Not every situation will lend itself to the previous decision-making model. In some business cases, decisions must be made under uncertain conditions. In such a case, the following technique may be used. This decision-making model may not produce as good a decision as the Military Decision-Making Model, which is very similar to the Scientific Decision-Making Model.

In this technique, we will still use a grid to lay out the decision table showing the states of nature and the decision alternatives. The payoffs for a craps table in a casino provide a good example of a payoff table. The craps table has various payoffs based on the number rolled and the probability of that number occurring. Obviously, the highest payoffs come from the hard ways because the hard ways have the smallest probability of occurring. Here is an example of a payoff table/decision matrix.

DECISION MAKING UNDER UNCERTAINTY			
Decision/State of Nature	Good Economic Conditions	Average Economic Conditions	Poor Economic Conditions
Expand Operations	150,000	75,000	5,000
Contract Operations	75,000	25,000	80,000
Maintain Status Quo	60,000	55,000	50,000

Example of a Payoff Table or Decision Matrix

For this decision using the payoff table above, the following criteria could be used: maximax, maximin, or minimin. Maximax is the maximum of the maximum payoffs—a very optimistic approach much like betting on the hard ways; maximin is the maximum of the minimum payoffs; and minimin is the minimum of the minimum payoffs. In the above example, these would be computed as follows:

Maximax: Maximum payoff for expanding operations is state of nature one—good economic conditions or $150,000; maximum payoff for contract operations is state of nature three—poor economic conditions or $80,000; and the maximum payoff for the maintenance status quo is state of nature one or $60,000. The maximum of the maximum payoffs is expanding operations in good economic conditions. Therefore, without any additional information, the decision for maximax is to expand operations.

Maximin: The minimum payoff for option one is poor economic conditions or $5,000; the minimum payoff for option two is average economic conditions or $25,000; the minimum payoff for option three is poor economic conditions or $50,000. Therefore, the maximum of the minimum payoffs is option three—maintain status quo.

Minimin: Using the same minimum payoffs, this decision is to look for the minimum of the minimum payoffs. The minimum of the minimum payoffs is to expand operations and hope for poor economic conditions.

DECISION MAKING UNDER CERTAINTY

The difference between decision making under uncertainty and under certainty is the addition of forecasts for the outcomes. Look at this updated payoff table with the addition of forecasted occurrence probabilities:

DECISION MAKING UNDER CERTAINTY				
Decision/State of Nature	Good Economic Conditions	Average Economic Conditions	Poor Economic Conditions	Expected Maximum Value
Expand Operations	150,000	75,000	5,000	
Contract Operations	75,000	25,000	80,000	
Maintain Status Quo	60,000	55,000	50,000	
	0.3	0.25	0.45	

Expected Maximum Value (Expand Operations) = (0.3*$150,000)+(0.25*$75,000)+(0.45*$5,000) = $66,000

EXPECTED MAXIMUM VALUES				
Decision/State of Nature	**Good Economic Conditions**	**Average Economic Conditions**	**Poor Economic Conditions**	**Expected Maximum Value**
Expand Operations	150,000	75,000	5,000	66000
Contract Operations	75,000	25,000	80,000	64750
Maintain Status Quo	60,000	55,000	50,000	54250
	0.3	**0.25**	**0.45**	

Decision/State of Nature	**Good Economic Conditions**	**Average Economic Conditions**	**Poor Economic Conditions**	**Expected Maximum Value**
Expand Operations	150,000	75,000	5,000	(B$5*B2) + (C$5*C2) + (D$5*D2)
Contract Operations	75,000	25,000	80,000	(B$5*B3) + (C$5*C3) + (D$5*D3)
Maintain Status Quo	60,000	55,000	50,000	(B$5*B4) + (C$5*C4) + (D$5*D4)
	0.3	**0.25**	**0.45**	

The formulas for this calculation are shown in the this frame.

EXPECTED VALUE WITH PERFECT INFORMATION AND THE VALUE OF PERFECT INFORMATION

What if you could have perfect information on what the future holds for your company and the economy? Does that information exist? It may exist for the products of your company assuming that the marketing folks are doing their jobs correctly.

If that information is available, what would you be willing to pay for it? We are not talking about insider trading information here; what we are talking about is better economic forecasting or product acceptance forecasting. If such information was available, the most you should be willing to pay for it is the payoff with the perfect information, lesser than the maximum payoff you would have without the perfect information. This would be the value of the perfect information (VPI).

Using our previous calculation for the expected maximum value, we would choose to expand our operations. Would we make the same decision if we had perfect information? If perfect information was available, we would obviously choose the state of nature that gives us the highest expected payoff. The calculation for the expected value with perfect information (EVPI) is the probability of that state of nature multiplied by each of the payoffs for that state of nature all added together.

When we calculated the expected maximum values, we used the probabilities and the payoffs across the rows for each alternative. The expected maximum value could also be called the expected value with no additional information. For the EVPI, we will use the probabilities and the largest payoff for each column or state of nature. Using the same payoff table, calculating for EVPI looks like this:

Decision/State of Nature	Good Economic Conditions	Average Economic Conditions	Poor Economic Conditions	Expected Maximum Value
Expand Operations	150,000	75,000	5,000	66000
Contract Operations	75,000	25,000	80,000	64750
Maintain Status Quo	60,000	55,000	50,000	54250
	0.3	0.25	0.45	
Expected Value with Perfect Information	45,000	18,750	36,000	99,750

For the first state of nature the calculation for the value of perfect information:
(0.3*150,000) = **$45,000**
For the second state of nature: (0.25*75,000) = **$18,750**
For the third state of nature: (0.45*80,000) = **$36,000**
So, **EVPI = 45,000+18,750+36,000 = 99,750**

The next step is to calculate the VPI. This is the value that a company would be willing to pay to get perfect information about the future of their product. Realizing that there is no perfect information, what we are trying to find is how much more we can make with better information and what the information is worth to us in the form of additional income. This could be a stock picking model, a new marketing model, or a forecasting model for the economy. This is not to be confused with insider trading information. Perfect information in this example could be marketing information that tells us what the market thinks of our product or could be a refined forecast of the future business cycles based on improved forecasting techniques or trends that have emerged. How much should you be willing to pay for this information? This is the value of perfect information. The calculation for this value is relatively easy:

The value of perfect information = the expected value with perfect information −
the maximum expected value:

VPI = EVPI − Largest EMV

Decision/State of Nature	Good Economic Conditions	Average Economic Conditions	Poor Economic Conditions	Expected Maximum Value
Expand Operations	150,000	75,000	5,000	66,000
Contract Operations	75,000	25,000	80,000	64,750
Maintain Status Quo	60,000	55,000	50,000	54,250
	0.3	0.25	0.45	
EVPI VPI = EVPI − Max EMV = 99,750 − 66,000 = 33,750	45,000	18,750	36,000	99,750

Therefore, in this example, an investor or company should not be willing to spend more than $33,750 to get better information.

Summary

Decision making includes the understanding that there are consequences that go along with the decisions. In this chapter, we looked at an idea of the consequences that goes along with making the decision, that is, to drive after drinking. The same is true for companies.

A model for comparing courses of action was developed in the chapter and a refined methodology was presented to assist leaders in making decisions under uncertainty and when more certainty is known.

Decision-making models are not designed to think for the decision maker. Decision-making models help the decision maker make a more informed decision. There is no exact science to decision making. A decision maker should use all information and tools at his/her disposal to help make the best possible decision while realizing that there are consequences to both good and bad decisions.

A decision-making model will not make the decision for you. The goal of a good decision-making model is to provide you with better information, thus enabling you to make a better decision.

Discussion Questions

1. Why is ethics important in decision making?

2. What company's actions prompted the passing of the Sarbanes–Oxley Act?

3. What is the goal of the Sarbanes–Oxley Act?

4. What are the variables that are included in decision making?

5. What is ethics?

6. Is there such a thing as situational ethics?

7. What is the maximax decision-making criteria?

8. Think about maximax as an optimistic decision criteria; is it possible to be disappointed if this criterion is the basis for a decision from a payoff table? Why?

9. What is the significance of the point of indifference?

10. What is the purpose of the EVPI?

11. How do you calculate the value of perfect information?

12. Using decision making under uncertainty, solve the following:
    The profit level for a furniture manufacturer using four different plants 1, 2, 3, and 4 and the demand level is A, B, and C. What decision would be made using maximax criterion?

Plant/Demand	A	B	C
1	200	350	600
2	250	350	540
3	300	375	490
4	225	275	603

13. If the following weights are added to the above table, what are the expected maximum values for each alternative and the value of perfect information for this decision?
    State of Nature A. 5
    State of Nature B. 35
    State of Nature C. 15

4 Quality and Operations Management

Everyone involved in the manufacturing of products or the provision of services is or should be involved in the quality of the product or service!

What is quality and what is the impact of quality or a lack of quality on operations management and the operations management chain? It could be that quality is like love; everyone has a different definition of what quality is in a product or service when they see it, but may have trouble defining quality. Ask a class of twenty-five students and you will get twenty-five different answers. Does quality have an impact on the supply chain? Does quality in the supply chain impact customer perceptions of your supply chain?

"If quality is to be managed, it must first be understood." (David Garvin)

One simple definition states, "Quality is a measure of goodness that is inherent to a product or service." Another definition from Webster's Dictionary defines quality as "the degree of excellence of a thing." Neither of these definitions provides clarity in the operations management chain of what quality is or the impact of quality on the outputs of operations. The American Society for Quality defines quality as "The totality of features and characteristics that satisfies needs." Even this definition leaves a little to be desired when looking at the operations management chain. Whose needs are being satisfied?

Perhaps a better working definition of quality for the study of operations management is: *fitness for use— as defined by the customer*. Telling the customer that you have a quality product or service is not enough; the customers have to experience the quality of the product or service for themselves. Obviously, the fitness for use of the product is fitness for use as the product was originally intended.

Using a screwdriver as a chisel will leave the customer thinking that the screwdriver is not a quality product as the handle of the screwdriver breaks when hit with the hammer. Conversely, using a chisel as a screwdriver will most likely leave the customer thinking that the chisel is not a quality screwdriver. Trying to drive a nail with a shoe will most likely result in a damaged shoe. The user of the shoe would be led to believe that the shoe is not a quality product—however, the shoe is not designed to be used as a hammer. One of my US Navy friends makes this point a little better. The Navy has ships that are designed to seek and destroy mines in the water. Not every ship is designed for this purpose but, "every ship can be used as a mine sweeper . . . once."

There are multiple facets of quality that impact the customer's perception of the product. Quality cannot be inspected in a product, contrary to the beliefs of many companies. Quality has to be designed into the product (we will look at this process in greater detail in the chapter on product development) and may very well be impacted by the process layout and manufacturing/service layout (we will look at this in greater detail in process development chapter).

Many companies have quality assurance offices, quality control offices, and quality inspectors. All of these are necessary for the assurance of providing a quality product or service to the customer. However, everyone involved in the design, manufacture, and delivery of a product is involved in the quality of the product. In the service industry, everyone associated with providing the service is responsible for the quality of the service. In the food service business, everyone from the manager to the buyer of the foods to the cooks to the servers to the host/hostess has a part in providing a quality service to the customer. In the retail world, everyone involved in retail operations management chain from the corporate buyers to the store managers to the sales persons to the delivery personnel have a part in providing a quality experience to the customer.

Dimensions of Quality. In order to adequately discuss quality, it is important to look at the dimensions of quality within the operations management chain.

The first dimension of the quality of a product is the reliability of the product. This reliability includes the availability of the system. When I was in the Research and Development process for the US Army the first time, the basic measure of a system was simply the reliability of the item. The reliability of the item was usually measured using the mean time between failures (MTBF). The MTBF is simply the average time between the breakdowns or failures of the product. When using the MTBF as a measure of reliability, the testing procedure simply averaged the times between the failures of the system.

As the systems became more complicated and new testing and measuring procedures were put into place for the products, a new methodology was adopted to look at the system reliability—systems availability. Systems availability takes into account the time necessary to repair an item. This repair time is called the mean time to repair (MTTR). When measuring the quality of a product using systems availability, the measurement looks like Formula 4.1.

Formula 4.1: Systems Availability

$$\frac{\text{Mean Time Between Failures}}{\text{Mean Time Between Failures} + \text{Mean Time to Repair}}$$

Example 4.1: Using the MTBF as the measure of the quality of the products or systems available would lead the company to choose product C since the MTBF is the greatest at 40 hours. However, when systems availability is used as the measure of quality, the choice of the quality product is now product D with a systems availability of 95.2%. Although this product breaks more often, the time to repair it is less, thus giving the customer more time of operation on average for the product.

Example 4.1: Systems Availability

	MTBF	MTTR	Systems Availability
System A	30 hours	2 hours	0.938
System B	25 hours	3 hours	0.893
System C	40 hours	4 hours	0.909
System D	20 hours	1 hours	0.952

The second dimension of quality is responsiveness. This dimension of quality is usually associated with a service or with the customer support provided by the company after the sale of the product. How responsive is the company to the needs of the customer after the sale of the product? Customer service seems to be a dying art form in most businesses today. So, the measure of the product may be more than just the product itself and include how well the company supports the customer when there is a problem with the product.

The same is true for service quality. How responsive is the company to unusual situations requiring service support? When I was finishing a basement in my house in Virginia, a nail for the paneling hit a water pipe. I knew the sound was not quite right when the nail hit the pipe and pulled the nail out only to reveal a hole in the pipe. This produced a nice little fountain of water where no fountain should be. After turning off the water, we called a plumber listed in the Yellow Pages with an ad for "24 hour service." Apparently, this company only had a 24-hour answer service and I was informed that they could be there the next morning. The next plumber ad in the Yellow Pages also advertised as "24 hour service." This plumber company had a plumber come on the scene within 30 minutes and he fixed my fountain. When the time came for finishing the bathroom for the downstairs, the first call was to the company that really did have the ability to respond to service outside the normal business hours.

In the retail industry, especially with the increasing numbers of Internet sales and the proliferation of e-commerce, the responsiveness of the company making the sale is a measure of the dimension of quality of the company. This is most evident when there is a problem or perceived problem with a product purchased over the Internet. In some cases, after a detailed search of the Web site to find a contact number, the result is a series of automated phone responses before the customer gets the opportunity to talk to a customer representative, who can discuss the problem and, in some cases, even more frustration before an acceptable solution can be reached and the problem solved.

The third dimension of quality of a product or service is measured by how the company solves a problem or provides a service. Is the company empathetic and caring about the customer or does the company act as if a favor is being done? A quality-focused company will show concern for meeting the customer's needs. How many times have you gone to a restaurant or retail store and the servers or sales persons simply act as if they are doing you a favor by being there?

The fourth dimension of quality deals with the knowledge of the company to help the customer with the use of the product or service. In the service and retail industry, can the person helping the customer provide the customer with enough knowledge to make the right choice? Cabela's is a good example of this. Cabela's boasts that they are "The World's Foremost Outfitter." In order to live up to that boast, Cabela's trains its employees to ensure that they have the necessary knowledge to assist the customer in choosing the proper gear for whatever outdoor activity the customer is interested in. Cabela's sales staff does not work on commission, which allows them to make recommendations on what the customer needs without the customer feeling like the sales staff is trying to make a bigger commission by recommending certain products. In the food service industry also, this is important. If you go into a restaurant, you expect the server to know about each item on the menu, if you have questions. This is a measure of the quality of the service. Here is an example of service quality: At the APICS International Conference in the Wynn Las Vegas resort in 2010, Francisco, a server at the evening reception, discovered that I really liked one of the hors d' oeuvres that they were serving. He then went and found another server with those particular hors d'oeuvres and sent the server to me. Francisco then went into the kitchen and got another tray of the item and brought it by my table several times. Francisco epitomized quality of service. No surprise when I talked with his supervisor and discovered this was the level of service that Francisco provided all guests.

If you call a help desk, you expect the person at the other end of the line to be able to help you. This is a measure of the company's quality. The last thing a customer wants to hear from a help desk is "That is a very good question, but I have no idea what you are talking about." Knowledge of products and service is a dimension of quality.

Another dimension of quality is the perception of the product. This may be influenced by advertising or the reputation of the product. There was a time in the IT world when no one questioned your purchase or the price if the product was IBM. The perception of Cadillac, Rolls Royce, and Rolex are intangible dimensions of quality based on reputation and advertising.

Another way of looking at the dimensions of quality is based on users, products, manufacturing, and values. User-based quality dimensions are simply based on the fact that the user is satisfied with the product. No matter how great or how good the quality of a product is according to the manufacturer, if the user perceives the quality as less than adequate, then the product is not a quality product. Conversely, if the user is satisfied with the product, regardless of the intended quality, it is still a quality product.

Product-based quality dimension is based on the product's attributes, which simply means does the product do all of the things that it is designed to do? As we discussed before, this is based on the prudent use of the product. Will the product's attributes meet the needs of the customer?

Manufacturing-based quality dimension is based on the ability of the product to conform to certain specifications. An example of this is the use of military specifications for a product. The ability to meet military specifications may be the order winner for a product and the determination of quality. Another way to look at manufacturing specifications as a measure of quality dimension of a product is to look at the requirements for it to work in a certain environment or for a specified period of time. The Sears Diehard battery, for example, used to advertise that it could be left on all day and still power the lights of Candlestick Park. Although the ability to light up Candlestick Park may be taking it a bit far, the ability to leave your car lights on and still be able to start the car was a strong selling point for the battery and set an expectation of specifications for the product.

Value-based product quality dimension is based simply on whether or not the consumer perceives that the cost of the product is a value for the customer based on his or her perceptions of the product.

GARVIN AND THE DIMENSIONS OF QUALITY

One of the Gurus for Quality in the twentieth century was David Garvin. He was one of the first to discuss the dimensions of quality. In his discussions, the dimensions of quality are similar to those already discussed, but are important enough to mention here.

1. The Performance Dimension: Does the product conform to basic operating characteristics? This is similar to our previous discussion on whether or not the product performs as intended when used by the prudent individual. If the product has certain basic operating characteristics set forth by the manufacturer, does it do these basic functions? Windows Vista is an example of this; if it really met all of the advertised functions, two things would not have happened. The first is the number of patches and changes required to make the system work properly. The second is that Windows 7 would not have been rushed to the market as quickly as it was.

2. The Features Dimension. Is there anything added to the basic characteristics or features? Does it do more than is required of the system? Here are a couple of examples. The first is my computer. My first computer was a Tandy 1000 with a single 5.25-inch floppy drive and an external 3.5-inch floppy drive. When it became available, I upgraded my computer to add a 300-baud dial-up modem (not long after Al Gore invented the Internet). In those days, all of Lotus 1-2-3 fit on one 3.5-inch floppy drive; the Tandy had a program called "Desktop" and when it came out, Harvard Graphics fit on a 3.5-inch floppy. Today, most people use their computer for graphics, spreadsheets, word processing, and accessing the Internet. Granted that the computers today are faster than my Tandy 1000, but, for the most part, computer users still only use their computers for the same things that my Tandy 1000 was used for. Is there an added features dimension of quality to my new laptop over the Tandy? That is a good question. My Tandy lasted 8 years before being replaced. Even then, it was not for lack of quality, but the update was dictated by the growing requirement for disk space that outgrew my dual floppies.

    The second example of the features dimension of quality where a product does more than required is one of my former cell phones. This phone was at the top of the line when I purchased it. When I got that phone, I was offered a package that allowed me to watch football games and NASCAR races on my 1.5-inch phone screen. This was a fascinating option, but when I tried to watch the Daytona 500 for fun on my phone, I was unable to determine which of the 43 cars going almost 200 miles per hour around the 2.5-mile track was leading, passing, drafting, or even in the race. This was a dimension of quality that was not needed—an extra feature that exceeded the requirements for the phone.

3. Durability. Will the product reach the advertised life expectancy before it has to be replaced? How durable is the product is a measure of product quality. Is your product like the "Energizer Bunny?" Does the product last as long as advertised? The Merriam-Webster dictionary defines durability as: "able to exist for a long time without significant deterioration."[1] This dimension of quality is evident in the "Lifetime Warranty" light bulbs. The advertisements for these bulbs lead one to believe that the bulbs will last a "lifetime." However, unlike the bulbs that have "an estimated life of 1000 hours," these bulbs do not have a set life expectancy. The "lifetime bulbs" I used in my garage lasted about 3 months. My first reaction was anger that my lifetime bulbs did not last a lifetime (whatever that was supposed to be). My second reaction was concern that my lifetime was soon coming to an end. Then I realized that the bulbs lasted their lifetime— unfortunately, their lifetime was not near what I expected when I bought them.

    Durability also refers to the ability of the product to perform under hard and frequent use while still meeting the specifications dimensions of the product. The Kevlar vests used by Soldiers and Police every

---

[1]durability. 2010. In *Merriam-Webster Online Dictionary*. Retrieved May 16, 2010, from http://www.merriam-webster .com/dictionary/durability

Photograph by Joe Waldenv

Figure 4.1: Sprint Mobile Communications Tower at a Kansas Speedway NASCAR Event

day in all climates and conditions; the users of the vests trust the quality of the materials and manufacturer to protect them day in and day out.

4. Reliability is the next dimension of quality according to Garvin. How well will the product operate over time? As discussed earlier, the reliability of the product is a measure of quality. We will look at reliability of products when we discuss product development and process development in the subsequent chapters. In order to ensure systems reliability for cellular phone coverage at NASCAR events, Sprint provides towers to help with the additional coverage needs at the events.[2] These towers were originally designed for emergency situations such as hurricanes and tornados. It will be interesting to see if Sprint provides this service in the future now that it is not the primary sponsor for the NASCAR cup series racing. The picture in Figure 4.1 is an example of these mobile towers.

5. Conformance. Are there preagreed-upon specifications? As a measure of the dimensions of quality, conformance looks at the required specifications for the product. As discussed earlier, manufacturing specifications may be stricter than consumer specifications. As quality is defined by the customer, if those specifications exceed normal specifications, they must be met in order to be considered a quality product.

   An example of conformity as a measure of quality is NASCAR. Every frame for every car that is allowed on the track is inspected by NASCAR technical inspectors to ensure that every part used conforms to the NASCAR specifications for tensile strength. This is to ensure the safety (another service dimension) and that the frames meet the prescribed thickness. After the inspection, Radio-frequency identification tags are placed in the frames by the inspectors, so that a later inspection can be done electronically to ensure no changes have been made in the frames.

6. Serviceability. How easy is it to repair, if necessary, how quickly can it be fixed, and how good are the repairs? If for some reason, the product needs service, whether from breaking or just scheduled service, how easy is it to repair or service the product. (We will look at this in greater detail when we discuss reverse logistics.) Another aspect of the serviceability of quality is the quality of the repairs. If the product needs to be repaired because it did not meet the durability dimension, how good are the repairs? This is another measure of quality. If the product is easy to fix, but the repairs are not of quality, then not only is the dimension of durability not met, but the dimension of serviceability is not met either and the product will never be seen as a quality product.

   In the late 1970s and early 1980s, Chevrolet had a car called the Monza 2 + 2. The Monza was a popular car in Europe and was rushed into production in the United States. The problem with this car (remember, Chevrolet was known as the "working man's car") was that to change the spark plugs required actually

---

[2]The towers were actually designed for use at natural disaster sites such as hurricanes to restore cell phone coverage when towers are destroyed. The mobile towers also provide a great backup at NASCAR events.

pulling the engine—which means "the working man" could not tune up his car without having an engine hoist (not something the average working man has in the tool box).

7. Safety. Is the product safe to operate and use? How safe is the product to operate? Even some products that are considered quality products do not meet this dimension of quality. Three-wheeled off-road vehicles meet most of the dimensions of quality, yet do not meet the definition of quality. Merriam-Webster defines safety as: "the condition of being safe from undergoing or causing hurt, injury, or loss."[3] Without picking on the ATV industry, the safety dimension of quality is not met if the number of accidents on ATVs is a measure of quality—even if the use of the vehicle may not be in the manner intended by the manufacturer.

8. Esthetical dimension of quality. This dimension is concerned with the look, the feel of the product, the smell of the product, or perhaps even the taste of the product, if the product is food. Several years ago, in the Dilbert comic strip, the Elbonians build an MP3 player that was 5-ft tall. Obviously, this does not meet the product specifications as discussed above. The solution was to add lips to the MP3 player to make it look like Angelia Jolie and then it was assumed that the esthetical dimension of quality would be met.

In the food service world, I can have the best food in the business, but if the smell of the facility is not esthetically pleasing, you will probably not want to enter my facility. There was a fish house in Wiesbaden, Germany, which was supposed to be one of the best in town. However, this particular fish house had the smell of day-old fish—a smell that I could not get past every time I walked toward the restaurant.

Another example of this is a Target store that opened in the past several years close to my house. This particular store had the restrooms at the front door. From a facility-layout perspective, this was probably a good idea; however, there were problems with the plumbing for the first several months. The store had a Starbucks in the front of the store, but because of the smell that resembled a port-a-potty, the desire to grab a coffee before shopping was not a good idea. The plumbing was eventually fixed and the esthetic appeal of the store was restored.

SERVICES AND QUALITY DIMENSIONS

There are seven basic dimensions of quality for services. Measuring the quality of services is a little more difficult than measuring the quality of products as the quality of services is more subjective than the quality of products.

The first dimension of quality for services is timeliness and the time to receive the service. From a supply chain perspective, this may be the measure of customer wait time. How long is the time that your customer orders a product from until they actually receive it? (We will look at this concept in greater detail when we discuss supply chain management.) Another aspect of this dimension of services quality is the time to complete a service. If the service manager at a car dealership's service department tells you that the repair job will take 4 hours, you expect the job to be ready in 4 hours and will most likely plan your return to the shop accordingly.

The same dimension of quality is applicable to the food service industry. How long does it take to get a seat at the restaurant, and then how long does it take to get your complete order delivered to your table? The airline industry is another example of this dimension of quality. Every airline is measured in on-time arrivals. If the airline actually posts transit times that are much longer than the actual flight time and they arrive early, is this really an on-time arrival or simply a misrepresentation of facts?

In the fast food industry, this dimension of service quality may very well be the differentiation between food chains. If one fast food restaurant can get you into and out of the store quickly with a complete order, they may have an advantage over their competition. McDonald's experimented with speed and order completeness in Missouri several years ago. In fact, it was a very successful experiment. They outsourced the order process to a call center in Colorado. The quality of the timeliness and order completion increased

---

[3]safety. 2010. In *Merriam-Webster Online Dictionary.* Retrieved May 16, 2010, from http://www.merriam-webster .com/dictionary/safety

dramatically. Customer satisfaction increased as a result of the decreased time in the drive-through line and increased order-completion rates.

Order completion is another dimension of service quality. How often have you driven off from a fast food restaurant only to find that the order was not complete or was not accurate? How many times have you received a shipment from an online retailer only to find that something is missing from the shipment? Order completion and perfect order fulfillment are measures and indicators of service quality, and will be discussed in greater detail when we discuss supply chain management.

Employee courtesy is another dimension of service quality. With the exception of "Dick's Last Resort," customers to restaurants and retail establishments expect to be treated with courtesy by the employees. Regardless of the quality of the product or service that the company is providing, the courtesy of the employees will determine if the customers stay or come back again. When I was in college, most of my clothes had to be tailored as I was preparing to enter the US Army. For some reason, at 5 ft, 5 in., and 195 lb, I was not able to buy ready-to-wear clothes off the rack. The tailor that I used was very competent, but complained every time I went to see him to get something altered. As soon as I could find another tailor close by, I switched tailor shops to one that seemed to appreciate my business. When you are providing a service, it is imperative that you remember the customers are paying for the service and you probably do not have a monopoly; therefore, customers should be treated with respect and not as if you are doing them a favor.

The consistency and accuracy of the service is another dimension of service quality. Does the service provider provide consistent service every time? If the provider is a tailoring service, do they provide quality tailoring consistently or do they only provide quality service sometimes? A shop close to Fort Leavenworth, Kansas, specialized in tailoring and sewing military insignia on military uniforms. When I was promoted in the military, I would buy new insignia for my Battle Dress Uniforms and before that my fatigues. The theory behind that was that the branch insignia and the rank insignia would be the same level of fade. My last promotion came in 2000. For that promotion, I took four sets of Battle Dress Uniforms into the sewing shop to have the new insignia and rank sewed on the uniform. Three of the four were done correctly and the fourth was sewed on upside down. Their quality was not consistent or accurate.

Another example of consistency and accuracy of service is In-N-Out Burger on the West Coast. This restaurant has a cult following that goes back to the beginning of the company in the 1940s. In-N-Out makes each order as the order is taken. The burgers are made from daily-ground beef and daily-cut potatoes are used for the French fries. Each order is then checked before giving it to the customer. To ensure the quality of the food, In-N-Out Burger only opens stores within a day's drive of its meat-processing plants and distribution centers.

Consistency as a service quality dimension also includes—does every customer get treated the same? However, there are exceptions to this dimension. In Las Vegas, the gambler willing to lose lots of money will get better treatment than those willing to lose $20 to $30 dollars. Is this an aberration to the consistency dimension? Not really. When the Super bowl was hosted in Phoenix in the mid-1990s, the management of the Las Vegas Casinos stratified their customer base and identified over 20 gamblers capable of losing over $2 million in a weekend, another 50 or so willing to lose about a million dollars in a weekend, and several hundred capable of losing over $500,000 in the course of the weekend. The casino operators targeted those gamblers and flew them to the game on a private plane, paid for their tickets, and brought them back to Las Vegas. The rationale was that if the gamblers were going to lose that much money, the operators wanted the gamblers to lose the money in their casinos. These gamblers got "comps" in rooms, tickets, meals, and airfare. I got a few free drinks. Was this consistent? Yes, if the casinos are going to stay in business, they have to cater to the folks willing to lose big money.

Conversely, if a food establishment is hard to get to and not easily accessible, it will not stay in business very long no matter how good the food is. For the company to stay in business, it has to have a service that is easily accessible.

How easy is it to get the service? This is another dimension of service quality. Cooter's garage in *The Dukes of Hazzard* was in the middle of nowhere, but everyone took their vehicles there. That is fine in the movies and on TV, but in the real world, a service—no matter how good—has to be accessible to the customer, if the service is going to survive. At the same time, the service has to be offered at times convenient to the customer. One installation that I was stationed at while in the US Army had a Post Exchange[4] that closed about the time that most soldiers on the installation got off work. Although the facility was easily accessible geographically, it was not accessible to the primary customers during the hours that the customers could access the store.

Responsiveness of the service is the final dimension of service quality. How responsive is the service provider to unusual situations? The plumbing company discussed above was able to respond to an unusual situation. This led to them getting not only more business from me, but also my recommendation when my neighbors worked on their basements.

DEMING AND QUALITY

There are numerous gurus of quality that influenced operations management theory and thought. There is a big difference between theory and execution. To paraphrase the military theorist Carl von Clausewitz, all things change when you go from the abstract to the concrete. In the world of the operations management chain, there are many theorists from the twentieth century that impact the theory of quality management, but the biggest concrete impact on the execution of quality is by Dr. W. Edwards Deming. Dr. Deming left the United States after World War II to help the country of Japan rebuild their manufacturing sphere after the devastation enacted on the country that was a result of the destruction Japan created during the war.

In the 1960s and early 1970s, "Made in Japan" meant poor quality. And then, overnight, it seems, "Made in Japan" stood for the epitome of quality around the world. When the United States became enamored with Japanese quality, everyone started wondering where they learned to produce such quality. The quality award in Japan is the Deming Prize. As more study of Japanese management philosophies and the quality movement took place, the name of Dr. Deming surfaced. Then, it was discovered that the Dr. Deming in question was an American.

Dr. Deming established his 14 points as a road map to quality in any organization. The work of Dr. Deming led to the Toyota Production System and what is now known as both Just-in-time and Lean (these topics will be discussed in greater detail in Chapter 12). His 14 points are:

1. Create a constancy of purpose. What is a constancy of purpose? If everyone is working on the same goal and same purpose, quality will be achieved. We talked about vision and strategy in Chapter 2. A leader with a clearly stated and understood vision and strategy will create a constancy of purpose in his or her workforce.
2. Adopt a philosophy of prevention. This is accomplished by designing a quality product rather than trying to inspect the quality into the product after it is produced. (We will look at product design and process design in Chapter 5.) Prevention means ensuring quality materials, quality processes, and a trained workforce. The quality of the product has to be built into the product and that starts with the design process.
3. Get rid of mass inspections. Mass inspections of products do not produce quality products. As we discussed above, the quality of the product will not be improved by inspections. However, having said that, there is a company in Missouri that knows that it has to inspect every product from one of its Asian suppliers because of quality problems. The testing and inspections do not improve the quality of the product; they simply identify the problems with the products before the items reach the consumer.
4. Minimize the number of suppliers. This sounds a lot like one of the principles of Just-in-Time that will be discussed in Chapter 12. Although many suppliers may be available for the materials to make a product, long-term relationships with fewer suppliers will help to bring the supplier into the manufacture of the products.

---

[4]The Post Exchange is a system that provides a department store operation at every military base. It started as a service to the soldiers in outposts as the United States expanded west and has remained a part of military life ever since.

5. Implement continuous improvement in the manufacturing system and in the workers producing the product. If a system of continuous process improvement is implemented in any corporation, the quality of the product or service will (or at least should) improve. At the same time, if the company is working to improve the knowledge and skill level of the workers, the level of the quality of the product or service will improve.

6. Train the workers. Look at the FORTUNE "Best Places to Work in America." The majority of the companies that make it to that list produce quality products or provide quality services. If you look at the companies profiled in this list, you will see that most of them provide more than the average training to their employees. The Container Store (a consistent member of this list) used to require several hundred hours a year for their employees to ensure that the employees could answer the questions of the customers.

    The Toyota North American Parts Distribution Center in Ontario, CA, has a very low employee turnover and requires over 80 hours a year in employee training to keep the employees up to date on new systems and provide refresher training to make sure the employees remain current on techniques and procedures in the distribution center.

7. Implement leadership development programs for new leaders. How often does a good worker get promoted to supervisor and then fails because no additional leader training is provided to the new supervisor? What Deming is telling us is not only do we need leadership in companies to provide quality products and services, but we also need to train those leaders in order to make sure that they are successful as leaders.

8. Get rid of employee fear. Why do employees have fear? Primarily because too many companies spend too much time trying to find employees doing something wrong rather than catching the employee doing something right. This mindset tends to produce less than quality products or services, as the employee focuses too much on not doing something wrong rather than focusing on producing a quality product or providing a quality service. This ties to another of the points—employee pride.

9. Get rid of the barriers between departments. As we will see in Chapter 5, breaking down the barriers between departments not only speeds up the product to market but also helps to have more involvement in the product design, resulting in a better-quality product.

10. No slogans. A slogan has never produced a quality product. This goes back to the constancy of purpose. If the leader of the organization is successful in communicating his or her vision and strategy to accomplish the vision, the employees will not need a slogan. Leadership is providing purpose, direction, and motivation to employees. If this is accomplished, a quality product will be produced or a quality service will be provided without a slogan.

11. Numerical quotas are not needed. What has been discovered over time with quota inspections is that if three inspectors are looking at a quota of items, problems occur. Initially, Inspector 1 does the inspections, as Inspectors 2 and 3 also do the inspections. After some time, either Inspector 1 decides that 2 and 3 will do the work or 2 and 3 figure Inspector 1 has checked the items and do not bother to do a good inspection. Eventually, no one is doing the inspection.

12. Improve worker pride. This one ties to the previous principle of eliminating employee fear. The key is to get your employees to understand that every product that they produce has their name on it.

    In a previous job, I was trying to get my mechanical workforce to put their name on their repair jobs. Because of their experience with getting beaten up for mistakes, they were fearful of putting their names on the jobs. In actuality, because of the electronic systems in place, I knew who was doing what on what equipment. It took over 6 months to get the attitude of pride and have the employees put their names on the jobs.

    This was not an original idea; I got the idea from the cars in Germany. Every Mercedes has a sticker with the signature of Mr. Daimler in the front window. Every job done has a signature on it—is it there because of electronic systems or because the employee is proud of what they did?

13. A quality program needs a program of training and education for the employees. There is a difference. Training is hands-on and is necessary in order to ensure proficiency. Education is a classroom program and also necessary—but, sometimes, hands-on training is needed to supplement the education. A well-trained

employee is much better equipped to make a quality product or provide a quality service than one that is haphazardly trained or assumed to be trained.

14. A sponsor. For any quality program, a company sponsor is needed to ensure the success of the program or project. This sponsor is critical to ensuring the implementation of the other points of Deming's process. Some companies call this a "champion for the cause." The bottom line is that for a quality program to work, there has to be a leader at the senior levels of the company, who supports the program. Jack Welch's support and leadership for implementing Six Sigma at General Electric is a good example of this.

THE COST OF QUALITY

Like freedom, quality is not free. There are costs to both good and bad quality. The costs of quality include the costs to prevent quality breakdowns. These include the costs upfront to design a quality product and the costs of training of the employees to produce a quality product. The cost of quality also includes the cost of sampling to ensure a quality product or process. This may very well include the test equipment and the labor costs for the sampling inspectors.

The costs of a lack of quality can be broken into internal and external costs. The internal costs of a lack of quality include stopping the line to fix a machine that has not been properly maintained, the cost of internal rework to fix problem products that are discovered in the manufacturing facility, and the possibility of having to downgrade the price of the product to sell it as a "second" in an outlet.

The external costs of quality include the cost of bringing the defective or broken product back from the customer (we will look at these costs in Chapter 13 when we discuss reverse logistics). External costs include warranty repairs, lost sales, and in some egregious situations—product liability law suits and settlements.

INTERNATIONAL STANDARDS FOR QUALITY: ISO 9000

> *ISO 9001:2015 sets out the criteria for a quality management system and is the only standard in the family that can be certified to (although this is not a requirement). It can be used by any organization, large or small, regardless of its field of activity. In fact, there are over one million companies and organizations in over 170 countries certified to ISO 9001.*[5]

This standard is based on a number of quality management principles including a strong customer focus, the motivation and implication of top management, the process approach, and continual improvement.

For companies that want to compete globally, the ISO 9000 series of quality management standards are a necessity. The basic tool for any ISO 9000 series certification is the process map. The process map will be discussed in greater detail in Chapter 5. The goal of the process map is to provide a visual display of the processes involved in the company's operations. The latest addition to the ISO 9000 series is ISO 9001:2008. The International Standards Organization describes this new standard as:

The ISO 9001:2015 lays down what requirements your quality system must meet, but does not dictate how they should be met in any particular organization. This leaves great scope and flexibility for implementation in different business sectors and business cultures, as well as in different national cultures.

1. The standard requires the organization itself to audit its ISO 9001:2008-based quality system to verify that it is managing its processes effectively—or, to put it in another way, to check that it is fully in control of its activities.

2. In addition, the organization may invite its clients to audit the quality system in order to give them confidence that the organization is capable of delivering products or services that will meet their requirements.

---

[5]https://www.iso.org/iso-9001-quality-management.html, accessed, June 22, 2017

3. Lastly, the organization may engage the services of an independent quality system certification body to obtain an ISO 9001:2008 certificate of conformity. This last option has proved extremely popular in the marketplace because of the perceived credibility of an independent assessment.[6]

This latest quality standard differs from previous standards that required an audit by an independent audit agency. The lack of auditors delayed the certification of many companies. The problem with this is that companies can now certify themselves without an independent audit team to validate the quality of the processes or products. This may very well be like the fox watching the hen house. With previous standards such as ISO 9001-2000, an independent audit was required.

The first step of the "certification" or compliance is to walk the process to document your as is situation. Once the process is mapped, validated, and analyzed, a destination situation can be determined. With the destination situation in hand, a leader can then develop the strategy and vision to reach the destination situation. This may very well include benchmarking operations against the best in class companies to help determine what the destination situation should look like.

The ISO 9000 series standards assess whether or not you or your suppliers really do what you say you do according to the process maps, standard operating procedures, and procedural manuals. Is the company customer focused? Are the employees involved in the quality initiatives and ensure a quality product is produced? The ISO standards provide a process-based approach to assessing and improving the operations of the company and its suppliers.

In addition to process maps, the Ishikawa or fishbone diagram is an important tool to assess quality issues and find the root cause of any potential quality problems. The Ishikawa diagram was first used by Kaoru Ishikawa. The four basic parts of the Ishikawa diagram are manpower, materials, methods, and machines. Usually, the causes of the problems or potential problems fall into one of these four categories. An Ishikawa diagram looks similar to this:

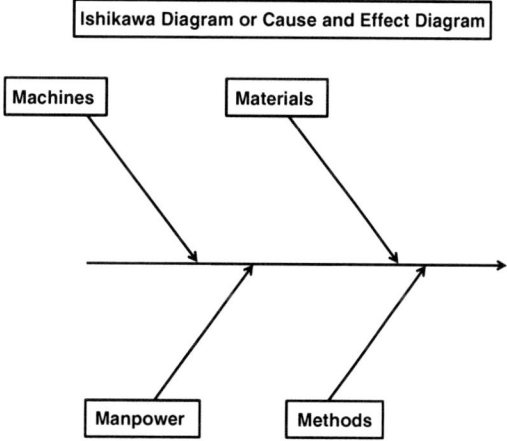

Figure 4.2: Ishikawa Diagram

With a process map and a blank Ishikawa diagram in hand, an operations manager can start the process of improving the quality of their operations.

SUMMARY

In this chapter, we looked at the foundations of quality and the definitions of quality. In defining quality, we looked at the dimensions of quality from the products and services perspectives. We also looked at the ISO 9000 series of standards to measure and improve quality. The quality tools of process maps and Ishikawa diagrams will be valuable to our discussion in Chapter 5 of the product and process design methodologies.

---

[6]Ibid. Accessed May 17, 2010

Discussion Questions

1. Why is quality important from an operations management perspective?

2. Recall a situation that you have been in, which would have benefited from the use of a process map.

3. Use your current job or a recent job and prepare a process map of the operations.

4. How could you use an Ishikawa diagram to improve your operations?

5. Look at an Annual Report for a company and review the report to see if the company is ISO 9001:2015 compliant for their quality programs.

6. Why is it important to be ISO 9000 compliant? Who cares?

7. Is ISO 9000 series compliance/certification an order winner or an order qualifier? Explain your answer.

5 Supply Chain Management

Supply Chain Management is a matter of vital importance to the company—the road to survival or ruin for the company. It is mandatory that it be thoroughly studied.

The APICS Operations Body of Knowledge states, "In the simplest terms, supply chain management is balancing or synchronizing supply with demand."[1] The Supply Chain Council describes the activities of the supply chain as going from the suppliers' suppliers to the customers' customers. In other words, it includes the activities of sourcing raw materials, sourcing components, delivering the materials or components to a factory, and once the products are made, the delivery of the products to the ultimate final customer. It also includes, as we will see in Chapter 16, getting the products back from the customer and replaced, repaired, or disposed of.

The APICS Dictionary defines supply chain management as: "The global network used to deliver products and services from raw materials to end customers through an engineered flow of information, physical distribution, and cash."[2] This definition is one of the better definitions of the overall supply chain because it hits on a key aspect that is overlooked by most supply chain definitions—cash flow. I do not care how good your supply chain design is; if you cannot get the cash from the customer in time to pay your suppliers and other creditors, you will not be in business very long.

After the Anthrax scare in Washington, DC, in 2001, the US Post Office that received the tainted letter was closed. The trickle-down problem from this closure was not discovered for about 6 months. It appears that the electric company that serves the District of Columbia had the payments for its services sent to a Post Office box in this closed down Post Office. About 6 months after the Post Office was closed, the electric company was trying to determine why it was losing money. The resultant research revealed that even though the Post Office building was closed to customers, apparently the mail was still being delivered there and the electric company's customers' payments were all at the closed facility.

Cash-to-cash cycle time is critical to supply chain success. This is a measure of how long after you receive payment for the products you sell that you pay your suppliers. In some cases, it may be a positive cycle time, which means your company is paying for the products before you receive them and sell them to the customer. If the cash-to-cash cycle time is negative, it means that the suppliers are paid after your company is paid by your customers. At one point, when Dell Computers was still in the assemble-to-order model in Texas, they had a negative 35-day cash-to-cash cycle time—in other words, Dell was paying their suppliers on average 35 days after their customers paid Dell for their new computer.

Most textbooks tell us that the term supply chain management first appeared in *The Financial Times* in about 1989. However, the term was actually used in a series of papers published in the United Kingdom in 1982 by R.K. Oliver and M.D. Webber to describe the future of logistics and transportation. The term did not really catch on until the mid-1990s. Prior to this point, the components that are now considered part of the supply chain management umbrella were stovepipe-managed functions that reduced the efficiency of the overall system.

---

[1] APICS Operations Management Body of Knowledge, 2nd edition, APICS, 2009, p. 21.
[2] APICS Dictionary, 15th edition.

Figure 5.1: The Evolution of Supply Chain Management

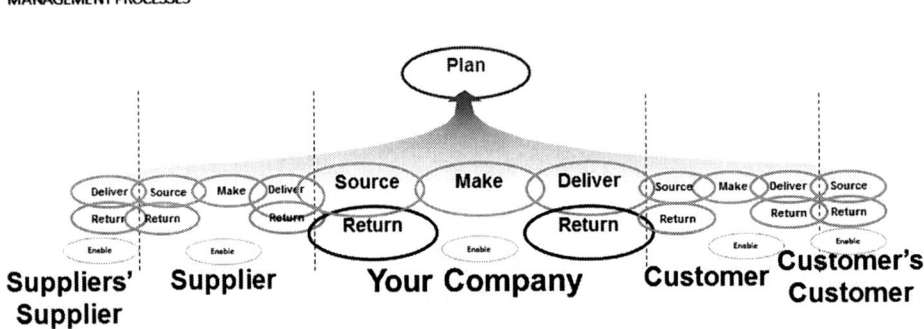

Figure 5.2: Supply Chain Operations Reference Model (Reference: APICS–SCC)

By the late 1990s, almost every company had adopted the concept of supply chain management. Figure 5.1 shows the evolution of the components of supply chain management. In the 1950s and 1960s, there were many stovepipe functions that led to fewer more efficient functions, but by the 1980s, the evolution in most companies had combined functions into fewer stovepipes.

In 1995, the Supply Chain Council was formed as a partnership between commercial companies and major consulting firms to establish standards for this new corporate function. The Supply Chain Council developed the Supply Chain Operations Reference Model (SCOR) to describe the supply chain. The SCOR model is designed to provide a cross-industry standard for supply chain operations and metrics to improve and benchmark supply chain operations regardless of the industry.

The SCOR model depicts six basic functions that the Council deemed to be inherent to every supply chain. The original model contained four functions—plan, source, make, and deliver. With Version 9.0 of the model, a fifth critical function was added—return. This version of the Supply Chain Council model appears in Figure 5.2. With Version 11.0 of the SCOR model released in 2013, the sixth basic function was added. This is the function of enable. This includes all those activities that help to enable the supply chain. The Supply Chain Council merged with APICS in 2014 to form APICS–SCC. The newest version of the model was released in 2017.

WHY IS SUPPLY CHAIN MANAGEMENT IMPORTANT TO THE OPERATIONS MANAGEMENT CHAIN?

Supply chain expenses account for the majority of the expenses of a company. From a customer perspective, the supply chain may be all the customer sees of the company outside of the Website. The late Peter Drucker, the management guru of the twentieth century, wrote in 1982 that logistics and distribution were most likely the last frontier for cost reductions in business. According to most studies, the rule of thumb for most companies is that it takes approximately 12 dollars in increased sales to equal the same effort to save one dollar in the supply chain operations.

The ability to successfully operate supply chain functions is closely watched by Wall Street. The inability to distribute goods to the customer is very closely watched by financial analysts. In 1999, Hershey's had a problem delivering chocolate products to customers during the Halloween season, significantly impacting their stock price and earning them a place on the *Supply Chain Digest*'s "Top Supply Chain Disasters of All Time." Toys R Us experienced similar supply chain problems with the delivery of toys for Christmas in 1999. Like Hershey's, this inability to meet customer due dates impacted their stock price and also earned them a place on the *Supply Chain Digest* list of disasters.

In order to achieve supply chain excellence, it is important to carefully plan (part of the SCOR model) the synchronization of all supply chain functions to help the company achieve a competitive advantage. Lowe's firmly believes that their supply chain operations provide them with a competitive advantage over their competition. Apparently, their competition believed so also. In late 2009, The Home Depot announced a major revamping of their supply chain operations in order to become more competitive. By 2016, this program had once again elevated The Home Depot to the top of the home improvement store ladder. The synchronization of activities and functions has to link the flow of information, materials, and cash in order to achieve a competitive advantage.

SUPPLY CHAIN INFORMATION AND SUPPLY CHAIN UNCERTAINTY

Supply chain globalization is one of the themes of Friedman's *The World Is Flat*. Friedman's theory is that the Internet and supply chain globalization, to include the outsourcing and off-shoring of operations, is what has leveled the playing field for all companies. As companies continue to globalize the supply chain operations of sourcing, making, and delivering of products (source, make, deliver from the SCOR model), there are inherent risks that accompany the complexity of global operations. The risks will be addressed in Chapter 16, Supply Chain Security. Along with these risks are the inherent complexities of global operations.

These risks include forecasting that will be discussed in Chapter 14. The longer the supply chain is extended, the impacts will be more to the overall forecasts throughout the supply chain. At the same time, the more extended the supply chain is, the chances for distortion of information along the supply chain becomes the greater. As we will see in later discussions of inventory management, this distortion of information is known as the bullwhip effect.

Other uncertainties in the supply chain come from customer-ordering patterns. With the advent of the Internet, customers can order from the store or from the Internet sites of the suppliers. Along with this comes the batching of customer orders by retailers rather than placing an order every time a customer places an order. The result is that suppliers get batched orders from retailers and individual orders from their corporate Web sites. The ordering patterns of the customers, coupled with the batched orders of the retailers, impact the ability of the suppliers to accurately forecast demand patterns. The result is the need to carry insurance in the form of inventory (this will be covered in greater detail in Chapter 12).

The flow of information in the supply chain will help to reduce some or all of the uncertainties associated with supply chains. As supply chains have become more complex and global, the need to pass information digitally and capture information digitally has become more important. Coupled with this increased reliance on information systems is a need to protect the cyber systems and information.

Today's supply chains require a centralized and coordinated information system. World-class communications is critical for supply chain success. FedEx has a world-class communications system that allows it track each package, every plane, and every truck and provides them the capability through their digitally assisted dispatch system to communicate with every driver. The BNSF railroad has a similar system to monitor the movement of every train in their system and communicate with the trains while in motion.

A world-class supply chain communications system will enable companies to integrate their distribution management system, inventory management system, and inbound transportation systems with the production management systems. Because so many systems are necessary for a successful supply chain, the lines between supply chain management and execution systems and enterprise resource planning (ERP) programs have become blurred over the past decade. The supply chain information systems have to provide visibility throughout the entire supply chain and provide the customer the ability to track the item through the delivery end of the supply chain once an order has been placed. Radio frequency identification tags (RFIDs) are one method of tracking items in the supply chain and the use of bar codes allows FedEx to track every single package and parcel shipped and provides the customers the status of their respective packages.

Information within the supply chain may be passed in the form of electronic data interchange (EDI).[3] The EDI is "the electronic communication of business transactions, such as orders, confirmations and invoices, between organizations. Third parties provide EDI services that enable organizations with different equipment to connect. Although interactive access may be a part of it, EDI implies direct computer-to-computer transactions into vendors' databases and ordering systems."[4] Prior to the advent of the Internet, EDI was transmitted via private networks and in set formats. The order forms used for online ordering put the transaction information into a set EDI format for use by the company.

Wal-Mart uses their information system to pass supply chain information through their networks and to their suppliers. Wal-Mart's information system is so sophisticated that they are linked to the Center for Disease Control in Atlanta, Georgia to pass information on pharmaceutical-related sales and issues. Wal-Mart is able to use the point of sale data at the stores to pass information to its headquarters at Bentonville, Arkansas, and from there to Wal-Mart suppliers to help reduce the friction and bullwhip effect in their supply chains. This allows Wal-Mart to consolidate sales data from all of the stores into one order to the suppliers.

The bullwhip effect gets its name from the fluctuations evident in the movement of a bullwhip (see Figure 5.3). You may have seen this type of whip used in some of the old cowboy movies. Basically, a bullwhip is about 8-ft long, made from braided strips of leather with a short (about 8 to 12 in.) wooden handle. A small movement at the handle causes huge fluctuations of the end of the whip. This analogy is applied to the supply chain where small movements in customer demand at one end of the supply chain leads to huge fluctuations at the other end of the supply chain. The better the flow of information in the supply chain is, the less distortion or fluctuations in the information flow results in less inventory in the system to cover the huge fluctuations previously seen in the supply chain.

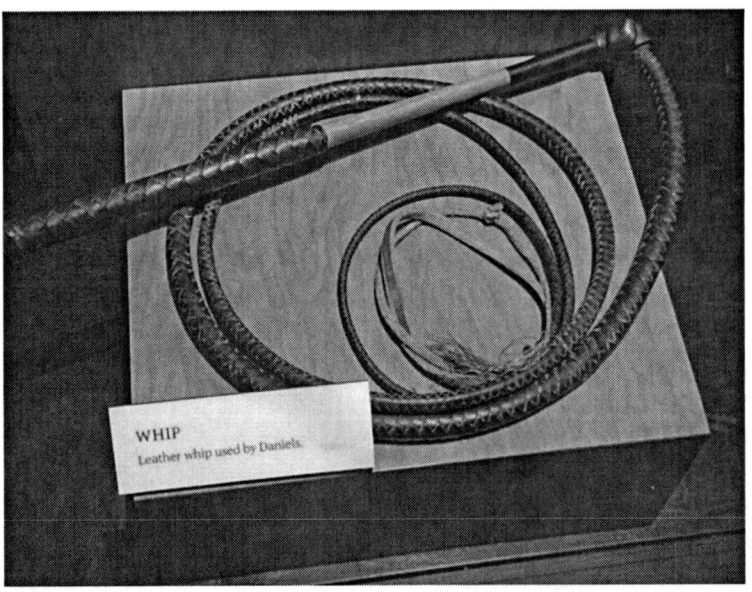

Photograph by Joe Walden

Figure 5.3: Bullwhip Used by Charlie Daniels on Display at the Country Music Hall of Fame in Nashville, TN

[3]The APICS Operations Management Body of Knowledge provides the following additional information on Electronic Data Interchange: "EDI is a way for a business to communicate with customers and suppliers. In North America, various industry groups establish and publish standards for standard transaction sets."
[4]Electronic Data Interchange, http://www.answers.com/topic/electronic-data-interchange, accessed August 16, 2010.

Another critical use of information in the supply chain is to keep accurate information on the levels of inventories in the supply room or distribution center. A good information management system will update the inventory availability and inventory levels with every transaction. Why is this important?

Here is a scenario that will help to make this aspect clearer. Suppose you buy an item from an Internet Web site. For most Internet retailers as soon as you hit the confirm key, the next screen you see is a confirmation of the availability of the item and the estimated shipping date if the inventory management system says the item is available. If the inventory management system updates the balance and availability with each transaction, the customer will know for sure that the item ordered is available. However, if the inventory management system does a batch update or, in some cases, a daily update, the items may have been sold and the inventory depleted before the update occurs. In this incident, the customer will receive the confirmation screen only to receive a message the next day that the item is not in stock and will be back ordered and shipped at a later date, if the customer does not cancel the item.

SUPPLY CHAIN INFORMATION AND ELECTRONIC COMMERCE

With the dependence on supply chain information management systems and the advent of the Internet, more and more companies moved from a strictly "brick and mortar" company to a hybrid company with both "brick and mortar" and electronic commerce capabilities, while a few other companies moved to strictly an electronic commerce operation.

Like our earlier discussion on electronic businesses and Clausewitz, some of the advantages of electronic commerce from a supply chain perspective sound great in theory, but do not sound as good when we move from the abstract to the concrete.

- Theoretically, the information systems available coupled with globalized supply chains connected via the Internet should provide companies with reduced prices and costs. The reduction in prices should come from the ability to increase competition for the raw materials and products as more suppliers become available via the Internet. The theoretical reduction in costs should come about as a result of the reduction in travel expenses and the ability to outsource manufacturing to developing companies. These theoretical cost decreases could be passed on to the consumer or retained as profits for the company. Additional cost reductions should come about as a result of automating previous manual systems and processes.

- Savings from automating manual processes assumes that the manual processes were actually necessary. If the processes are not needed under the automated system, there will not be any savings to the supply chain. All too often, when automated systems are put into place, there is not a good analysis of left of baseline and right of baseline requirements, resulting in unnecessary automated processes.[5]
Savings from automation also assume that the proper system is implemented. If the new ERP program does not improve the overall supply chain operations of the company, then there will be no cost savings. For example, Digital Equipment Company spent approximately $35 million on an ERP system only to find out that the new system was not as good as the old system.

- Electronic commerce has enabled supply chain companies to shorten order cycle times by enabling customers to place orders online. Prior to this, the only options for ordering items from a company were to order from the catalog, order and pick up at the retail facility, or place the order at the distribution center or factory. Supply chain information systems shorten this ordering process thus, shortening the entire customer order cycle time. Reducing the customer order cycle time produces more satisfied customers, thus producing more commerce.

---

[5]For every conversion from manual to automated processes, a detailed analysis is required of all the processes. The first step is to determine if the processes are value-added and needed under the system (known as a left of baseline analysis). After nonvalue-added processes are eliminated, a test run is necessary before going "live" and then a detailed analysis of the new automated system is needed to make sure everything worked as planned and is a necessary step in the process (known as the left of baseline analysis). When the US Army went to a more modern automated supply chain system in the mid-1990s, a careful analysis of the processes and a process walk determined that some of the processes that were included in the automated systems were outdated and not needed with the new system. This required an Engineering Change Package to update the new system without having the unnecessary processes.

Bar Codes and RFID Tags

Before the use of bar codes and RFID technologies to track items in the supply chain and provide "visibility" in the supply chain items, they were tracked, inventoried, and ordered using 80-card column punch cards as shown in Figure 5.4. The problem with the punch cards was that they came in a box of several hundred cards to the box. For a warehouse with several thousand items to be inventoried, it required printing/punching prior to the inventory. Usually, the punch card "printer/reader" was not in the same location as the warehouse. This resulted in having to transport the boxes of cards to the warehouse. On one particular day in Hawaii, I watched a box of cards get blown out of the hands of the warehouse worker, who was transporting the cards. As strong as that wind was, I am convinced that the cards were scattered all across the islands.

Bar codes made their appearance in the early 1960s. The US Army started the use of bar codes to track and inventory equipment. Bar codes are a series of vertical lines and spaces. The Universal Product Code (UPC) has a series of 13 digits. Prior to 2005, the United States and Canada used a 12-digit product code, but moved to the UPC. The first two digits of the UPC are the country codes (00 through 13 represent the United States- and Canada-based companies); the next five digits represent the company code; the next five digits represent the product or article code; the last digit in the 13-digit UPC is a check digit assigned to verify that the bar code has been properly read or copied (Figure 5.5). The UPC is a one-dimensional bar code meaning it can only be read in a certain sequence. The use of the bar code enables the company to capture point of sale data that can be used to reduce some of the uncertainty in the supply chain and provide information to suppliers. Figure 5.6 is an example of a two-dimensional or 2D bar code that can be read from multiple angles. Bar codes are also used for item-identification purposes as shown in Figure 5.7.

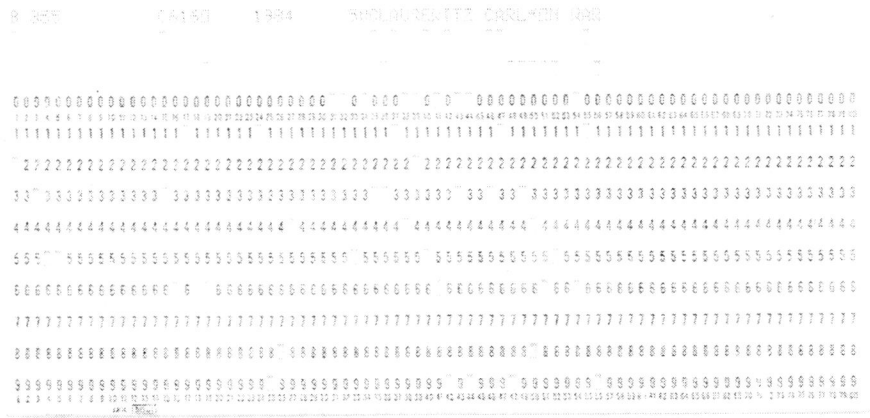

Figure 5.4: 80 Card Column Punch Card

Figure 5.5: Example of 13-Digit UPC

Figure 5.6: 2D Bar Code (Also Known As a QR Code)

Figure 5.7: Identification Bar Code

RADIO FREQUENCY IDENTIFICATION TECHNOLOGY AND SUPPLY CHAIN INFORMATION SYSTEMS

The RFIDs are discussed in Chapter 8; these tags have a large part to play in today's supply chain systems. The use of RFID tags has been the promise of the industry for several years as the best way to track and identify items in the supply chain. The use of RFID not only provides the benefits of scanning that the bar codes provide, but also enable quicker and more accurate inventories through the use of the scanners. The problem with RFID tags is two-fold. The first major problem is the cost of the tags and the infrastructure to read and store the tag data. This is no small investment. The second problem is that RFID tags cannot be read through liquids, can only be read from close distances, and may not be compatible with products such as cell phones.

Gillette started a program in 2001 to track Mach 3 razors in the supply chain. The company was losing visibility of the product and money. The cost of the tags was about $0.75 a piece, making the test an expensive one. However, the company discovered that the losses were not a result of internal or even external theft. The test with the razors revealed that the expensive razors were being misshipped to retailers. As is usually the process in supply chain issues, the customers that received too many were not complaining and the customers that were shorted were quick (as they should be) to identify a short shipment. This test enabled Gillette to solve their supply chain problem.

INFORMATION BENEFITS AND DRAWBACKS

A good supply chain information system will enable the company to replace inventory with information. This always sounds like a bold claim. How is it possible to sell the customer a product if all we have is information? The goal is not to get rid of inventory all together, but if a company can get better information of their supply chain operations and between their supply chain partners, the need to have excessive piles of inventory to cover the fluctuations in information flow in the supply chain will be reduced. If the need for the piles of stuff is reduced throughout the supply chain, then as the inventory levels decrease across the supply chain, it gives the illusion that the inventory has been replaced by information. Actually, it is not an illusion; the better and the more accurate the information is, the ability to reduce inventory is enhanced and supply chain costs are reduced.

Better supply chain information systems lead to a better flow of information. This leads to better collaboration between supply chain partners. Better information flows, better collaboration, and reduced variability in the supply chain lead to shorter cycle times to make and distribute products. Shorter cycle times lead to greater customer satisfaction, and this usually leads to higher profit levels.

However, there are downsides of sophisticated supply chain information systems. The first is that they are more vulnerable to cyber security issues. As we will see in Chapter 18, supply chain security is a very large problem in today's supply chains. Cyber security risk is an ever-increasing problem. Another downside of e-commerce and supply chain information systems is that more and more companies are learning that just having a great Web site is only part of the success equation. The other half of this success equation is the ability to get the product delivered to the customer. There is a direct link between the capability of the supply chain information system and success of the company.

SOURCING—FINDING SUPPLIERS, CULTIVATING SUPPLIERS, PARTNERING WITH SUPPLIERS

"Sourcing decisions are important within the supply chain and rely on standards and policies being maintained."[6]

As purchased supplies, parts, components, and materials account for almost half of all manufacturing costs, it is important to pick the right suppliers and sources of supply. It is equally important to collaborate with suppliers to share information for reducing the variabilities in the supply chain, while also trying to cultivate your suppliers.

---

[6]APICS Operations Management Body of Knowledge, 2nd edition, APICS, 2009, p. 12.

Just what does cultivating suppliers mean? Part of the cultivation process is to get suppliers to work with your company. It also includes working closely with the suppliers to get win–win terms and better products. By working with the suppliers, it strengthens the supply chain. Because the supply chain is only as strong as its weakest link, by working with suppliers and helping suppliers develop their employees and understanding the needs of your company better, the company ensures that they are not the weakest link. Cultivating suppliers means seeking to understand what drives them and establishing long-term relationships with the suppliers.

Partnering with suppliers makes sense when a holistic view is taken of the supply chain. In the days when all of the functions of what is now called a supply chain were under separate silos, partnering was not always sought with suppliers. When the entire supply chain is viewed as interdependent, it becomes obvious that supply chain partners should work together. As we saw in the product-development phase, partnering with suppliers may very well produce better-quality products.

Sourcing is important whether it is for purchasing raw materials, component parts, or services that the company needs in the process of manufacturing products. Sourcing is also important in the form of outsourcing when a company makes the strategic decision to outsource processes or services that are not deemed to be the core competencies of the company. Outsourcing has become a strategic decision based on the outcomes of the SWOT analysis as discussed in Chapter 2.

One of the concepts of Just-in-Time is the idea of establishing long-term relationships with suppliers. This is the concept of single sourcing. Single sourcing is often confused with sole sourcing. So, it is important to explain the difference between the two.

Single sourcing occurs when there are multiple sources for the product, raw material, or service. However, even though there are multiple suppliers or sources of supply, the company or purchasing agents choose to go with one supplier. This has advantages and disadvantages. The obvious advantage is the partnering with one supplier. The fortunes of both companies may be tied to this partnership and single-sourcing decision. The biggest disadvantage of single sourcing is putting all of your eggs in one basket. If there are multiple sources, but the company chooses to use only one source, and that source goes out of business or has financial difficulties as several automobile manufacturers recently discovered, there will be a big problem. If the company does not do any business with the other available suppliers or sources and then is forced to do business with them, the company may find out that the capacity is not there to meet the needs for manufacturing or may end up paying more for the product or service than was originally budgeted for.

Ok, so what is sole sourcing and how does it get confused with single sourcing? Sole sourcing is when only one supplier or source of supply is available for the commodity or product that the company needs. The limit to a sole source may come as a result of a patent or scarcity of the commodity or product.

Especially in government contracting, there is a misuse of the concept of sole sourcing. The term sole source is often used when, in fact, there is a desire for single sourcing, but as a way to get past government contracting regulations. Although legal, it is not necessarily ethical. Here is an example from a recent posting to the Federal Business Operations Web site. One particular US government office wanted a course in leadership for its executives. In order to bypass the guidelines of the Federal Acquisition Regulation for competition and bidding, this particular agency stipulated that this contract was to be a sole-source contract as only one company had taught this particular course in the past. A little research revealed that this particular course had only been taught once before. Was this sole-source company the only company capable of teaching a leadership development course for new executives? Of course, not. But since this course had only been taught once before, by stipulating that the company had to have taught the course before made this a de facto sole-source contract, when it should have been a single-source decision. Care is needed in sourcing to ensure that ethics are applied to the supplier sourcing decisions.

DISTRIBUTION

This is the supply chain function most frequently referred to as logistics. Distribution is the physical movement of products forward in the supply chain. It includes the movement between storage facilities and from storage facilities to the end users. The receipt, storage, picking of the product, and the shipping of the products are part of the distribution functions. In order to be successful in today's supply chain operations, speed is critical in distribution operations.

Under the distribution umbrella is the operation of warehouses and distribution centers. Warehousing and distribution are often used interchangeably. They are not the same thing and should not be used as interchangeable terms.

Warehouses focus on the storage aspect of the distribution umbrella. Warehouses are usually smaller than distribution centers. Warehousing is not a new industry. Prehistoric drawings indicate that early man stored food to get through the long winters. In Biblical times, Joseph ran the warehouses for the Pharaoh in Egypt, leading to the Israelites' journey to Egypt and the resultant Exodus led by Moses back to Israel. History is filled with stories of warehousing of various goods and food stuff.

Warehouses can take the form of product-focused warehouses such as a cold-storage warehouse for food or a dry-storage warehouse for items with longer shelf lives that do not require wet or cold storage. Warehouses can also be long-term storage facilities. These facilities may be collocated with a distribution center or feed the distribution centers, but should never be confused with distribution centers.

Distribution centers focus on the movement of the goods through the supply chain. Some of the largest industrial buildings are distribution centers. The average new distribution center today is in excess of one million square feet. In 1998, at the Warehousing Education and Research Council Annual Conference in Anaheim, California, a large number of distribution executives were heard to complain that warehousing was going to become obsolete as a result of the advent of the Internet and online retailers selling direct to the consumer. It was similar to Chicken Little running around crying, "the sky is falling in."

These executives were partially right. Warehousing and distribution, as they were known in the 1990s, went away, but resurfaced as a totally reformed industry. The advent of the Internet and the ability of the customer to order individual products online changed the distribution industry in two large ways. The first change in the distribution industry and distribution centers came as a result of the individual customer order quantities.

With customers ordering directly from the companies' Web sites, a new organization for the distribution centers was required. Now distribution centers were required to have a single-item pick area, a case lot pick area, and pallet storage or bulk storage. A single-item pick area is where distribution workers can pick individual items to meet customer orders for eaches. This is an addition to the traditional case lot pick areas to support retail store orders and the pallet storage or bulk storage areas in the facility supports the restocking of the case pick and single-item pick locations in the distribution center.

The second impact on the distribution centers as a result of Internet Web sites is the addition of a returns area as a result of customers returning items ordered over the Internet that did not meet their needs. The impact of reverse logistics will be discussed in greater detail in Chapter 16.

The addition of the single-item picking area and the returns processing areas to the distribution centers not only added more responsibilities to the distribution centers, it also added a requirement for more space in the distribution centers. So, the executives may have been wrong about warehousing and distribution going away, but, in a way, they were right in saying that distribution centers and distribution operations have changed dramatically with the advent of the Internet.

One other large change has come about in distribution centers. This change is the concept of postponement. The change started with the increased competition in the distribution industry as a result of third party logistics providers—known as 3PLs. These companies focus only on distribution and warehousing operations. The door was opened when companies realized that distribution and storage was not a core competency.

Postponement is a value-added service provided by the distribution center. These value-added services may be as simple as placing price tags on the products before shipping from the distribution center. Cabela's does this for their stores before shipping items from their distribution centers.

Postponement in the distribution center for the apparel industry takes on a different value-added service for the distribution center. In earlier days in the apparel industry, clothing items were put in boxes and shipped flat to the stores. When the clothes arrived at the store, they had to be pressed or steamed and placed on hangers to make them presentable to the customers. The distribution centers started storing the items in the distribution center on hangers and on racks. This enables the distribution centers to deliver garments on hangers and ready for display at the stores.

Part of the confusion between distribution centers and warehouses comes from the fact that both type facilities are managed by sophisticated automated management systems that are simply referred to as warehouse management systems or WMS. These automated systems started out for the management and automation of warehouses and as warehouses starting morphing into distribution centers, the name of the system did not change.

These systems have become very sophisticated over the past 15 years. A good WMS will not only provide the distribution center with instructions on what should be placed where in the center (this is known as slotting[7]), but will also provide the workers with the picking lists. A pick list provides the workers with the instructions of what items on the shelves need to be "picked" and prepared for shipment to the customer. The newer WMS will also provide the workers with the packing instructions, and a good WMS will also provide the loading plan for the outbound trucks.

In addition to automating the receiving, storage, picking, packing, and shipping of the goods in the warehouse or distribution center, a WMS may provide management of the outside storage areas and may also offer a system for time and attendance accounting. In one implementation, we used the WMS in conjunction with an RFID system to track workers' arrival and departure times as well as tracking productive time and break times. These data not only identified nonproductive activity by some of the workers, but they also enabled the distribution center to forecast employee requirements and scheduling needs.

TRANSPORTATION

A very important part of the supply chain umbrella is transportation. The US Army transporters have a saying, "Nothing happens until something moves." This is true in the commercial supply chain. You can have the best distribution center, manufacturing facility, and the best product on the market, but if your company cannot deliver the product due to a lack of transportation assets, your supply chain is a failure.

The supply chain is a system of interrelated activities. The key here is that the system is a chain of operations that depend on each other to be successful. Transportation is part of this system of interrelated activities. In the transportation world, there are modes of transportation and transportation nodes.

The modes of transportation include railroads, highway transportation, water transportation nodes (to include ocean movements and barge movements), and air transportation. The nodes within the transportation network are the locations where shipments are placed on one of the modes of transportation. Nodes include rail sidings, ocean terminals, rail terminals, airports, distribution centers, and cross-docking facilities.

Transportation may take the form of intermodal operations. Intermodal operations are simply freight moving by more than one mode of transportation. Intermodal could be rail to truck, ocean carrier to truck to rail to truck, or even truck to air to truck. International freight most commonly becomes intermodal freight as the ISO 20- and 40-ft containers move from a ship docking on the West Coast to a train for movement toward the East and then by truck to the distribution center or retail facility.

Railroads Rail has been a critical piece of the distribution system of industrialized countries since the nineteenth century. Depending on which account you believe in, there are somewhere between 92,000 and 150,000 miles of railroads in the United States alone (Figure 5.8). The delta between the two numbers is based on the serviceable amount of rail. Railroads provide a relatively inexpensive and reliable mode of transportation. Today's rail operations are more reliable than in the 1960s. During the 1960s, there was a freight company known as Railway Express Agency. The problem with this company was that more freight disappeared than was actually being delivered—this gave the entire rail industry a bad name.

There are certain commodities that can only move by rail. Coal is an example, and some chemicals can be more safely transported by rail than by truck. Having worked for the railroads for a short time, I know that the major rail companies are working hard to become more user-friendly. BNSF, for example, established a contract in 2004 to work with the US Military to provide better services, while determining the real transportation requirements. The use of double stacking of rail cars is another example of efforts to improve service. Another

---

[7]Slotting is the process of placing items in the distribution center or warehouse. Slotting may be either random where any vacant slot can be used for the next inbound item or the slotting may be dedicated slotting. In dedicated slotting, every item has a set location in the facility, which leads to worker familiarity of the locations. In random slotting, the primary advantage is that spaces do not sit empty waiting for its assigned goods to be replenished. This helps to optimize space utilization, but also takes away the advantage of the dedicated slotting of knowing where items are always located.

Figure 5.8: Rail Operations in Barstow, CA

example of the rail companies working with their customers to improve service is the covered, bi-level car carrier rail cars. The automobile companies complained to the rail companies about the damages that their cars were incurring during the shipment from the West Coast to other parts of the United States. With the threat of losing this lucrative business, the rail companies designed the covered car carrier to protect the cars while in transit on the trains.

One of the disadvantages of rail is that it is slower than other modes of transportation. Although weight-wise, the majority of freight in the United States moves by rail, rail movements are considered inflexible. Rail is considered inflexible because in order to use rail as a mode of transportation requires a rail siding. While a truck can deliver almost anywhere, a shipment by rail requires a rail siding in order to off-load the shipment.

On the flip side, the advantages of rail include the fact that, as mentioned earlier, certain commodities and oversized products can only move via rail. With the advent of the ISO shipping containers in the late 1970s, the use of rail for intermodal shipments increased dramatically. Because of the cost, intermodal shipments can move across the country on rail cheaper than trucking the goods across country. Another advantage of rail is the concept of trailers on flatcars or moving semitrailers on the flatcars and then hooking a tractor to the trailer at the off-load site.

The rail network of the European countries is very dependent and a highly important part of the supply chain in moving goods from the major ports, such as Rotterdam, to the inland customers. In South Africa, the rail is getting better as a result of the infrastructure improvements to support the recent World Cup games. In 2008, the rail service was considered so unreliable that some companies were crunching numbers and planning for the reality of operating their own rail companies to move their freight.

Road/Truck Transportation. The majority by volume (not weight) of the freight in the United States moves by truck. The trucking industry is divided between truckload (TL) and less than truckload (LTL) companies. Truckload companies only move full truckloads of freight. Customers receive a flat rate for the entire truck. This rate for the full truckload is less than the cost of shipping less than TLs. This is possible because the customer is only having the products delivered to one location.

The LTL firms charge the customers a piece rate based on the weight and cube of the items. The LTL firms usually consolidate multiple shipments to form a full load. The LTL is advantageous to those companies that do not need to hire a full TL for their products. The LTL companies can team up with freight consolidators, such as Freightquote.com, to get full shipments. Companies like Freightquote.com[8] use computer software programs to match the excess shipping capacity of shipping companies with shipping requirements of customer companies to provide a win–win–win situation. The shipping companies win because they get full loads and fill up their excess capacities to help optimize profitability. The customers win because they get basically TL equivalent

---

[8]For more information on freightquote.com go to www.freightquote.com

rates for their shipments. Further, Freightquote.com gets a commission for matching shippers with customers. Over the past few years, Freightquote.com has moved into matching shipping requirements for international and intermodal shipments in addition to LTL and TL shipping.

The advantage of truck transport over rail transport is the ability to move smaller packages and the ability to deliver to almost any site as long as material handling equipment and a dock or mobile ramp is available. The disadvantage of truck transport is that certain items are not transportable by truck. The advantages of truck are the disadvantages of rail and the advantages of rail are the disadvantages of trucking. Another problem with trucking in the twenty-first century is the aging of the truck drivers. The projection is that there will be a shortage of thousands of drivers within the next 10 years.

Small Package Carriers and Air Transport. Prior to Federal Express starting operations in 1973, the only way to send a package relatively quickly was via the US Postal Service's airmail. This process was not always compatible with the "air mail" services of other countries, and, in 1979, it still took in excess of 4 days to ship a letter airmail from North Carolina to Hawaii.

Federal Express (now known as FedEx) was formed by Frederick Smith in 1971 and started providing express shipments in 1973. FedEx established its headquarters in Memphis primarily due to the weather in Memphis. As FedEx expanded its operations through expansions and acquisitions, the services and options to deliver "the world on time" increased. To ensure the overnight delivery promise, FedEx controls all operations from their World Wide Operations Center in Memphis in the facility previously housing the Holiday Inn Reservations Center. This facility has multiple, large-screen displays of weather, flights, and package shipment information.

FedEx flies an empty plane from the Northwest United States daily down the West Coast and then across the country to Memphis as a precaution and an empty plane from the Northeast United States down the East Coast and across to Memphis as backup in case one of the scheduled FedEx planes is forced to make a precautionary landing or has mechanical problems. These planes help ensure that FedEx can deliver the "world on time."

As operations are expanded to international deliveries, "the world on time" can be defined by the customer—the options include next day morning, next day before 10:00 a.m., before noon, afternoon, second day, and now FedEx ground. One of the value-added services that FedEx now provides is customs clearance for international shipments. In fact, in the Memphis Hub for FedEx, there is an entire floor dedicated to customs. Amazingly, the most confiscated item coming through Memphis appears to be Cuban Cigars. The work of the customs folks for FedEx could be reduced with the opening of trade with Cuba.

United Parcel Service (UPS) recently celebrated their 100th Anniversary. Although started in 1907, it was not until 1982 that UPS started offering second day air service in addition to its package service. Another small package carrier, DHL, was originally formed in 1969 in California. In 1998, DHL was purchased by the Deutsche Bundespost, the German postal and communications company.

The growth of Internet companies coupled with the desire of customers to have their products "now" have led to the growth of the small parcel and air transport companies. These companies offer the ability to ship relatively small packages (usually under 400 lb) with relatively accurate shipping and delivery. In addition, the ability to track the packages not only makes this service popular with customers, but also increases customer expectations and satisfaction. Some of the companies offer better online tracking than others.

Small parcel shippers offer this service at a relatively high cost when compared with other modes of transportation. However, this is relative. If the customer wants a product tomorrow or needs the product by tomorrow, then the question becomes, "is it better to pay for premium air transportation or let the customer go somewhere else?"

Water Transport Water transportation is one of the oldest forms of transportation and may take the form of barge movements as shown in Figure 5.9 in Honolulu Harbor. It has been used with great frequency in the United States on the inland rivers and throughout Europe to clear the major ports and move goods inland to the interior countries. Water transportation may take the form of ocean shipments as shown in Figure 5.10, coming into the Port of Charleston, South Carolina. Ocean shipments are the most common form of international shipping with over 500 million containers (20-foot equivalents) moving around the world on ships.

Photograph by Joe Walden

Figure 5.9: Barge Movement

Figure 5.10: Ocean Movement

Photograph by Joe Walden

Some products have to be moved via water. The sheer volume of materials coming out of Asian Countries prohibits movement via air. The Panama Canal recently completed construction of new, wider locks to accommodate the larger vessels moving this cargo around the globe. When it was constructed in 1912 to 1913, the canal was built to accommodate the widest military ships at that time. This constraint from 100 years ago limits the size of ships through the canal to about 5,000 containers. The expanded canal now accommodates ships up to 14,000 containers. After the construction started on the new canal locks, Maersk Lines introduced a new cargo ship that can move up to 18,000 twenty-foot equivalent containers. The pictures in Figures 5.11 and 5.12 show ships moving through the canal, and Figures 5.13 and 5.14 show the construction of the new canal channels and locks.

The advantage of water transportation is that it can move bulky items internationally and intranationally. Water transport is inexpensive compared with trying to ship items internationally via air, and obviously movement between continents is easier and, in some cases, only possible using water. The disadvantage of water movement is that it is slower than other modes of transportation. This disadvantage became exacerbated in 2009 when the Maersk Lines announced that they could save $1 billion (USD) by cutting transit speeds in half. This immediately doubled the shipping times and, at the same time, increased dramatically the amount of goods in transit and not available to the customers. Couple this decrease in shipping speeds with the slowdowns resulting from security concerns and Somalia pirate attacks, and the movement of goods via water becomes a longer supply chain with increased risks.

Photograph by Joe Walden

Figure 5.11: Movement through the Panama Canal Miraflores Locks (Atlantic to Pacific Transit)

Photograph by Joe Walden

Figure 5.12: Movement through the Panama Canal Gatun Locks (Pacific to Atlantic Transit)

Photograph by Joe Walden

Figure 5.13: Construction of the New Panama Canal Gatun Locks and Channels (May 2013)

Photograph by Joe Walden

Figure 5.14: Construction of the Gatun Locks (January 2014)

Pipelines. One other mode of transportation should be discussed to complete the transportation aspect of supply chains—the movement of products via pipelines. Although experiments have been ongoing for years to move slurry coal via pipelines, the most common use of pipelines is for liquid products such as water or petroleum products. The advantage of pipelines over other modes of transportation is that the pipeline can be put in place and move large quantities of liquid products over any type of terrain and in almost any weather condition.

Photograph by Joe Walden

Figure 5.15: Pipeline Running through Leavenworth County, Kansas

The use of pipelines is relatively secure except when folks take pot shots at overground pipelines similar to what happened in Alaska a few years ago. When this happens, there are problems. Security is not always assured, as the US Army discovered during the war in Vietnam—during this operation, the Army lost as much product to pilferage and theft as it delivered every day.

Pipelines have a relatively high initial cost for digging the foundation and laying the pipeline. However, after the pipeline is in operation, the costs of operations are low. A little pipeline maintenance is needed occasionally as seen in the James Bond movie, *Diamonds Are Forever*, in the early 1970s. An occasional welding job inside the pipeline is needed and some minor preventive maintenance is needed on the pipeline and its pumps, but, for the most part, the pipeline needs very low maintenance. There is a pipeline that runs through Leavenworth County in Kansas (Figure 5.15), and the Central European Pipeline provides product throughout the European continent.

SUMMARY

In 2005, Thomas Friedman wrote *The World Is Flat*. This *New York Times* best seller postulated that the globalization of supply chains has significantly contributed to the "flattening" of the world. The globalization of supply chains has opened the doors to many companies and countries through the use of the Internet. The opening of trading partners and trade agreements has helped to extend supply chains. The European Union is a good example of a trading partnership/trading bloc that has helped to globalize operations by creating stronger bonds and using the trading blocs to help take advantage of economies of scale to improve supply chain operations.

The downside of globalized supply chains is tied to security and quality. The sheer numbers of containers moving around the world contribute to supply chain security issues as do the extended supply chains that are more open to terrorist interdiction and disruption of the supply chain. Sourcing from unknown sources around the globe can and, in some instances, definitely create quality issues and concerns.

Everything is supply chain–related, from sourcing to delivery of the finished product. The Supply Chain Council describes the supply chain as reaching from the suppliers' suppliers to the customers' customers and includes the basic functions of planning, sourcing, making, delivering and the new function of returning products from the intended user back into the system. Everything we do in any part of the operations management chain is related in some form or fashion to supply chain operations whether or not we are in the business of providing goods or services to the customer. In order to be successful in the operations management chain, a company has to be successful in the supply chain.

Discussion Questions

1. What is the difference between warehouses and distribution centers? Or, are the two terms interrelated?

2. Many discussions of supply chains use the terms logistics and supply chains interchangeably. Is this accurate or are the two different? If they are different, how do they differ?

3. What are the advantages of the different modes of transportation?

4. Logistics was derived from the military as a concept. In today's supply chain, what function is closely associated with the military logistics concept of moving supplies and personnel?

5. What is intermodal transportation?

6. How has the distribution center been impacted by the increase in customers ordering direct from the manufacturer via the Internet?

7. What is the mode of transportation most common for international shipping? What impact does this have on the supply chain?

8. What are the functions of the Supply Chain Council's "Supply Chain Operations Reference" Model?

9. Describe the supply chain?

10. What does cash-to-cash have to do with supply chain operations?

11. What is a warehouse management system and how does a WMS impact supply chain operations?

12. What is the difference between single sourcing and sole sourcing? Define each of the concepts.

13. What part does information have in the operation of supply chains?

14. Is security a concern with information systems?

15. What is the role of bar codes in today's supply chains? If so, what are the risks?

16. What does an RFID tag provide supply chains with that a bar code does not? If no improvement or advantage, why would you use an RFID tag?

APPENDIX 5A: SUPPLY CHAIN METRICS

This appendix provides some of the most common supply chain metrics.

a. Perfect order fulfillment: This metric measures how well a company's supply chain supports the customer. There are six parts of the perfect order fulfillment calculation:

1. Right product: Percentage of time that the right product is delivered to the customer. If you order a red computer and a blue one arrives, this is not the right product; if you order a large shirt and a small arrives, this is not the right product. For example in 5A.1, this computer was ordered as a red computer and the shipping box said red on the outside. A blue computer is not the right product.

2. Right Place: This is the percentage of time the right product is delivered to the right place. How can you deliver to the wrong place? This could be due to a misprinted address label, could be delivered to the wrong house, or stuck in the wrong mailbox. Although a package stuck in the wrong mailbox is not necessarily the shipping company's fault, from a customer's perspective, this is still a supply chain issue. For example, several years ago, a package was accidentally placed in the wrong box by the USPS. Apparently, the receiver of the product decided she would open the box and she liked the products; so, she kept them. This cost the shipping company poor will with the right customer, and they eventually had to refund the cost of the item.

3. Right Time: This is the percentage of time that the product shows up at the time promised. If you order online and opt to have next day delivery because you really need the product tomorrow and the product does not arrive tomorrow, then the company has missed this part of perfect order fulfillment. If you pay FedEx for next day morning delivery and it shows up next day afternoon, this is not the right time delivery.

Figure 5A.1: Right Product?

4. Right Condition: Did the product show up damaged or not working properly? If so, this is a violation of the perfect order fulfillment category of right condition. If you take your new plasma television set out of the box and the screen is damaged, but the box is not damaged, not only is this not the right condition, but it would indicate that the TV was damaged before the protective wrap was applied and before it was put in the box.

5. Right Quantity: This is simply the percentage of time that the quantity ordered equals the quantity shipped. If you order three new shirts, but only receive two, then this counts against the right quantity metric. Several years ago, Gillette was having an issue with this metric for Mach 3 razor blades. They invested in RFIDs to track their products only to find that the distribution center staff was misloading the boxes. Unfortunately, the company that received the extra razor blades never complained, only the company that received the shortage quantity did.

6. Right Billing/Invoicing: Did the company bill you for the product and price that you agreed upon? If you order a textbook and opt to only receive a used version, but you are charged for a new textbook, this is not right billing. If you order a product for $19.95 online, but the credit card bill reflects a $49.95 amount, this is not the right billing.

   The calculation of perfect order fulfillment measures the percentage of time that the supply chain takes "perfect" care of the customer.

b. Inventory Accuracy. This is a measure of how accurate your inventory system is. The calculation is the number of items that match the record inventory count when a physical count is conducted divided by the total number of items (SKUs) that are counted. Why is this important? Inventory that a company cannot account for is lost money. The higher the inventory accuracy, the better control of the inventory that the company has.

c. On-Time Delivery. This measures how well the company meets the customers' required delivery dates, assuming that the company agreed to that required date. The calculation is the number of items delivered on time divided by the total number of items shipped.

6 Program Management and Project Management

Project management and program management are often used interchangeably. These are not interchangeable terms. A project is a onetime operation. According to the APICS Dictionary, a project is "An endeavor with a specific objective to be met within predetermined time and dollar limitations and that has been assigned for definition or execution."[1] The APICS defines a program as: "a coordinated set of related projects usually including ongoing work."[1] A program may run forever. "Project management is a carefully planned and organized effort to accomplish a specific (and usually) one-time objective, for example, construct a building or implement a major new computer system."[2] This chapter will focus on project management and the tools that the operations manager needs in order to be a successful project manager.

The first discussion of a project management topic really comes in 33 AD. A documented comment from that time said a person would be called a fool if they started a building (a project) without having enough money to finish it. Here are some examples from the past several years that seem to show that this particular lesson from 2,000 years ago has not been fully learned by builders today. All three of these facilities were started in 2007 to 2008 as new resorts/mega resorts in Las Vegas and then ran out of money during the recession. The construction depicted in Figure 6.1 was to replace the old Westward Ho Casino, the Stardust Hotel and Casino, and the New Frontier Hotel and Casino. The projected completion date after the restart is now early 2019.

Figures 6.2 and 6.3 show another building started at about the same time was stopped, and then finally completed in 2015. The builders for the building in Figures 6.4 and 6.5 ran out money and the proposed mega-resort has been in the current state of completion (or lack of completion since 2010).

The first written account of project management comes from "An Essay Upon Projects" written by Daniel Defoe in 1697. This paper on project management starts the discussion with "The building of the Ark by Noah, so far as you will allow it a human work, was the first project I read of."[3] Defoe goes on to use the building of the Tower of Babel and describes the tower project as "for indeed the true definition of a project, according to modern acceptation, is, as is said before, a vast undertaking, too big to be managed, and therefore likely enough to come to nothing." Defoe demonstrates a very good understanding of projects given the amount of information known at the time.

The first "modern" article about project management appeared in the *Harvard Business Review* in a 1959 article, "The Project Manager." While not necessarily modern, it is modern when compared with Defoe's writing in 1697. The first Department of Defense publication to guide military project managers was published by the US Air Force in 1964, which parallels with the expansion of the US Space Program and the associated projects under that program umbrella.

Project management is an industry unto itself, has its own published body of knowledge, and has its own certifying body—The Project Management Institute. This institute serves as the clearing house for project management concepts and practices, and provides the certification as a project management professional.

---

[1]APICS. (2013). *APICS Dictionary*, 14th ed. Chicago, IL: APICS.

[2]Lonergan, K. 2010. All About Project Management. http://managementhelp.org/plan_dec/project/project.htm (accessed October 22, 2010).

[3]http://www.gutenberg.org/files/4087/4087-h/4087-h.htm (accessed October 22, 2010).

Figure 6.1: Major Construction Project in Las Vegas Started in 2008—Projected Completion 2020

Figure 6.2: Incomplete Building 2012

Figure 6.3: Finally Complete after 8 Years, 2015

Photograph by Joe Walden

Figure 6.4: From This Angle, the Resort Appears to Be Near Completion. This Particular Building Was Started in 2007. This View Is from 2016.

Photograph by Joe Walden

Figure 6.5: From the Backside of the Building, It Is Obviously Not Close to Completion. As of January 2016, Discussions Have Centered on a Complete Demolition of the Building and Starting Over

Project management is defined by the Project Management Institute as: "Project management is the application of knowledge, skills, tools, and techniques to a broad range of activities in order to meet the requirements of a particular project."[4] Wikipedia defines a project as "a temporary and one-time endeavor undertaken to create a unique product or service that brings about beneficial change or added value."[5] A project is a onetime operation with a defined beginning and a defined end. This chapter is designed to give the potential project manager the knowledge, skills, and some of the tools necessary to successfully lead a project.

Thus far, we have emphasized that projects are a onetime operation. Programs on the contrary are not onetime operations. Programs may go on forever, and some government programs seem to go on forever even after the program has outlived its intended purpose. A program could conceivably have thousands of projects under the program.

---

[4]Source: Project Management Institute, https://www.pmi.org/pmbok-guide-standards/lexicon (accessed May 29, 2018).
[5]http://en.wikipedia.org/wiki/Project_management

PROJECT PLANNING

A project must have a plan in order to be successful. A survey of professional engineers showed that the lack of a project plan was the second most common reason for project failures. The only factor more prevalent than a lack of planning was simply not following basic management principles by focusing on the systems vice the plan and the goals of the project. A good plan will help prevent having a constraint in the areas of personnel and resources after the project is started.

The first document that drives the project planning is the statement of work. This document describes the goals of the project, the time frame for completing the project, and the work to be performed. A poorly written statement of work will lead to project frustration and maybe even the inability to complete the project on time and within budget. A good statement of work will help the project leader to identify the manpower requirements, help establish a valid budget, and show the relationship among the activities in the project. In addition, the statement of work should specify the completion date of the project. Without this completion date, one of the critical aspects of a project is missing. The statement of work enables the project leader to analyze exactly what is being asked for and determine the real resources requirements and develop a valid time line for completion of the project.

Once the statement of work is analyzed, the project leader can develop the objectives for his/her project team. The project leader can establish the precedence of events and the associated time frames for each event, and from that listing of events, the project leader can forecast the completion time frame for the project. From a good statement of work, the project leader will be able to do a detailed mission analysis of the project and identify all tasks—those that are specified in the statement of work and those tasks that may not be specified, but are implied. An implied task is one that the project leader knows from experience that must be accomplished in order to complete the specified tasks. For example, if the specified task is to pour the foundation for a building, there are some implied tasks such as grading the land, putting the forms in place, and roughing in the plumbing before the foundation can be poured. The more specific the project statement of work is, the more detailed the planning and allocation of resources will be.

Determining the implied and specified tasks enables the project leader to determine what the US Military calls a "troop to task analysis." This analysis is necessary for the project leader to select the proper skills and personnel for the team as well as determine the right number of members to have on the team. Too many team members may lead to project failures and too few project team members may lead to project delays and not meeting the project deadlines. By carefully analyzing the statement of work, the project leader can develop a work breakdown structure that details exactly what each team member will do and may even be able to break the project into modules to assist in scheduling and completing the project on time.

Determining the right mix of personnel is also important to ensure the team is functional. One of the problems with project teams is that they are not permanent members of the team. The team members belong to another operation, department, or program. This creates a matrix management organization and a challenge for project leaders. The challenge here is that the team members know that their annual performance appraisals will be written by someone other than the project leader. Therefore, their allegiance is to their real boss because that boss determines the success or failure of their careers. This is not an insurmountable challenge, just one more consideration when choosing teams and team members.

PROJECT CONTROL

Project control involves all the activities to ensure the successful completion of the project. The success of the project is based on the detailed analysis and identification of all important tasks. Once the tasks are identified, it is important to make sure the order of precedence is established to make sure supporting activities are completed before the next activity starts. Back to our example of pouring the foundation—all of the implied tasks must be completed before the task of pouring the foundation can be started.

The next step is developing the budget for the project. The statement of work should provide the maximum amount the company is willing to spend on the project, but that does not mean that the entire amount needs to be spent on the project. The analysis by the project leader will enable the development of the budget. Once the budget is established, project controls are necessary to ensure that the project is completed within or even

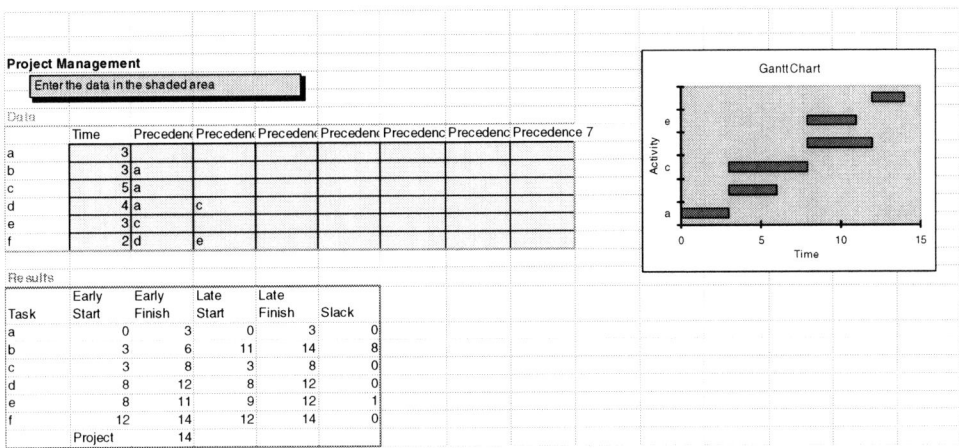

Figure 6.6: A Gantt Chart Developed Using Excel

under budget. One of the greatest sins of project management is busting the budget for the project. The only worst sin of project management is not completing the project within the specified time frame.

GANTT CHARTS

One of the common methods of providing project control is by the use of the Gantt chart. Developed by Henry Gantt early in the last century, these charts have been in use for projects for almost 100 years. The Gantt chart is a simplistic approach to project management. The chart is a bar chart that is easy to understand. Using the bar chart, a company can quickly identify if they are on schedule or behind schedule. The television show, *Extreme Makeover—Home Edition*, used Gantt charts to track their progress in building a new home for the featured family. On this show, the goal is to demolish an outdated home or a home that did not meet the needs of a family and then rebuild a dream home within a week. Project control is critical for the completion of the house. The Gantt chart allows the project leader to quickly check the day and hour and see if the team is on track.

Before the days of computers and automation, the Gantt chart was critical in the control of projects such as the Interstate Highway System and the building of the Hoover Dam. The chart shows the time frames and the amount of work that should be completed in that time frame. Although over 100 years old, it is still a popular tool for project control because of its simplicity and ease of reading. In order to develop a Gantt chart, the project leader needs to know the tasks, the time to complete each task, and the order of precedence for the tasks. Figure 6.6 shows an example of a Gantt chart.

PERT/CPM CHARTS

There are two other commonly used techniques for tracking and controlling projects. The Critical Path Method (CPM) and the Project Evaluation and Review Technique (PERT) are very similar. Both provide a network diagram of all the actions necessary to complete a project. The CPM and PERT diagrams are a little more complex than the Gantt chart.

The CPM was developed in 1956 by Remington Rand. The CPM provides tradeoffs between project duration reduction and the increases in project costs and activities. The CPM uses deterministic times and shows the times on the nodes of the network. Figure 6.7 shows the CPM diagram that corresponds with the Gantt chart in Figure 6.6. The CPM shows a "Dummy" activity—the "Dummy" is an activity that does not impact the critical path, but must be completed before the next activity can be started. The CPM diagram also tells if there is any slack in the network. Slack is where moving the activity forward or backward will not impact the completion time. There is no slack on the critical path. In the diagram below, the critical path is A–C–D–F. Any slack that will allow for an earlier or later start time will not be on the critical path. So, in this example, there is no slack for A, C, D, or F. The CPM network calculations are shown in Figure 6.8.

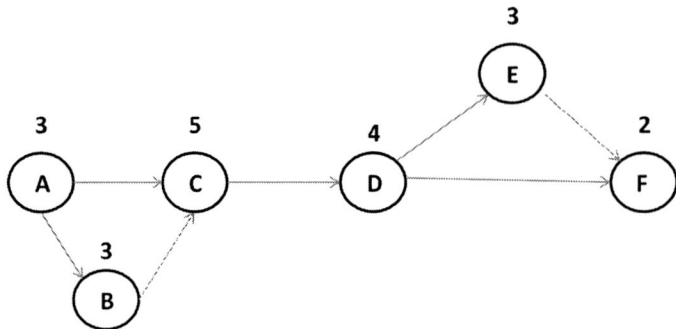

Figure 6.7: The CPM Diagram

ACTIVITY	EARLIEST START	LATEST START	EARLIEST FINISH	LATEST FINISH	SLACK	CRITICAL ACTIVITY
A	0	0	3	3	0	YES
B	3	11	6	14	8	
C	3	3	8	8	0	YES
D	8	8	12	12	0	YES
E	8	9	11	12	1	
F	12	12	14	14	0	YES

Figure 6.8: Using the Management Scientist Software to Calculate Slack, Earliest Start Times, and Latest Start Times for the CPM

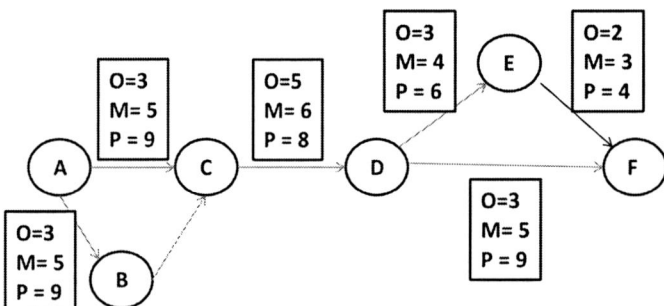

Figure 6.9: PERT Chart

For the diagram in Figure 6.7, the completion time is 14 periods. The project cannot be completed in a shorter time without changing the inputs and resources for the project. The critical path is the longest pass through the network.

The PERT was developed in conjunction with the US Navy for the building of the Polaris Submarines in the 1950s. The PERT chart provides three time forecasts to account for uncertainty in completion times. There is a lot of discussion about the differences between a CPM and a PERT chart—most of this is centered around the concept of the activity on the node or the activity on the arrow. What really separates the two diagrams is the number of time estimates provided. This is the biggest difference between the CPM and PERT diagrams. The PERT has an optimistic time, a pessimistic time, and a most likely time. In addition, the PERT diagram has the time estimates on the arrow in contrast to the node as in the CPM diagram. Either diagram will enable the project leader to control the operations. Figure 6.9 shows a PERT diagram with the time estimates. As there is a range of time estimates for the PERT network, the equation in Formula 6.1 is used to calculate the estimated completion time for the entire network.

Formula 6.1: Calculation of Estimated Time for the PERT Network

$$\text{Estimated Completion Time} = \frac{(\text{Optimistic Time} + (4 \times \text{Most Likely Time}) + \text{Pessimistic Time}}{6}$$

For example, using the times to complete A–B, the estimated completion time for that activity shown in Figure 6.9 will be (3 + (4 × 5) + 9)/6. Therefore, the estimated completion time for activity A–B will be 5.33 periods.

From a customer's perspective, the Gantt chart or the CPM chart is better as they allow the customer to know exactly when the project will start and when it will end. From a supplier's perspective, the PERT chart is better since it provides the supplier with a greater range of times to complete the project and with some flexibility.

PROJECT CRASHING

This has to be part of the initial project planning phase. Can the project be finished sooner than planned? The project is running behind schedule, can we finish it on time? The answers to these questions come from the concept known as project crashing. Project crashing is a methodology to reduce the project completion time by expending additional resources. The crash time is the amount of time for an activity that can be reduced. However, there is usually a cost for crashing a project as more resources are added to the project. The closer a project is to the planned completion time, the greater the cost to crash a project. The goal of project crashing is to complete the project earlier or on time at a minimum cost. Reducing a project's length is acceptable as long as the cost of crashing the project does not exceed the indirect costs. In some projects, there is a penalty assigned to not completing on time. In this case, there is a trade-off analysis necessary to determine if the penalties for not completing on time exceed the costs of crashing the project.

In 2012, there was a major heating/ventilation/air conditioning (HVAC) upgrade to Murphy Hall at the University of Kansas main campus. This project was supposed to be a 2-month project. However, asbestos removal caused some delays in the project. The project manager decided that the cost of crashing the project by paying union scale overtime was actually more expensive than paying the daily penalty for not finishing on time.

Another consideration in the contracting world for projects is the rise in looking at past performance as a criteria for winning new proposals. A company that habitually chooses to pay a penalty rather than crash the project may find themselves on the outside looking in on future projects.

LIFE CYCLE MANAGEMENT

Life cycle management is part of the project management umbrella. Life cycle management looks at the long-term costs of the project and not just the short-term costs. In some organizations, this is known as the care and feeding of the project. Life cycle management would look at the life of a product if the project charter was to develop a new product for the company. The project is focused on the product development; however, a successful project leader will also focus on the lifetime costs of the product to the company.

Life cycle management looks at the acquisition costs, the development cost, the production costs, and the costs to sustain the product after it is introduced to the public, and may also include the costs of disposal of the product at the end of life of the product.

SUMMARY

This chapter provided an overview of project management. Projects are onetime operations with a defined beginning and defined end. Project management success depends on the initial statement of work and the planning involved before starting the project.

Projects can be controlled through the use of Gantt charts, PERT diagrams, or CPM diagrams. The Gantt chart provides an easy-to-use visual display of the activities and project completion progress. Without delving into the activity on arrow vs. activity on node discussion, the CPM and PERT diagrams provide the same display with the biggest difference being the deterministic times of the CPM and the three time estimates for the PERT network.

Discussion Questions

1. How does the PERT Chart differ from the CPM Chart?
2. What does the Gantt chart do for a project manager?
3. What purpose does the statement of work provide?
4. What is the "troop to task" analysis for project management?
5. What is the difference between projects and programs?
6. What are the goals of project management?

7 Product Design

Why is product development important to the operations management chain? What is product development? What about process design? Don't most textbooks discuss these two topics as separate chapters? Actually, most textbooks do address these as separate issues and in separate chapters. However, as the goal of this book is to address the entire operations management from a real-world perspective, we will address these two interrelated subjects together in the same chapter. The two topics are interrelated because they impact each other. The design of the product and the design of the process should be worked on concurrently. The goal of this chapter is to show the importance of both design functions to the overall operations management chain and to each other.

Product development is tied to the strategy of the company as discussed in Chapter 2. A company's future products are not only strategic decisions, but also have to be in sync with the overall strategy and focus of the company. Obviously, if the company is focused on reducing carbon footprints and producing environmentally friendly products, the company will not want to produce ozone-depleting products.

Product development and the ability to continually produce new products to meet the needs of the customer may be the company's competitive advantage. For example, Rubbermaid has a goal of 300 new products to be developed each month. All of these products will not see the shelves of stores, but the ability to continually produce new products offers a competitive advantage for Rubbermaid. 3M encourages employees to experiment round the clock to produce new products. The Post-it Notes was a result of one of these experiments. The employee was not trying to create the Post-it Notes, but it did turn out to be a very profitable "mistake."

The product design has a primary goal of producing a quality product that meets the needs of the customer. The product design operation is where the ideas for the product are generating; it is where the look of the product is conceived; it is where the components of the product are decided. This part of the operations management chain is critical to the success or failure of the company. If a quality product is designed, tested, and produced in a production process that is well designed, and if the product meets the needs of the customers, the company will be successful.

In order to design a product that meets the customers' needs, we need to know what the customer wants. The first step of the Motorola Six Sigma methodology is to "define the customer, define what the customer wants and define how we can do it better than the competition." So, how do we define what the customer wants? What if the customer needs a service and not a product? This chapter will look at this concept also.

Complicating the product design process is the fact that customers are demanding new products at an alarming rate; these products seem to have decreased product life expectancies with increasing technology demands along with other complexities. The availability to consumers of a wider variety of products through the Internet also fuels the demand for new products. All of this means that the company has to be more flexible than in the past. Remember that flexibility was discussed as a way to position the company competitively.

The product design process should provide the company with the desired appearance of the new or improved product. The latest trend has been for "*new and improved.*" There is no way that a product can be both new and improved. If the product is new, there is no reason to improve it already. And if the product is improved, does it not imply that the product has been around and was deemed to need an improvement to keep it competitive in the marketplace?

Part of the product development process is to not address how the product will look, but how the product will be supported after the sale. A product design that does not consider this aspect may end up costing the company more over the life of the product than the company is planning for. The product design has to also consider the life cycle of the product. This includes not only the marketing, sales, and support of the product, but also the forward and reverse logistics infrastructure to deliver and bring the product back, if necessary.

Another aspect of the product design is to plan from the beginning the end-of-life aspect of the product and what actions the company will eventually have to take to phase out the product and when support for the product should be stopped. Somewhere in the life cycle of the product, demand for the product will decline and may even stop. This has to be considered as part of the product design process. The Giga Pet is a good example of a short life cycle.

The Giga Pet became the "have to have" product in 1995. Every child had to have one. When we came back from Germany in July 1995, it was the toy of choice for every child—some children had as many as 10 on their belt loops. This was a great product for the summer. The Giga Pet shown in Figure 7.1 had a puppy that had to be fed, watered, bathed, and played with on a regular basis. As the child played and fed the puppy, it grew to be a full-sized dog. The problem came when school started and the dog was not fed and watered as was done regularly. Initially, as school started, mom and dad helped by playing with the dog, but for those children with 10 Giga Pets, this became a chore. The result was that when the child came home from school, the dog was dead. This was traumatic for the child. Of course, the Giga Pet could be restarted, but when it died again, the thrill wore off. The result was the forecasters did not see the end of life of the Giga Pet and continued to produce the product. The Giga Pet went from the end caps and a price of $19.99 to the Dollar Tree and 99 cents–only stores.

The appearance of the product (how it will actually look) may dictate the materials needed for the product or may be impacted by the materials available to make the product. The product design process will not be the only determinant of how the product will look like; how it looks may be determined by the performance specifications for the product and may be influenced by the dimensions or tolerances of the materials that will make up the product. Conversely, the materials needed to meet the desired tolerances may dictate the appearance of the product. Furthermore, how the product is supposed to be used may very well dictate the appearance of the product itself. Also, where the product being designed is going to be used may very well dictate the design of the appearance of the product.

The design of a service is not that different from the design of a product. The same planning process is necessary to design a product or a service. Both design processes require the designer to understand what the customer wants in order to provide the customer with a product or service. What benefits should the customer get from the product or service? How will we determine that? A good service or product design will determine how to match the answers to these questions with a service or product that will meet the customers' needs or wants.

The goal of the design process should be to not only design a service or product that meets the needs of the customers, but this product or service should also be designed to be provided or produced as efficiently and cost effectively as possible. Remember the primary reason for being in business is to make a profit. If a

Photograph by Joe Walden

Figure 7.1: The Giga Pet

company cannot make a product efficiently and in a cost-effective manner, the company cannot make a profit. The same is true of services; if the company cannot provide the service in a cost-effective manner, the company will not be in business very long.

A quality design process will focus on getting the product to the market as quickly as possible. There is a difference between speed to market and haste to market. Speed to market is important. Speed to market means getting a quality product to the market as quickly as possible. Haste to market is getting a product to market quickly, but not with a quality product. Certain software companies are real good at getting products to market quickly, but they may not be quality products. This results in many revisions to the product to make it better. Apple recently did this with the iPhone 4G. To get the product to market quickly, Apple rushed the new iPhone to market knowing that there may be a problem with the reception. Seems in a haste to get this new product to market, they knew that the reception was possibly flawed because of the placement of the antenna at the edge of the phone. If held in a particular way, this antenna would be blocked thus, preventing reception. The fix? Give each user a cover that will enable the reception no matter where the phone is held. This is haste to market. Almost every example of haste to market vice speed to market results in a reverse logistics operation and after-sales service support. Speed to market vice haste to market results in fewer, if any, revisions to a product.

THE STEPS OF PRODUCT DESIGN

Although most textbooks will lead you to believe that product design is a sequential and lockstep; for an effective product design, the following steps must be conducted as close to concurrently as possible.

Traditional product design has all of these steps working in sequence. Concurrent product design breaks down the barriers between departments (similar to one of Deming's 14 points) and works with cross-functional teams to help speed the product to production and to the market. We will discuss this in greater detail later in this chapter.

- **Idea Generation**—Where do the ideas for products or services come from? What role does the voice of the customer play? Can you create your own market?
- **A Feasibility Study**—Can we make this product with the specifications that the customers want?
- **Prototyping and Testing**—Building the initial prototype of the product and testing (and maybe revising and retesting).
- **Finalizing the Design and Planning for the Production Process**—Will the process be a make to order, make to stock, assemble to order, assemble to stock, or a project. Will the product be mass produced, mass customized, or one at a time?

Let us look at each of these parts of the product design individually. Although we will look at the steps individually, they are interrelated and need to be not only synchronized, but must be conducted as close to concurrently as possible.

Idea Generation. Ideas can come from almost anywhere. Your suppliers should be able to assist in getting ideas for improvements to the current product or new products based on the availability of different materials. Another source of ideas should be your sales force. These are the people that should have the ear of the customer. Therefore, the sales force should be the best source of what the customer wants, which should then drive the generation of ideas for new or improved products.

One source of ideas for products may be trade shows. There is no shortage of trade shows in the operations management chain; everything from new product shows to emerging product shows to experimental trade shows. These shows allow company representatives to see what other companies are doing and can gauge the interest in the products from the number of people at each of the booths at the shows. Unfortunately, my experience of watching people at trade shows is that too many attendees are more interested in what is being given away for free rather than trying to find out what the emerging trends or products are.

As we will see when we discuss reverse logistics, every company should be mining data and information from the returns process. This information should include why the product is coming back. Also included in this information are customer thoughts about the product and customer complaints. Another source of new product or improved product information from returns comes from warranty work. What is lacking in the current product and how can we improve the product or come out with a new product to solve these problems?

Field tests and trial users provide companies with not necessarily the ideas for new products, but provide feedback on which products the customers prefer thus, giving the company an idea on which products to move forward with. Golf companies use this technique frequently. Several golf equipment companies allow golfers to "join" the companies' testing panels. The companies then randomly select from this pool of testers to send them new and trial equipment for testing. Thus far, in over 9 years of being on the testing panel, I have had the opportunity to "test" a golf glove. And I was allowed to keep the glove even though I "did not like it." I did not like it because they sent me a "Men's Large." There were enough fingers in the gloves to make another glove as my normal golf glove is a Men's Small. My friend had the opportunity to test a new Driver. This club was very nice. My friend could really hit the ball with this new club—it still sliced badly, but with this club, he could slice it farther.

McDonalds' use field testing to determine the acceptability of new products. For example, they tested the McRib sandwich in the Midwest. Why? Barbecue is a big deal in the Midwest. Ribs are very popular in the Midwest. Therefore, if the McRib could not sell in the Midwest, there was no reason to try to sell it elsewhere. They did the same for the breakfast burrito. This was tested in the Southwest with the theory that if a breakfast burrito cannot sell in the Southwest, then it will not sell in the Northeast either.

McDonalds' have tested other products and promotions worldwide, but although they have done well in other places outside the Mainland United States, they are not staples in the Mainland. In Germany, you can buy a Big Mac and a beer. In Hawaii, you can buy eggs, spam, and rice for breakfast. Although this sells well in Hawaii, it has not made its way to the Mainland United States yet.

It used to be a common practice to place field testers of different products in the package with the Sunday newspaper. These products included cereals, soaps, dishwashing detergent, and washing powders. The goal of these testers was to get customer feedback on the product by enticing the customer to buy more of the product and capture that data from the use of the attached coupon.

The most common method of generating ideas for new products and services comes from the Research and Development departments of the larger corporations. The problem with R&D is that when the economy goes south as we saw in the 2008 to 2010 recession, companies have a tendency to cut R&D expenses to save money and improve the immediate bottom line.

Reverse engineering is one method of getting ideas for products or ideas of how to make a product better and less expensive than the competition. Japan is noted for this. In the 1960s and early 1970s, "Made in Japan" meant that the product was junk. Then, after a couple of decades of taking US-made products apart and reverse engineering the products, the stamp "Made in Japan" become synonymous with high quality. China is doing the same thing now.[1]

Benchmarking may be beneficial as a means to generate ideas for improving products or processes. Benchmarking is not commercial tourism. There has to be a goal of the benchmarking process. Benchmarking starts with the corporate admission that the company may not be the best at what they are doing and start the search for the "best in class" companies. If you are benchmarking products, you have to go to a competitor to benchmark against. However, if you are benchmarking a service, you may be able to go outside your industry to benchmark.

Southwest is a good example of going outside their industry to benchmark services. Southwest has learned that to be successful in the airline industry, it is imperative to have people in the seats and the planes in the air. Planes sitting on the ground can cost an airline several thousand dollars an hour. So, Southwest went to NASCAR to observe pit crews. Their rationale was that (at the time) if a Winston Cup team could change four tires, make a track bar adjustment, add a round of wedge to the springs, and add 22.4 gallons of fuel in 13.9 seconds, just maybe they had some ideas that could be translated to turning planes around quicker. If the planes could be turned around quicker, more people could be flying and more dollars could be made. They also went to Formula 1 Racing to observe their refueling operations as Formula 1 and Southwest used the same fuel nozzle for refueling operations. This is a good example of thinking outside the box for benchmarking.

---

[1]For more on this practice and the adaptations made by Chinese companies, read *Dragons at Your Door* by Ming Zeng and Peter J. Williamson, Harvard Business School Press, 2007.

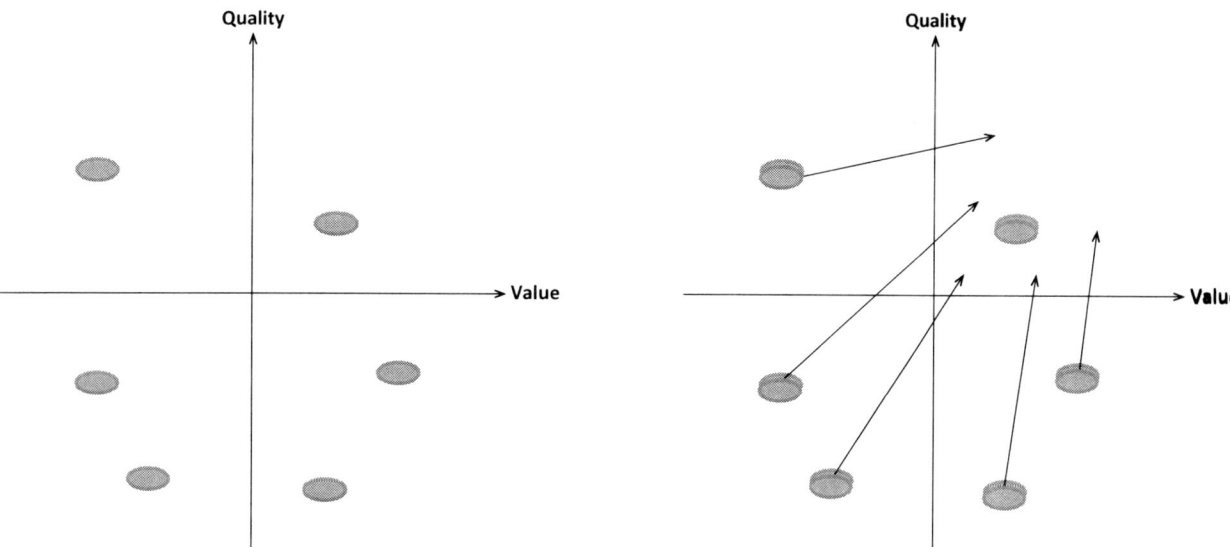

Figure 7.2a: Example of a Perception Map

Figure 7.2b: Shaping the Perceptions of Potential Customers

Figure 7.3: Options for Cheerios

Photograph by Joe Walden

One final technique for determining customer desires and wants is through a perception map. Customer perceptions can be placed on an "X,Y" axis chart. The goal of the perception is to get the product into the upper right-hand quadrant, so that it is perceived by the customer as beneficial to them and a value for the price. Look at Figures 7.2a and 7.2b. During the product development process, a strategy must be developed to shape the perceptions of the potential customers so as to move the perception to the upper right-hand quadrant so that the customers perceive the product to be of high quality and high value. A perception map to get the customers' perceptions of breakfast cereals could be responsible for the plethora of cereal options. The more options available, the better the probability that the perceptions of the customers will be positive and in the upper right-hand quadrant. Cheerios used to have one flavor of cereal; as Figure 7.3 shows, Cheerios now has multiple options for their breakfast cereal influenced by perceptions and the need to design different products.

Feasibility Study. What is a feasibility study and why do we need one here? The *World English Dictionary* defines a feasibility study as, "a study designed to determine the practicality of a system or plan."[2] So, the reason

---

[2]feasibility study. (n.d.). *Collins English Dictionary - Complete & Unabridged 10th Edition.* Retrieved August 01, 2010, from Dictionary.com website: http://dictionary.reference.com/browse/feasibility study

a feasibility study is needed at this point in the product development cycle is to determine the practicality of producing this product. In order to do an effective feasibility study for our product, we may need to **segment our market** to determine the feasibility of producing the product for different segments of the market. General Motors used to be very good at segmenting their markets. They had Chevrolet, the "working man's car"; Pontiac, which is gone now; Oldsmobile which has been gone for a while now; Buick; and Cadillac, a winner of the Malcolm Baldrige National Quality Award, considered the top of the line car.

Part of the feasibility study has to consider the **economic analysis** of the product. In other words, can we make this product or provide this service and make a profit? If not, we cannot stay in business. This does not mean that occasionally the company will not offer a loss leader to entice customers into the store, but we cannot design a product that will lose money out of the gate. Although when I watch the management of some of the local professional sports organizations that are in business to make money, I wonder whether they will offer a product to the customers that can make a profit or whether the owners bypassed the feasibility study and economic analysis.

While conducting the economic analysis, one of the questions that must be asked is can we produce this product and sell sufficient quantities of this product to make a profit? If so, how do we find point (we have to cover all of our fixed costs and variable costs)? This is the breakeven point. Equation 7.1 is the breakeven point calculation. The goal is to cover all of the expenses for this product (see Equation 7.2)—this is another way of looking at the breakeven point.

Equation 7.1: Break Even Point Calculation

$$\text{Break-Even Point} = \frac{\text{Fixed Costs}}{\text{Sales Price} - \text{Variable Costs}}$$

Fixed Costs = Sunk Costs (incurred even if nothing is made)
Sales Price = At what price can this product be sold?
Variable Costs = labor, electricity, materials, operating costs

Equations 7.2: Another Look at the Breakeven Point Analysis

$$\text{Total Costs} = \text{Total Revenues}$$

Example 7.1 Breakeven Analysis

A company wants to design and build a new surf board. The fixed costs (FC) for the company are $50,000; the variable costs (VC) for this product (materials, labor, and overhead) are $100 per surf board; the projected sales price ($S) is estimated to be $600 each.

$$\text{Break Even Point} = FC/(\$S - VC)$$
$$\frac{\$50,000}{\$600/\text{board} - \$100/\text{board}}$$
$$= 100 \text{ boards}$$

Example 7.2 Total Revenues Analysis

Using the above data, we can do a revenue analysis for breakeven analysis using Equation 7.2:

$$\text{Total Costs} = FC + VC(x)$$

$$\text{Total Revenues} = \text{Sales Price}(x)$$

$$\text{Equation 7.2: } \$50,000 + \$100(x) = \$600(x)$$

$$\$50,000 = \$500(x)$$

$$100 = (x)$$

The next part of a good feasibility study is to determine whether the company has the **technical skills** available to make the product. Although the company may have the capability to produce the prototype, this part of the feasibility study will determine whether the company can produce more than just the prototype or may determine if the company may be capable of designing a product and they did not have the capability of producing even the prototype. Part of this process has to be to determine whether the company can produce the product with the technical specifications of the design.

Part of the breakeven analysis has to include what to do if the company cannot make the required quantity to breakeven. Most texts will tell you that at that point, it is simple—do not make the product. However, in reality, the analysis should include looking at the fixed and variable costs—is it possible to reduce those through leasing vice buying or by buying used equipment rather than new. Can the sales price be altered a little? Can someone else make the product with the same quality we expect, but less expensive? Once all of these options are exhausted, then the company may opt to not make the product at all.

Risk Analysis. The last part of the feasibility study has to be a risk analysis of the product. In other words, can the company produce a safe product? What is risk analysis and why should you conduct a risk analysis and how should the analysis be conducted? The risk analysis has to consider how the product may be used and not just the intended usage. A good risk analysis has to look at the probability of something going wrong with the product and if it does, what are the severities of the impacts? Part of the product development risk analysis has to include identifying all of the possible hazards. If a hazard is discovered, waiting for the problem to hit the front pages of *USA Today* or on CNN's Headline News is not a good idea. If a problem is identified during the testing and development, it has to be addressed before the product is introduced to the public. In the 1970s, Ford developed the Pinto. The Pinto apparently had a problem with the location of the gas tank at the rear of the car, which would burst into flames when experiencing a rear-end collision. The problem was known, but not fixed before the Pinto (see Figure 7.4) was introduced—the result was deaths and lawsuits and the removal of the Pinto from the Ford Fleet.

The steps for a risk analysis should follow this outline as provided by the US Army.

- **Identify the Hazards**—What are the potential hazards for this product? This analysis has to consider not only if the product is used as intended, but must also consider the potential hazards, if the product is not used as intended. For example, while designing a toy for small children, the designer must consider if children will put the product in their mouths and the associated hazards such as choking.
- **Assess the hazards to determine potential risks**—After identifying the hazards, it is important to determine the probability of the hazard occurring and the impact if the hazard does occur.
- **Develop controls and make risk decisions**—What controls need to be put in place to help mitigate, minimize, or even eliminate the hazard. One option to eliminate the potential hazard may be to decide not to produce the product. If the decision is made to produce the product and the hazard cannot be eliminated, the lawyers will have to be part of the control process to write the small print to accompany the product inserts.

Photograph by Joe Walden

Figure 7.4: The Ford Pinto

- **Implement controls**—Once the risk decisions have been made, controls must be put in place to ensure that the hazards are minimized or eliminated throughout the design and testing as well as during the manufacture process.
- **Supervise and evaluate**—This step makes the risk assessment similar to a continuous process improvement program. The goal of this phase of the risk assessment process is to make sure the decisions and controls are actually working. This is analogous to "we only do well what the boss checks." This step of the risk analysis process is the quality control check. Theoretically, all of the risk assessment steps will be completed before the preliminary design is finalized.

Prototype Design Process. Concurrent to the risk analysis and feasibility study is the design of the product. We have already established that part of the design process has to determine how the product will look. Now, we need to build the prototype. Once the prototype is completed, it is time to start the testing process. This process may identify some hazards in operations that were not considered or identified during the risk assessment.

The testing of the prototype and having the problems or hazards identified may lead to revisions to the design or scrapping the project all together. Sometimes, as requirements change or problems are identified, the prototype has to be redesigned and then retested. Sometimes, the product gets stuck in a testing do-loop.

Here is an example of the testing do-loop and changing requirements. In the late 1980s, the US Army was developing, testing, and ready to produce a new variable reach forklift. This military forklift was similar to the blue forklifts shown in Figure 7.5. The forklift passed through the prototype development based on the requirements submitted by the potential users. This forklift was ready for manufacture and issued to the units in the field. This was going to be the Rolls-Royce of forklifts. It was hardened against chemical attacks, nuclear attacks, and it had an enclosed cab with air conditioning and heat.

Then, Saddam Hussein invaded Kuwait in August 1990. This act started what became the Operations Desert Shield and Desert Storm. After the buildup, the short war, and the redeployment process were complete, the Army decided what they really needed was a variable reach forklift that was capable of being shipped in a standard 8×8×20-ft container. This would allow the forklift to be shipped in a container with the other containers and then be ready to roll out and unstuff the other containers. This required the designers to go back to the prototype design, make some alterations, and retest the redesigned prototype.

When I returned to the R&D operations for supply chain equipment in 1997, the same folks that were working on this forklift were finally ready to move the item from the testing stage to actual operations in the field for the Army. Some department of the Army Civilians invested a large part of their careers moving this forklift through the design, prototype, testing, redesign, retesting, redesigning, and final approval of the forklift.

Reliability, Availability, Maintainability. The first time I was in the R&D operations for the US Army, the focus on designing equipment was on the reliability and maintainability of the equipment and not on

Figure 7.5: Example of Variable Reach Forklifts in Action in Kuwait, April 2003

the availability. In retrospect, this was interesting since we had a team of RAM (reliability, availability, and maintainability) engineers that were supposed to analyze every product that we designed.

Reliability is usually expressed as a probability that the product will actually perform the stated time length as well as the designed and intended function during that time period. This is important to the design of the product and the claims the company will make about the product. Reliability also measures the mean time between failures (MTBF)—the average time between breakdowns or failures in the system.

Computing the reliability of a system is much like the computation some of us are familiar with from high school physics. Capacitors in parallel provide a reliability that is actually less than any of the capacitors individually. The reliability of each capacitor is multiplied by each of the other capacitors. For example, if three capacitors are in parallel with reliabilities of .95, .94, and .90, respectively, it would result in a reliability of 0.8037. This is similar to the old Christmas tree lights. If one bulb went out, the entire string would not light up and every bulb had to be tested to find the bad bulb.

Conversely, if capacitors are placed in parallel, the actual reliability is greater than the capacitors individually. This is similar to the newer Christmas light strings that bypass the burned out bulb with built-in redundancy and finding the bad bulb becomes very easy. Part of the design process is to consider whether the added expense of built-in redundancy will make the product more reliable.

Example 7.3

If two capacitors are placed in parallel with reliabilities of .95 and .92, respectively, they will have a reliability of the first capacitor plus 1-the reliability of the first capacitor multiplied by the reliability of the second capacitor (.95 + (.92(1−.95)). In this example, the reliability of the two capacitors will be: .95 + .92(.05) =.95 + .046 =.996. This increase in reliability is the result of built-in redundancy; if the first capacitor fails, the second one will kick in.

Maintainability tells the company and the customer how easy it is to maintain a product or a piece of equipment. The maintainability of the product may include how much it will cost the customer to fix the product or how much it will cost the company to repair the product, while it is still under warranty. The metric of maintainability is the mean time to repair (MTTR)—the average time to fix the product if it breaks or fails.

Availability is a combination of the reliability and maintainability. Availability describes the total time the product is available to the user. In the 1980s, the Chevy Monza 2 + 2 was reliable, as the MTBF was lengthy, which is a good aspect, but to change the spark plugs required pulling the engine to reach the plugs. This made the MTTR rather lengthy. The metric for availability is systems availability. Formula 7.3 shows the calculation for systems availability.

Formula 7.3: Systems Availability Calculation

$$\text{Systems Availability} = \frac{\text{Mean Time Between Failure (MTBF)}}{\text{MTBF} + \text{Mean Time To Repair}}$$

Example 7.4

A product sampling shows that the MTBF for the prototype A is 200 hours. During the testing, this product experienced several failures that resulted in an MTTR of 25 hours. The prototype B experienced an MTBF of 275 hours and the failures of prototype B resulted in an MTTR of 50 hours.

Based on the MTBF alone, the testing would have led the decision makers to choose prototype B. However, using the systems availability equation would lead the decision makers to choose prototype A.

Calculations: Prototype A: Systems Availability = 200/(200 + 25) = .89

Prototype B: Systems Availability = 275/(275 + 50) = .85

That product design may very well be the order winner, which provides the competitive advantage. Here is an example of an order winner in the design phase—Figure 7.6 is an example of order-winning advantage and taking the customer into account in the design process. The label of the bottle of wine in Figure 7.6 is printed not only in normal print, but also has the label printed in Braille.

Photograph by Joe Walden

Figure 7.6: Braille Label

While the product design is ongoing, the process design must be ongoing as well. These are related events. If the two are not conducted concurrently, the company may find that they have a great product and a good prototype, but do not possess the ability to produce more than one of the items.

Process Design—How the Product Will Be Made and Product Design. The goal of the process design phase is to design a process of manufacturing the product that is as simple and cost effective as possible. This may mean making the process from raw material to finished product or assembling the product from subassemblies or from modules. As the product is designed and the product design reaches the desired end state, detailed drawings or blueprints should be developed.

From these blueprints, a logical production design can be developed that may drive the facility design we will discuss in Chapter 10. The product design and the blueprints will help develop the requirements for the tools and equipment needed to make the product. At the same time, the product design and blueprints will also help determine the sequence of events or activities in the manufacturing process.

Traditional Product Design and Concurrent Product Design. Traditional product design is a lock-step process that moves from idea generation to engineering to manufacturing to marketing to supply chain and to production. This could be a lengthy process that could be sent back to the previous step for any reason thus, making the process longer.

Concurrent product design is a rather recent concept that has the goal of getting a quality product to the customers faster. Concurrent product design puts all of the players at the table together. When creating the concurrent design team, it is important to have representatives from all of the stake holders' departments. By placing the right people on the team concurrently, the barriers between departments are broken down and the "do-loops" that hinder product development are short circuited.

A good concurrent design team will have the engineers, the R&D folks, the manufacturing and marketing departments, and the supply chain elements on the team. Accountants need to be on the team to conduct the breakeven analysis and because of the nature of today's society, the concurrent design team also needs to have lawyers on the team to help draft the small print about the possible side effects or potential hazards from misuse. Some of the identified side effects of drugs advertised on television appear to create severe problems than the original problem itself. It is also a good idea to improve the design of the product to get the suppliers and potential customers involved in the process.

DESIGN FOR SIX SIGMA (ALSO KNOWN AS DESIGN FOR MANUFACTURE)

Design for Six Sigma is different from the traditional Six Sigma DMAIC steps. The goal of the design activity is to design a quality product. The goal of an individual design process is the eventual product that the team is designing. In order to design the right product, it is important to know what the customer wants (very similar

```
┌─────────────────────────────────────────┐
│          Design For Six Sigma             │
│  • Define—the goals of the design activity│
│  • Measure—customer input to determine    │
│    what is critical to quality from the   │
│    customers' perspective—what are        │
│    customer delighters? What aspects      │
│    are critical to quality?               │
│  • Analyze—innovative concepts for        │
│    products and services to create value  │
│    for the customer                       │
│  • Design—new processes, products, and    │
│    services to deliver customer value     │
│  • Verify—new systems perform as expected │
└─────────────────────────────────────────┘
```

Figure 7.7: Design for Six Sigma

to the first step of Six Sigma—define the customer, define what the customer wants) and how the customer defines quality.

As shown in Figure 7.7, designing for Six Sigma or designing for manufacture includes trying to minimize the number of parts included in the manufacturing process. This may be accomplished by assembling the product from modules or subassemblies, designing the product for easier assembly, and designing the manufacturing process to minimize material handling.

VALUE ANALYSIS

Before selling the product on the open market, the company should conduct a value analysis. The goal of this analysis should be to determine if the product is perceived as a value for the price according to the customers. In assessing the value, the company needs to determine the following:

- Is there something within the product that the customer can do without? Today's computers are good examples of this. The average computer user today uses the computer for word processing, graphics, spreadsheets, and communications. There is much more that most computers can do that are not used by the average user. For the most part, today's average computer user employs his/her computer for the same purposes that my Tandy 1000 did almost 25 years ago. My Tandy 1000 had a desktop software package that had word processing and spreadsheets. This was supplemented by Lotus 1-2-3 and Harvard Graphics. Both of these programs fit on one 3.5-inch floppy disk. After Al Gore invented the Internet, the addition of a 300-baud modem allowed me to access the Internet. And yet, every year, a large number of users buy new computers because of the advertising for the new bells and whistles that they may never use.
- The value analysis should identify if the product is perceived as not worth the price—this may drive a different conclusion to the breakeven analysis calculations.
- Is there a less expensive material or component that could be used in the manufacture of the product that will increase the value or reduce the cost of producing the product?
- Can someone else make the product cheaper or better or faster? We will discuss the options for this in Chapter 8 when we discuss the make or buy decision process.
- The analysis should identify if there is another product that does the same function that is already on the market. If so, the design process needs to consider how to make this product with more value additions or more reliable and durable.

DESIGNING FOR THE ENVIRONMENT—NEW TREND, NEW FAD, OR NEW NAME FOR OLD PROCESS?

Designing products for the environment is nothing new. In 1970, Clemson University was trying to design a Coke bottle that would disintegrate on the side of the road after being thrown out of a vehicle. This was before littering fines became enforceable. The problem was that they could not keep the bottle from disintegrating on the shelf—not a good thing for grocery stores.

The latest fad—okay, hopefully not a fad, but a long-lasting trend, in manufacturing is to design and build products that are environmentally friendly. This is a good thing because we only have one planet to leave behind for the future generations. Designing the product that can be made from recycled or recyclable materials is an example of designing for the environment. Designing the process to make the product to use less energy is an example of designing for the environment. Or designing the packaging for the product to use fewer materials is also designing for the environment.

The Green Laws in Europe are designed to force companies into considering the environment in the design and manufacturing processes. The Europeans have been more environmental-conscious than the Americans for decades. While stationed in Europe in the mid-1990s, it was clear that there was concern for the environment just from the amount of items that were part of the mandatory recycling program—some of which are not recycled in the United States even today.

Here are some examples of environmental design issues. Hewlett Packard and Xerox have determined that it is cheaper to pay for customers to return printer cartridges than it is to make new cartridges. On the flip side of this view is the disposal of carpets. Every year, there are approximately four million pounds of carpets (all manmade products and recyclable) that are dumped into landfills.

SUMMARY

The goal of the design process is to provide a quality product that meets the needs of the customers in a cost-effective and efficient manner. While designing the product, it is important to consider the RAM of the product and to design a product that will meet the necessary specifications, while ensuring that the product does not fail due to poor product design.

It is the responsibility of the company to assess the needs of the customers and then determine whether the company can profitably make the product and at what point will the company start to make a profit from the product.

While designing the product, it is imperative to consider how the product will be made or assembled and how the product and the production process will impact the environment. A concurrent design team should get the quality product to the market quicker with fewer, if any, necessary revisions to the product.

Discussion Questions

1. Why is designing for the environment becoming more important? Is this a recent occurrence? Provide examples of designing for the environment.

2. If a product has FC of $1,000,000 with VC of $200 per item with a sales price of $1,500; what is the breakeven point? Why is this important?

3. Using the data from above, what are the total costs at the breakeven point?

4. What are the goals of the product design process?

5. Should the product and production plan be developed consecutively or concurrently?

6. What is the difference between traditional and concurrent product design?

7. What is Design for Six Sigma and how does it differ from the Six Sigma process discussed in Chapter 4 (Quality)?

8. Can the design process provide the company with a competitive advantage?

9. What is the difference between availability and maintainability?

10. What is meant by the term mean time between failure?

11. What is meant by the term MTTR?

12. If Product A has an MTBF of 175 hours and an MTTR of 25 hours; Product B has an MTBF of 250 hours and an MTTR of 60 hours; and Product C has an MTBF of 150 hours with an MTTR of 20 hours, what is the systems availability of the products and which one should the company select for production?

8 Production/Process Design

The process design strategy sets the corporate strategy for the production of the products that were designed in the product design process. Part of the process design may include how vertically integrated a company wants to be. Vertical integration is defined as: "When a company expands its business into areas that are at different points of the same production path."[1] In the 1980s, Anheuser Busch tried to become completely vertically integrated and own the entire supply chain and operations management chain. They moved into the bottle- and glass-making business, can- and aluminum-making business in addition to the beer-making business as was discussed in Chapter 2; once they realized that their core competency was making beer, they divested themselves of the other aspects of the operations management chain.

The production or process design is critical to the future of the company and the profitability of the company. The product of this design phase may very well determine the future capital investments in equipment and facilities. How the product is to be produced may dictate the flexibility to produce other products.

Per our previous discussions on strategy and processes, the production process can take the form of mass production, continuous production, assemble to order, make to order, batch processing, or projects (one at a time production such as dams, planes, or bridges).

PLANNING THE PROCESS AND DESIGN

One of the products of the product design process is the **blueprints.** The product design should produce detailed drawings of the proposed products. These blueprints will allow the design team to properly design the process to produce the product and should provide the producer an idea of the skills needed to make the product.

From the blueprints, the design team can determine all of the components of the product. This list of components is known as the **Bill of Material (BOM).** The BOM is much like the ingredients listing on a recipe card for baking a cake. They both serve the same purpose. Bills of Material can be flat BOMs, which only list the primary parts or assemblies. A multiple layer or indented BOM shows the components of the assemblies and may be detailed down to the screws and washer level. According to the APICS Body of Knowledge, a Bill of Material is defined as: "The BOM is the document that specifies the components needed to produce a good or service. It lists the parts, raw materials, subassemblies, and intermediates required by a parent assembly. A BOM specifies the quantity required to make one item, specifies units of measure, and quantifies phase-in and phase-out dating."[2]

The next piece of planning data that comes from the product design process will be the **assembly chart** also known as a product structure diagram. The assembly chart is like the diagram in the shelves that my daughter and I put together recently. Inside the box was the BOM (a listing of all the parts in the box), the assembly chart that provided a graphic of what the shelves should look like as they were assembled, an **operations process**

---

[1]vertical integration. (n.d.). *Investopedia.com.* Retrieved August 03, 2010, from Dictionary.com website: http://dictionary.reference.com/browse/vertical integration

[2]*APICS Operations Management Body of Knowledge Framework*, 2nd edition, APICS The Association for Operations Management, 8430 West Bryn Mawr Avenue, Suite 1000, Chicago, IL, p. 51. For more on the Operations Management Body of Knowledge or APICS—The Association for Operations Management go to http://www.apics.org

chart that listed each of the steps in the shelves assembly, and a **routing sheet**. The routing sheet showed the proper sequence of events to assemble the book shelves from the ingredients listed in the BOMs.

Using the original analogy of baking a cake, a good recipe card not only lists the BOMs to make the cake, the recipe card has a picture of the finished product, the assembly chart or steps in the baking of the cake, and the routing sheet that shows the proper sequence of what to do to assemble and then bake the cake. Just as these diagrams and listings are important in baking a cake, they are just as important in manufacturing or assembling a product.

MAKE OR BUY DECISIONS

An analysis of the product design may lead the company to decide to not make the product themselves. Designing the product may be a core competency, but actually making the product may not be a core competency. Before looking at why the company should not consider outsourcing, it is important to understand that in some situations it is not feasible to outsource. For example, if there is a barrier to making a make or buy decision such as "Buy American" or "Buy European." In some businesses, there may be "classified" or proprietary information such as the "Colonel's 11 herbs and spices" in Kentucky Fried Chicken that precludes outsourcing.

Let us take a look at some of the criteria that may lead a company to decide to outsource their manufacturing to a third party provider.

Cost. Can someone else make the product cheaper with the same quality? It may be beneficial to outsource the manufacturing of the product. One company that provided portable equipment batteries discovered that another company could not only make their batteries cheaper than the parent company could, but could also make the batteries with the same quality. A little more research proved that the outsource company could also apply the company's labels to the batteries before shipping. The battery company was able to transform the manufacturing plant to a larger warehouse, create a workout room for employees, and establish a day-care facility within the original plant location for the employees.

Capacity. If a company does not have the capacity to make the projected demand of the product, it may be an effective strategy to outsource the manufacture of the product. We will look at capacity decisions in greater detail in a later chapter. This may be a temporary decision for short-term spikes in demand or could very well be a long-term outsourcing decision based on forecasted increases in demand that exceed the capacity of the company.

Quality. Can another company make the company's product better than the designing company? If another company can make the product and make it better, why not outsource? However, if the quality improvement creates a price that prohibits the value proposition, then obviously it is not wise to outsource.

Speed. Can someone else make the product faster? The second part of this question is—can they make it better or cheaper than the designing company? If the cost is not increased, if the quality is the same, and the product can be produced faster and delivered to the customer faster, then it is logical to outsource the manufacture of the product.

Expertise. Does the company that can make the product faster or cheaper actually have the expertise to make the product? In the late 1980s, the US Army in conjunction with a major company developed a "Flameless Ration Heater" for the Meals, Ready to Eat (MREs). This one product actually made the MREs edible. The manufacture of this product was given to a small business set aside (a contract specifically set aside for a small, disadvantaged business). Then, Operation Desert Shield kicked off and the requirement for this product skyrocketed. The small, disadvantaged business that was originally given the contract did not have the expertise or the capacity to make the required amount of product and the contract was given to the company that helped develop the product.

Barriers to Make or Buy. In some instances and in some industries, the decision to make or buy is blocked by legal or other means that prevents a company from outsourcing its products or components. For example, the Department of Defense contractors may not outsource their product components or parts to certain countries that are on the "do not buy from" list. Another example of not being able to make this decision is if the company has proprietary data or proprietary components that they do not want to lose control over.

EQUIPMENT SELECTION/PROCESS SELECTION

Part of the production and process design is the selection of equipment. This is another reason that the process and product designs need to run concurrently. If the product design identifies new or specialized equipment that must be ordered, it is imperative to get the equipment ordered as soon as possible. You never know when there will be a long lead time for the equipment.

When I was a young officer at Fort Gordon, Georgia, the installation decided to outsource the maintenance of all facilities as a test for outsourcing commercial operations. Seems the mechanic who was responsible for maintaining the air conditioning systems for the block that I was working on was not offered a job by the incoming contractor. It also seems that this individual knew that the air conditioning system for the block was not functional when he was let go in February. As he was not offered a job, he did not think it was his job to worry about something that would not be needed until long after he was gone. So, when the thermometer topped 95° and 95% humidity (as is common in Georgia in the summertime), it was discovered that this block of buildings that were built with windows that did not open because the "modern" HVAC system had no air conditioning. The real kicker was the lead time for the part was over 4 months since it was only made in Sweden. Although a little different, that same principle is important when buying new equipment.

When considering the purchase of new equipment, there is always some risk and uncertainty. The first consideration always seems to be the purchase cost of the equipment. Because of this, some companies choose to piecemeal their purchases. This is similar to the old Johnny Cash song, "One piece at a time." In the Johnny Cash song, he worked at the Cadillac factory and took home one piece at a time. The problem came when they tried to put the car together after about twenty years. All of the pieces did not fit. The same thing happens when ordering equipment one piece at a time vice ordering all of the equipment at one time—by the time the last piece of equipment is purchased, it may not be compatible with the earlier purchased equipment.

Another consideration that may lead to a make or buy decision point may be the operating costs for the equipment. This may also play into a decision point if the operating cost in energy costs does not sync with the company's goals of being green.

If a decision is made to buy new equipment, there may be some annual savings realized by using more modern equipment. There may also be some government revenue breaks or tax rebates for using more environmentally friendly and modern equipment.

PROCESS ANALYSIS

The goal of process analysis is to analyze the processes to determine if there is waste or no value addition in the process. The usual tools for this are process maps, flowcharts, and process charts. This is done with the understanding that every process adds cost, but not every process adds value. And as we stated in Chapter 1 that one of the goals of operations management is to add or create value, it is important to know which processes are adding value and which ones are simply adding cost. If a process does not add value to (a) the customer experience; (b) the quality of the product; or (c) the bottom line profits, why do it?

According to the APICS Operations Body of Knowledge, process mapping is: "a visual form for documenting the details of a process. Depending on the map's objective, the level of detail will vary. Process maps can take many forms, including flowcharts; relationship maps; cross-functional maps; and supplier, input, process, output, customer (SIPOC) diagrams."[3] A simple process map is shown in Figure 8.1. A process map serves several purposes, the first of which is applicable to this discussion—providing a visual picture of the process. The second important function of a process map is to use it as a teaching tool for new employees on the processes of the company. Here is a simple example of a process map for receiving operations.

---

[3]*APICS Operations Management Body of Knowledge Framework*, 2nd edition, 2009, APICS The Association for Operations Management, 8430 West Bryn Mawr Avenue, Suite 1000, Chicago, IL, p. 33.

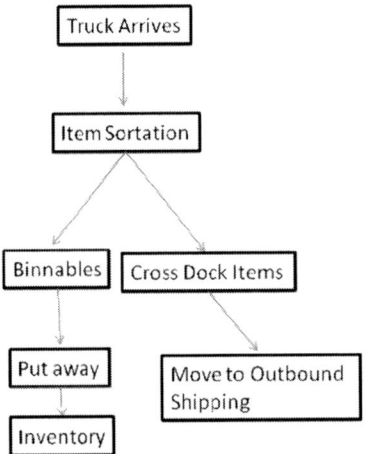

Figure 8.1: Sample Process Map

The goal of the process redesign operations is to get the waste out of the process. At the same time, as the waste is identified and eliminated, thus streamlining the process, the process map links the processes to value creation. Once a process map is developed, the next step is to start capturing data and placing dates and time stamps on the process map. This will further enhance the ability to use the process map to improve efficiency and benchmark the processes against industry standards and company past performance to determine whether the changes are actually improvements. Remember not every change is an improvement. The goal of the process mapping is to identify improvements you can believe in and not simply change.

Another, less costly method of improving the process is to personalize the process. Here is an example of personalizing the process. This is a process called "naming the aisle." Naming the aisle is a simple process to talk about and relatively easy to implement. In a distribution center, each aisle has a location placard at the end of the aisle. By placing the team names that are responsible for the maintenance of the aisle or the team leader's name on the aisle and then putting the metrics such as picking accuracy, inventory accuracy, and orders picked per hour on the end of the aisle adds pride to the workers. This also adds a little internal competition to see which aisle is better. The combination of pride and competition improves the overall operations of the process.

Another method of improving the process is through the use of Six Sigma. The goal of Six Sigma is to reduce variability in the process. If the variability is reduced, the process should be improved. Motorola introduced the world to the Six Sigma concept in the early 1980s with the steps of:

Define
Measure
Analyze
Improve
Control

This methodology became known as the DMAIC method. Although Motorola introduced Six Sigma, General Electric received more attention with their use of Six Sigma. Even with the publicity that GE received for its use of Six Sigma, it was not until Jack Welch tied the implementation of Six Sigma to the bonuses of the executives that Six Sigma became successful in both the manufacturing and services sector of the company.

The US Army introduced a similar program to improve its supply chain processes in 1995. This program was called Velocity Management. The methodology for Velocity Management was define, measure, and improve. The D-M-I methodology was basically "Six Sigma light." Like Six Sigma, this program sought to reduce the variability of the supply chain and, as a result, significantly improved the customer response by the supply chain systems.

Improving the process is also possible by simply varying the entry point of looking at the process. A different entry point provides a different perspective of the situation. The US Army conducted an After Action Review of the initial supply chain operations for Operation Iraqi Freedom approximately 1 year after the invasion started. The first point here is that the After Action Review should have been conducted closer to the event to get a good review of the processes to improve them.

Every senior leader that spoke at the After Action Review had a different perspective and from each perspective, they felt that what they did was good, but everyone else came up short in their performance. Amazingly, there was overlap in the areas of responsibility, so the different perspectives were parochial in nature and not true perspectives. So, when changing perspective, it is important to get a true perspective of your own and not a jaded perspective or parochial point of view.

When Lieutenant General Gus Pagonis left the US Army and became the Vice President of Supply Chain Operations for Sears, he made each of his employees spend time in a store or distribution center on a regular basis. The point of doing this was to make sure the employees could see from other perspectives the actions based on their decisions and allow them to modify policies based on their work experiences.

When I was in Kuwait, I regularly jumped on a forklift to unload trucks, move supplies, and load outbound trucks. By seeing things from the workers' perspective, I was able to understand the impacts of certain events on the operations, such as the rain impacts on a largely outdoor, unpaved facility and heat and dust-related impacts on operations. I also put on coveralls and crawled under vehicles at the US Army National Training Center in the Mojave Desert to see the impacts of policies on maintenance to better understand how to support my customers. Some policies look good at the corporate office, but do not translate well from the abstract to the concrete and result in vague or imprecise guidance at the worker level.

The recent hit television show, *Undercover Boss*, seeks to do the same thing—provide CEOs a different perspective of their operations. The result of the bosses going undercover to actually do some of the work at different locations seems to have provided great insights to improve operations. One of the ideas that may come out of changing perspectives and varying the point of entry into an operation may be a change in automated systems.

Before moving to a new automated system, it is imperative to evaluate the systems and the current operations. By evaluating and documenting all current activities, it may become apparent that some of the current processes may not be needed in an automated environment and are thus, nonvalue-added with the new systems. The analysis may point toward the use of an enterprise resource planning program or ERP.

ENTERPRISE RESOURCE PLANNING PROGRAMS

The main goal of an ERP system is to take all of the old stovepipe databases and information systems into one enterprise-wide information system. Once all of these systems have been consolidated, data mining is possible and the ability to hide information and data is eliminated within the company. This allows the company to have all employees working from the same data and forecasts. Figure 8.2 shows the feed of all other databases to the ERP system.

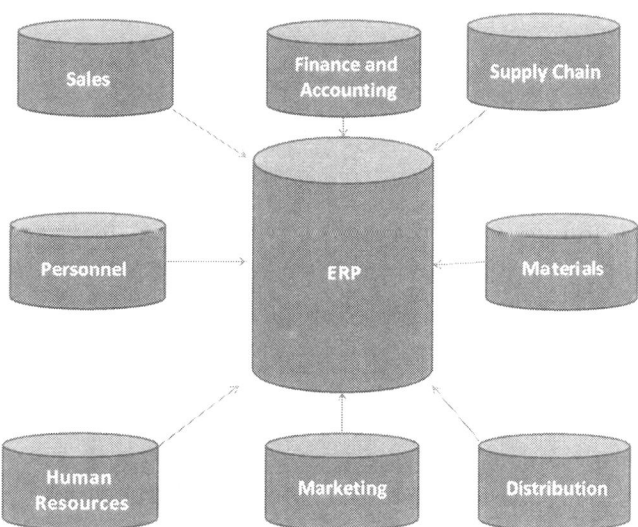

Figure 8.2: Example of an ERP Database

SAP (systems, applications, and programs) is the largest provider of ERP software with over 43% of the market as of 2006. Oracle is also a strong player in providing ERP systems. Oracle realized several years ago that they needed a good personnel and finance module for their ERP systems. Rather than develop a new set of software modules, Oracle purchased PeopleSoft and incorporated what was at the time the best available standalone module into their system.

The ERP is not always the end-all solution to systems and process improvements. Although it is getting better, for every good news story on the implementation of ERP systems, there is always a horror story or a company such as Dell that spent millions of dollars only to pull the plug and go back to the old system. In 1999, Hershey's implemented an ERP system. The result was missing the majority of their Halloween candy shipments due to a glitch in the software. This incident placed Hershey's on the Supply Chain Digest's list of the worst supply chain disasters of all time.

RADIO FREQUENCY IDENTIFICATION (RFID) TAGS

The RFID tags have been around for over 20 years. In the late 1980s, the US Army looked at using what was then being called MITLA chips or microprocessor technology with logistics applications to track the shipment of supplies and equipment worldwide. In 1994, the US Army started tracking the shipments of materials and supplies using the SAVI tags as shown in Figure 8.3.

The research into the use of this particular tag started after the completion of Operation Desert Storm (the First Gulf War). When this particular operation was complete, there was over 27,000 twenty-foot equivalent (TEU) containers on the dock at Dhahran, Saudi Arabia, with no clue what was in them or who they belonged to. The US Army wanted to reduce or eliminate this problem for future operations. With the RFID tag, the Army was able to track every shipment from origin until final destination.

This particular tag is an active tag. An active tag is always on and can be read from up to 300 ft with an interrogator. With the proper software, this particular tag can be fed into the ERP system and tracked worldwide, thus giving the company using the tags supply chain visibility. The downside of this tag is that it is relatively expensive. This is relative when compared with the cost of losing a shipment or a customer due to a lost or misrouted shipment.

The tags getting the most attention over the past thirteen years is the passive tag. Wal-Mart, with great fanfare, announced that as of January 1, 2005 every supplier would have to start using RFID tags down to the item level. The Department of Defense made a similar announcement at about the same time. Wal-Mart quietly backed off their demand to only include the top 100 suppliers to two distribution centers and, in 2009, announced that they would apply tags to shipments that suppliers did not tag and charge the companies for the tags. Actually, this worked out to the advantage of the companies. In 2013, Wal-Mart did not admit defeat with their initiative, but did announce that they would charge suppliers per pallet that was not tagged. The cost of this charge was much smaller than the cost for smaller suppliers to buy the tags and the infrastructure to write the tags.

Photograph by Joe Walden

Figure 8.3: SAVI RFID Tag on a Pallet in Kuwait

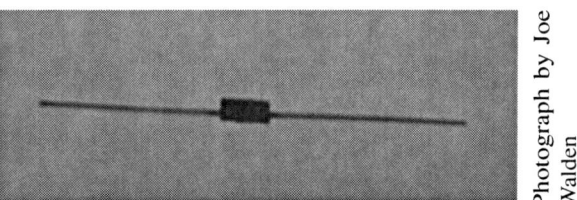

Photograph by Joe Walden

Figure 8.4: Michelin RFID Tag for Tires

In July 2010, Wal-Mart announced a program to place RFID tags in jeans and other clothes to "improve inventory accuracy." This same concept was attempted in 2006 by United Colors of Benetton with a great outcry of invasion of privacy by their customers in England. This outcry led to abandonment of the program.

The concerns about invasion of privacy is not a new concern with RFID tags although passive tags need to be activated by a reader and can only be read from about a foot away. California has considered several laws to let customers know if the product that they are buying has an RFID tag and, if so, give the customer the option of having it disabled. The concern is: if I can read the tag, who else can read it? Figure 8.4 is a picture of a tag developed by Michelin to track and inventory tires. Another use of this tag was to let customers know if there was a recall or if they needed to rotate their tires. Again, the concern is that if they can read the tags, who else can read it and can someone track my vehicle to see where I am going and where I have been.

COMPARING TWO PROCESSES

What if there are options for the production processes? There is a rather simple calculation for choosing the best process based on cost analysis. This calculation compares the two processes to determine which process will provide the lowest total costs based on the forecasted production levels. Equation 8.1 shows the calculation for the point of indifference. The point of indifference is that production point where the total costs for either process are equal.

Equation 8.1: Point of Indifference

$$\text{Point of indifference} = \text{the point where:}$$

$$\text{Fixed Costs}_A + \text{Variable Costs}_A\ (x) = \text{Fixed Costs}_B + \text{Variable Costs}_B\ (x)$$

Where x = demand quantity or forecasted production level

Example 8.1 Using Equation 8.1

Process A

Fixed Costs = $250,000
Variable Costs = $50/item

Process B

Fixed Costs = $350,000
Variable Costs = $35/item

Step 1: Set up the Equation 1 equations to set Process A and Process B equal to each other to solve for x (forecast production quantity and point of indifference)

$$\text{Fixed Costs}_A + \text{Variable Costs}_A(x) + \text{Fixed Costs}_B + \text{Variable Costs}_B\ (x)$$

$$\$250,000 + (\$50)(x) = \$350,000 + (\$35)(x)$$

$$(\$15)(x) = \$100,000$$

$$x = 6,666.6667 = 6,667$$

Items must be rounded up to a whole number as a partial product is not feasible or possible. Therefore, the point of indifference is at a production level of 4,000.

Step 2: Insert the point of indifference into the Equations to determine the best process: If the forecasted production level is 6,000, the lowest total costs are calculated:

Process A

$= \$250{,}000 + (\$50)(x)$

$= \$250{,}000 + (\$50)(6{,}000)$

$= \$550{,}000$

Process B

$= \$350{,}000 + (\$35)(x)$

$= \$350{,}000 + (\$35)(6{,}000)$

$= \$560{,}000$

Step 3: Select the process with the lowest total costs. In this example, the company should select Process A. Based on this calculation, if the forecasted production had been 7,000, Process B would be chosen.

Process A

$= \$250{,}000 + (\$50)(x)$

$= \$250{,}000 + (\$50)(7{,}000)$

$= \$600{,}000$

Process B

$= \$350{,}000 + (\$35)(x)$

$= \$350{,}000 + (\$35)(7{,}000)$

$= \$595{,}000$

SUMMARY

The selection of a process for production of the product designed in Chapter 7 may impact expansion decisions, investment expenses, or may very well drive the make or buy decision process.

The selection of processes and equipment for the production of a product must be conducted concurrently with the design of the product, if the goal of getting a quality product to the market as quickly as possible is to be met by the company.

Discussion Questions

1. Why is the process development process important to the operations management chain?
2. What is the goal of process design?
3. What is the importance of the point of indifference?
4. If a company has the option of choosing between two processes for the production of their product, calculate the point of indifference with the following data:
    Product A: Fixed Costs = $500,000; Variable Costs = $125 per item produced
    Product B: Fixed Costs = $750,000; Variable Costs = $75 per item produced
5. If the forecasted production for the above data is 9,000 units, what process should the company select?
6. Research RFID tags and explain the size and capability differences between active and passive tags.
7. What aspects should a company consider if making a make or buy decision?
8. What is ERP and why is it important?
9. What documents comprise the recipe card for a product?
10. Create a process map of any process that you are familiar with.
11. What is the purpose of a process map?
12. Why is it important to relook the breakeven point calculation as part of the process design steps?

9 Productivity

What is productivity, and why does it matter in operations management? As mentioned in the introduction to operations management, productivity is one of the measures used by Wall Street to compare competitiveness between companies. Productivity is also used to measure the competitiveness of countries.

The Bureau of Labor Statistics defines productivity as:

> Productivity and related cost measures are designed for use in economic analysis and public and private policy planning. The data are used to forecast and analyze changes in prices, wages, and technology. There are two primary types of productivity statistics:
>
> - Labor productivity measures output per hour of labor.
> - Multifactor productivity measures output per unit of combined inputs, which consist of labor and capital, and, in some cases, intermediate inputs such as fuel.
> - Data on output per hour and unit labor costs are available for the U.S. business sector, the nonfarm business sector, and the manufacturing sector. These are the productivity statistics most often cited in the news. In addition, output per hour and unit labor costs are available for over 400 selected industries in manufacturing, mining, utilities, wholesale and retail trade, and services.[1]

The *APICS Dictionary* defines productivity as: "An overall measure of the ability to produce a good or a service. Productivity is a relative measure across time or against common entities (labor, capital, etc.). In the production literature, attempts have been made to define total productivity where the effects of labor and capital are combined and divided into the output" (Blackstone, 2013).

APICS defines labor productivity as: "A partial productivity measure, the rate of output of a worker or group of workers per unit of time compared to an established standard or rate of output" (Blackstone, 2013).

Machine productivity is defined by APICS as: "A partial productivity measure. The rate of output of a machine per unit of time compared with an established standard or rate of output" (Blackstone, 2013).

Productivity is simply a measure of outputs divided by inputs. The calculation for productivity looks like Equation 9.1:

Equation 9.1: Productivity

$$\text{Productivity} = \left(\frac{\text{Outputs}}{\text{Inputs}}\right)$$

Changes in productivity are measured as shown in Equation 9.2. Changes in productivity include two inherent assumptions. The first assumption is that the quality is the same or better in the second period over the first period. Think about that—if the output increases, but the quality is less requiring downgrading of prices or rework of products, then there really is no improvement in productivity. The second assumption built into productivity increases is that someone is actually buying the products. If no one is buying what you are

---

[1]Bureau of Labor Statistics. http://www.bls.gov/bls/productivity.htm, accessed September 16, 2016.

making, then are you really more productive? No! Someone has to buy your product—remember, you are in business to make money.

Equation 9.2: Change in Productivity Calculation

$$\text{Change in Productivity} = \frac{\text{Output Current} - \text{Output Previous}}{\text{Output Previous}} \times 100$$

Example 9.1

Last year, the company produced 1,000 items; this year, the company produced 900 items with the same level of inputs. Their change in productivity is:

$$((900 - 1,000)/1,000) \times 100 = -10\%$$

SINGLE-FACTOR PRODUCTIVITY

Single-factor productivity looks at one particular aspect of inputs. This could be labor, dollars, hours, or materials. Single-factor productivity is calculated by dividing the outputs by one of these inputs. For example (see Example 9.2), a company may want to know the number of products that they are producing per employee (a common Wall Street metric). If the company wants to know how many items are produced per dollar of labor invested, they would calculate this metric using the technique in Example 9.3.

Example 9.2

A company produces 5,000 items per week; there are 3 employees.

$$\text{The single-factor productivity is } (5,000/3) = 1666.67 \text{ items per employee}$$

Example 9.3

A company produces 5,000 items with a labor investment of $30,000. Their productivity is:

$$(5,000/30,000) = .1667 \text{ items per labor dollar invested}$$

MULTIFACTOR PRODUCTIVITY

Multifactor productivity is another way of looking at the outputs of company. This technique looks at more than one factor of inputs. For example, a company may want to look at the productivity of the inputs of labor dollars and materials dollars. Look at Example 9.4.

Example 9.4

The BW Company wants to determine their productivity using the following inputs information:

$$\text{Labor dollars} = \$45,000$$

$$\text{Materials dollars} = \$10,000$$

$$\text{Outputs} = 200,000 \text{ items}$$

$$\text{The multifactor productivity is: } (200,000/(\$45,000+\$10,000))$$

$$= (200,000/\$55,000)$$

$$= 3.63 \text{ items/labor and materials dollars invested}$$

MAKING SENSE OF PRODUCTIVITY NUMBERS

Who cares about productivity? Why does it matter? Everyone in operations management should be concerned with productivity. How much are we getting for what we are investing? With constant efforts to reduce costs and improve profitability, a small increase in the outputs from the same or less inputs will link to increased profits.

Most textbooks suggest that productivity increases when a company gets smaller. This usually happens through drawdowns, planned reduction in operations, or forced layoffs. Think about this. Having been with several companies when they went through reductions in size or forced layoffs, what I saw was an increased concern about being laid off causing a decrease in productivity. One company I worked with as a consultant went through a series of layoffs that resulted in the salaried employees work weeks expanding from 40 hours a week to almost 60 hours a week. The company bragged that their productivity had increased after the layoffs. When looking at the outputs compared with the number of employees, it may be true that the productivity increased. However, when comparing the output with the number of hours worked, the actual productivity went down.

Another inaccuracy put forth by most textbooks is the idea that productivity increases when a company expands. This may be true in the long run, but, in the short run, there is a decrease in productivity as the best workers spend time training the new workers. The best producers are not working at peak productivity while training the new workers and the new workers are not up to the productivity rates of the experienced workers for the duration of the learning curve.

Productivity in a company does increase when nonvalue-adding processes or activities are eliminated. Remember all processes add cost (thus adding to inputs), but not all processes create value (adding to the outputs). Productivity also increases when a company comes up with a technological breakthrough.

However, not all technology breakthroughs increase productivity. Think about PowerPoint. It does make life easier for presentations, but it also takes away from productivity in some offices from the constant changes to presentations and the addition of "sexy" graphics to make a simple point. One boss, many years ago, kept a group of employees changing a single slide trying to find the perfect color for a graphic. Or think about e-mail. How much time is spent daily reading and sending e-mails that may or may not be of value. How much time is wasted daily on surfing the Web during office hours?

COMPARING PRODUCTIVITY BETWEEN PLANTS

It may be advantageous when trying to improve operations to look at the productivities of different plants, determine which plant may need improvements or, if needed, which plant may need to be shut down to improve the company's overall productivity. Take a look at Example 9.5.

Example 9.5

The Skylar Company has three plants producing their products. The plants are in Kansas City, Raleigh, and Melbourne. The information for the plants is shown in this matrix:

	Kansas City	Raleigh	Melbourne
Output/month	15,000	14,500	15,500
Labor cost $	3,000	4,500	2,500
Materials cost $	10,000	10,000	10,500
Overhead $	2,500	3,500	2,000
Total inputs	15,500	18,000	15,000
Productivity	0.97	0.81	1.03

Based on this analysis of productivity, the plant in Melbourne has a higher productivity measure of items produced per dollar invested. This being the case, the company management should look into what Melbourne is doing different or more efficient than Raleigh or Kansas City. The solution may be to use personnel from Melbourne to train the workers at the other plants. The solution could be as simple as changing procedures, or it may be as drastic as closing the least productive plant and move operations to the more productive plants. It is important to remember when comparing the productivity between plants, companies, or countries that the output has to be a quality output, and someone has to be buying the product or service for it to be true productivity.

SUMMARY

Although this has been a very short chapter, it is important to understand the calculations for productivity and the use of productivity measures to improve operations. Productivity measures the outputs divided by the inputs. This may be a single-factor measure or a multifactor measurement.

Productivity can be improved by getting more outputs from the same or less inputs through the reduction of nonvalue-adding activities or processes. But it is important to remember the two assumptions built into the productivity change calculations for improved productivity: Quality is the same or improved, and someone is actually buying the products being produced.

Productivity can be a measure of competitiveness between companies or countries and is also a metric used by Wall Street to analyze companies. Productivity can also be a way of looking at multiple operations to determine which plants or stores need improved operations or even shut down.

The Bureau of Labor Statistics summarizes the use of productivity: "How can we achieve a higher standard of living? One way might simply be to work more, trading some free time for more income. Although working more will increase how much we can produce and purchase, are we better off? Not necessarily. Only if we increase our efficiency—by producing more goods and services without increasing the number of hours we work—can we be sure to increase our standard of living.

That's why BLS produces labor productivity statistics every quarter that tell us how well we are improving our economic efficiency. These measures compare the amount of goods and services we produce with the number of hours we work."[2]

Discussion Questions

1. A company has a machine that produces 6,000 nails per hour. An upgrade is available that will allow the machine to produce 6,600 nails. What would be the increase in productivity with this upgrade?

2. The AEB Company spent $25,000 on materials last month. From these materials, they produced 35,000 surf boards. What is their materials productivity?

3. The AMB Company wants to look at total productivity (multifactor) and compiled the following information for last year:

Output last year	275,000
Labor cost $	330,000
Materials cost $	125,000
Overhead $	36,000
Total inputs	491,000

---

[2]Bureau of Labor Statistics. http://blogs.bls.gov/blog/2016/08/09/why-this-counts-productivity-and-its-impact-on-our-lives, accessed September 15, 2016.

4. If AMB compiled the following data for this year, what is their change in productivity?

Output this year	285,000
Labor cost $	325,000
Materials cost $	120,000
Overhead $	40,000
Total inputs	485,000

5. What is the relationship between nonvalue-adding processes and productivity?

6. Why are some intended improvements in technology not necessarily a cause for increased productivity?

10 Facility Layout Design and Location Analysis

Facility layout design is critical to the success of the operations management chain. The layout may dictate the profitability of the company and should be carefully considered during the product and process design phases. The layout should not dictate the processes, but the other way around; the processes should dictate the layout. Customer locations may dictate the location of facilities and the location may dictate part of the layout plan. For example, a cross-docking and trans-loading facility, as shown in Figure 10.1, should be located close to major rail networks and major road networks.

The major goal of facility planning is to minimize material handling within the facility, regardless of the type of facility being planned. If material handling can be reduced, the opportunity to mishandle, mislead, or damage the product is minimized. If the material handling can be reduced, costs can be reduced and if costs can be reduced, one of two things can happen: either the profits for the company can be improved or the price for the products can be reduced.

The next goal of the layout design process should be to layout the facility to improve the efficiencies of the space and workers. In a distribution facility, the most of the worker's time is spent moving from one location to the next picking location. If the layout can be designed to better utilize the space and employees' time more effectively, the amount of time spent walking from one location to the next can be reduced. Almost every distribution center manager complains that there is not enough space in the facility. Why? This is because most facility managers measure their space on the square footage of the facility vice cube footage utilization. Everyone in the business falls into this trap. Look at a *Modern Materials Handling* Magazine,[1] and you will see articles about distribution centers—almost each one of them lists the square footage of the facility. Efficiently utilizing the space of the facility may mean utilizing the cube footage of the facility. Only very few distribution centers or warehouses stack supplies and materials one pallet high; therefore, cube footage may provide more space. Furthermore, placing similar items close to each other in the facility may very well reduce the movement in the facility thus using employee time more efficiently.

Photograph by Joe Walden

Figure 10.1: Cross-docking and Trans-loading Facility—Located near Major East–West and North–South Roads and Major Rail Yard

---

[1]Go to http://www.mmh.com for more information on Materials Handling and facility layout models.

In order to more efficiently layout the facility, it is necessary to eliminate bottlenecks in the facility. This is much easier to do when designing a new facility than when inheriting an older facility. We will look at the Theory of Constraints in more detail in the discussion of Just-in-Time. However, it is imperative to get rid of all bottlenecks in the facility to produce a more efficiently run facility. Any bottleneck will reduce the efficiency and effectiveness of the operation. The principles of the Theory of Constraints and the principles of Just-in-Time—reducing waste—will improve the efficiency of the facility.

If waste is removed from the operations, there will be less movement. If there is less movement, we have achieved the primary goal of the layout design: reducing the need for material handling. If reducing material handling is achieved, the need for material-handling equipment is reduced and, therefore, the costs of operations are reduced and again profits should be improved.

A good facility layout should consider the interactions and communications between the workers and management. If communication is improved, the quality of the outputs will improve. If the management can communicate directly with the workers, less will be lost in the communications process. One facility that I was in recently had all of the management on the second floor with two-way mirrored glass on the walls so that they could look down at the workers. This provided the management team with visibility of what was happening on the shop floor, but violates the idea of facilitating communications.

The World Wide Operations Center for BNSF Railroads[2] has the same layout design. The BNSF facility is an awesome facility. From the floor (and from the windows on the second level), everyone can see the large screens that show the location of every train on the system and the contents of the trains as well as a weather screen and a listing of freight by commodity. The problem is that when on the operations floor, you feel like big brother is always watching and the ability to communicate face to face is severely reduced. Conversely, FedEx[3] has a World Wide Operations Center in Memphis, Tennessee, which is similarly set up on the operations floor—large screens with tracking for every plane and the FedEx Weather Station. The difference is that the offices are on the operations floor to facilitate communications.

The final goal of the facility design process is to facilitate reduction of the manufacturing cycle time. Or in a distribution facility, the goal of the layout design is to reduce the processing times in the facility to bring down the customer wait times for the products the customers have ordered. If the facility is laid out for efficiency, it should also improve responsiveness to the customer.

At the same time, that the design should improve the efficiency of the operation; if it is a service operation, the goal should be to maximize the exposure of products to the customers depending on the type of operations. In some operations, it may be better to design the process so as to minimize the travel and movement of the customer through the facility.

Grocery stores have the concept of maximizing exposure of the products to the customer. Almost every grocery store has the same layout. You go into the store and the fresh fruits and vegetables are on one end of the store, the meats and seafood are along the back, the frozen foods and breads are in the middle, and the dairy products are at the other side of the store. Even the Wal-Mart Supercenter grocery layout concept has the same basic layout; only, it is a from front to rear rather than a left–right or right–left orientation.

Starbucks stores are laid out to maximize the exposure of the products such as cups, accessories, coffees, and teas to the customer before reaching the counter to order a drink or pastry. Another coffee chain needed assistance with their layouts in 2005. This West Coast chain was looking for suggestions from consultants to improve the sale of the complementary items to their coffees and teas. Figure 10.2 shows their typical layout and analysis of the layout.

The first observation of this layout is that the customers could enter by either of the doors without ever seeing the cups and mugs for sale or the coffees and teas for sale on the shelves. This violates the idea of maximizing exposure to the products. The next problem with this layout is that after ordering the drink, the customers go to the pickup area to get their drinks. Located by the pickup area at A was the menu of what drinks were available. This probably should be placed in clear view of the ordering area and not where you pick up the drinks. After picking up the drinks and getting cream and sugar at B, the customer could leave without seeing the other items for sale.

---

[2]For more on BNSF go to http://www.bnsf.com
[3]For more on the operations of FedEx go to fedex.com

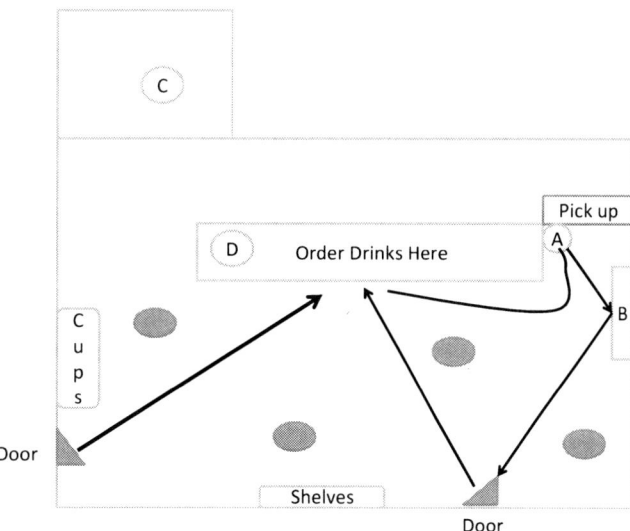

Figure 10.2: Coffee Shop Layout

If the customer came in through the door on the bottom of the diagram, they could reach the ordering area without ever seeing the pastry area at D. The area shown at C was actually a tasting area that featured the newest flavors and the coffees of the day. This area was not clearly marked and was not obvious to the customers, and, therefore, not really utilized thus leading to the loss of the marketing value of the area.

OTHER CONSIDERATIONS FOR LAYOUT PLANNING

Safety and Security. Safety always has to be a consideration in the design of the facility or its layout. A company can design the most efficient production layout, but if it places the employees at risk or the product at risk from the layout, it cannot be implemented. Granted providing a quality product with the least amount of movement and material handling is important, but the most important asset that any company has is its employees. If the safety of those employees is put at risk, the design is a no-go.

In California, the Occupational Safety and Health Administration (Cal OSHA) has certain rules and regulations laid down that may or may not be applicable in other areas of the country. However, these rules to protect the workers may be applicable in other states and in other countries that have earthquake threats. The Cal OSHA requires distribution centers that stack materials at more than two pallet positions high to be bolted to the ground for earthquake protection. This is important when designing a distribution center or warehouse layout. Why? Once the pallet racks are bolted down, it is not only not practical, but also possibly not cost effective to move the racks—so, it is important to get the racks in the right place the first time.

It is also important to consider security of the facility and the controlled access for visitors and employees as part of this design process. Most facilities have a controlled entrance, and may have security guards at the entrance to ensure that employees are coming and going from the controlled access point. The other reason for this controlled entry point, besides the safety and security of the employees, is to ensure that a dishonest employee is discouraged from taking stuff out of the facility.

Product Quality. Obviously, as the process design is for producing a quality product, the layout of the facility has to support that goal. If the layout design's primary goal is to minimize material handling, the corollary benefit of this goal is that the chances of producing a quality product are improved if the product is handled as little as possible. The fewer times a product is moved, the smaller is the probability that it will be damaged or misrouted, thereby, reducing the impacts on the quality of the product.

If a product needs a certain environment for production such as a painting facility or the manufacturer of computer chips, there may be impacts on the layout and/or the location of the facility. For example, at the

Harley–Davidson Plant in Kansas City, Missouri, the painting of the gas tanks is in a controlled environment that contains an air dam to blow particles off the workers to prevent defects in the paint. This process also has restrictions on the foods that the workers can eat to prevent defects in the painting of the tanks.

Flexibility for Future Operations. Every plan should include a consideration of the future of the operations. Whether it is a manufacturing facility that needs to consider future products or variations of the same product or a distribution center that needs to consider future storage requirements and product configurations as well as the ability to expand capacity in the future, the company has to consider posturing for the future.

In the mid-1990s, Grainger designed and built a new distribution center in Fontana, California. By 2001, this facility had outgrown its capacity and needed to expand the operations. However, in the 5+ years that the facility was open, the facility had become blocked in—there was no place to expand the facility. Grainger decided to design and build a new facility a few miles down the road in Mira Loma, California. This time the facility was built larger than the current capacity by about 1.5 times. This allowed the company to slowly expand into the facility as the need arose. The other flexibility that Grainger built into this facility was to buy the land around the facility to allow for the flexibility of future expansion and prevent being blocked in again.

TYPES OF LAYOUTS

Process Layout. A process layout places all of the like machines in the same area of the facility. As processes are completed, the products are moved to the next process. In the facility diagram below (Figure 10.3), each of the areas shown represents the groupings of like machines or processes.

In order to improve the layout of a facility, it is necessary to analyze the flow of materials or a work in process from one process to the next. This flow analysis may show that the layout is flawed and not producing an efficient use of personnel and is causing an inordinate amount of moving of the materials and work in process. Take a look at Figure 10.4. This example shows a similar process layout that may not be so efficient. Look at the flow of the materials and work in process through the facility. This analysis shows that the layout may not be as efficient as it could be and may be requiring more material handling and movement as is necessary or should be necessary. This layout has work in process moving across other process sectors. This is not an efficient layout. The goal of the process layout analysis is to find the optimal layout that will meet the goals of layout design.

Product Layout. The product layout is the traditional, linear manufacturing layout. Raw materials or subassemblies enter at one end of the manufacturing line and a finished product comes out of the other end of the product layout.

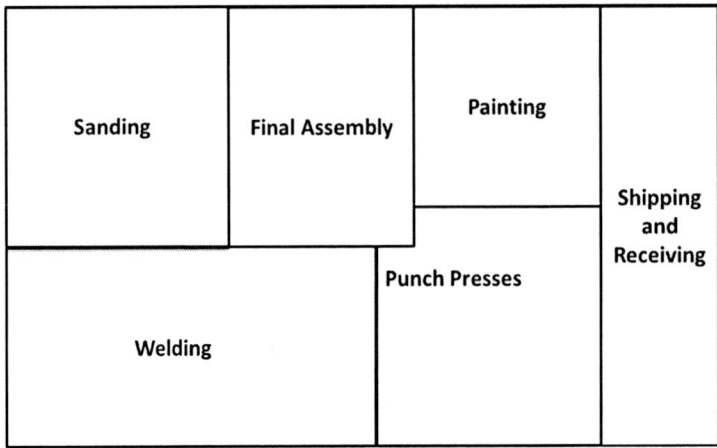

Figure 10.3: Process Layout Example

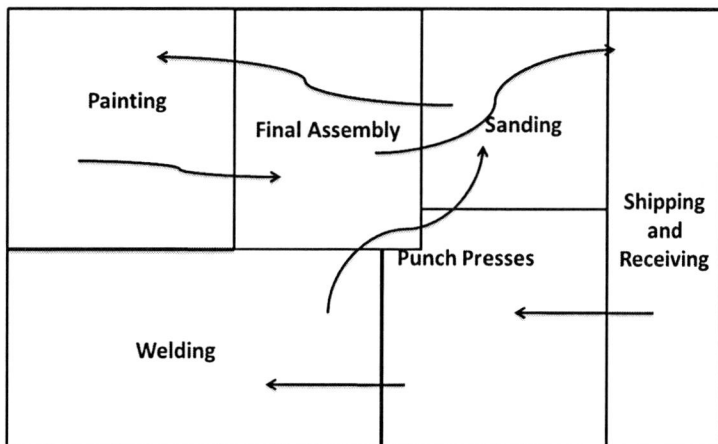

Figure 10.4: Process Layout

The first thing that has to be considered in designing the product layout is to know or determine the assembly order as stated in the process charts we saw in Chapter 8. This is important in order to make sure that the layout is in a logical format based on what needs to be done first. (We will see this same methodology when we look at the Critical Path Method and Project Evaluation and Review Technique for Project Management.)

The next step in the product line design is to consider if work stations or work cells will be used for the product line. Either way, the design has to consider how much work will be assigned to the work station or work cell to ensure a smooth flow through the line without delays or a buildup of work in process. In order to do this, it is important to measure the cycle time for the entire line (Harley–Davidson knows it takes 54 minutes for one bike to be made on one of their product lines). Then, the cycle time for each work station or cell must be calculated.

Cellular Layout. What is a cellular layout? A cellular layout is an attempt to balance the line and reduce material handling through a facility. This can only be accomplished by measuring the cycle times for each cell to ensure that the cells are balanced internally and externally. A cellular layout groups like machines into a cell. This sounds a lot like the definition of a process layout and may very well be a process layout within a product layout. Parts families may be grouped together within the product line and passed from one process cell to the next process. This produces a hybrid layout or a line within a line production.

The advantages of a cell are all based on proper planning and analysis. To achieve the benefits of cells requires balancing within and between cells. When properly designed, the cell will minimize the need to constantly change set ups along the product line by grouping the like activities together much like the process concept.

Cellular layouts, although perceived by some advocates of Just-in-Time as the best way to produce goods and services, may not be appropriate for all products or services. If there are not enough processes or enough parts families in the operation, it may not be feasible to move to a cellular layout. Computer models are great for analyzing the available data to determine whether or not cells are right for the product or service.

Cellular layouts are not just for manufacturing. Cells can be seen in services and retail operations also. When I lived in Hawaii, there was a family-owned store in Waipahu, Arakawa's, which was broken into cells based on the "family member" that ran that particular department. The family saw this as efficient, but from the customer's perspective, the need to pay for items at every cell was seen as a bit inefficient.

In the fast-food industry, cells play a big part. In hamburger fast-food restaurants, there are cells that focus on the making of French fries, a cell that focuses on "grilling" the burgers, another cell that focuses on putting the burger together, and another cell that is focused on taking the customers' orders. The goal is to reduce the customer wait time and improve efficiency of the operations.

Project Layout. Project layouts are fixed position layouts. Remember the discussions on projects earlier in the text that projects are onetime operations. In a project layout, it is not feasible to have a product layout. The manufacture of airplanes is an example of a fixed position or project layout. It is not feasible to have an assembly line for such a large product. Usually, in a fixed position layout, the largest costs are the variable costs associated with bringing highly skilled labor into the operation and then taking them back out after they have completed their work. The materials are brought to the product assembly area in time for the laborers to apply them. Conversely, the fixed costs for the production are relatively low.

Hybrid Layout.   The Harley–Davidson Motorcycle and Powertrain Assembly Plant in Kansas City, Missouri has a hybrid layout. The manufacture of the gas tanks is a process layout—from the cutting of the blanks to the forming of the gas tank halves to the welding to the paint operations. Once the tanks and the powertrains are complete, the remainder of the assembly is a product line with four assembly lines—three basic models (V-Rod, Sportster, and Dyna Glide) and one custom-made (Screaming Eagle) assembly line. On the custom-made line, each bike is made by one craftsman rather than the standard assembly line used for the three basic models.

PROCESS DESIGN

Now that we have the basic layouts defined, it is time to look at the methods for determining the optimal layout.

Block Diagramming.   Look back at Figure 10.4. A block diagram could be applied to the layout. The goal of the block diagram is to establish, with quantifiable data, the number of items moving from one process or machine to the next process or machine and what if any are moving backward to be redone. Figure 10.5a shows a facility looked at recently that could have used a block diagram to determine the optimal layout based on flow analysis and quantifiable data to determine which processes should have been placed adjacent. This particular facility was "focused on Lean initiatives." However, the primary goal of Lean, as we will see later, is to reduce waste. One of the wastes that Lean seeks to reduce or eliminate is the waste of movement. This particular facility could have improved operations by using the data, which they had available, and a block diagram.

In this particular aircraft parts repair and rebuild facility, items came in through each of the three doors and went to area A, area B, or area C for initial analysis and repair. Then, the items moved from the initial area to one of the other two areas for additional work and then to one of the other areas for more work before being shipped out to the customers.

Using the quantifiable data of the movements from one area to the next, and analyzing the data to determine the movements between adjacent areas, a more optimal layout is possible. Look at Figure 10.5b and the redesign based on adjacent sector movements. This new layout not only allows for movement from each area to the other areas without passing through area B in the middle, which slowed operations. The new design also provides an area strictly for quality assurance and shipping, which was handled throughout the facility in the previous design.

Figure 10.6 shows the US Navy's methodology for determining the flow of materials between departments in a distribution center. The chart allows the organization to create an easy-to-understand methodology to establish the flow from department to department.

Figure 10.7 shows another method from the US Navy to establish activity between departments. This chart shows the affinity between departments: the activities with three lines have strong movements between the departments meaning they have to be in close proximity, the activities with two lines have substantial movement and, therefore, should be in close proximity to each other, the activities with one line have some movement, and those activities not connected at all have no movement and, therefore, have no need to be closely located in the facility.

Relationship Diagrams.   One of the most common relationship grids is the Muther's grid. This technique was originally developed by Richard Muther. The relationship grid is designed to be used when quantifiable data are not available. Therefore, this technique is not used if the data shown for the block diagram or the affinity diagram are available. A relationship diagram is based on someone's opinion of what should be located close to other activities. In 1980, the warehouse that I was responsible for was destroyed by a large tropical storm in Hawaii. Although this warehouse was a showplace warehouse that was included in every distinguished visitor's tour in Hawaii, there were some areas that could be improved. The data were not available to show what moved from where to where. So, my smart guys developed a rough draft relationship diagram. We were not aware of

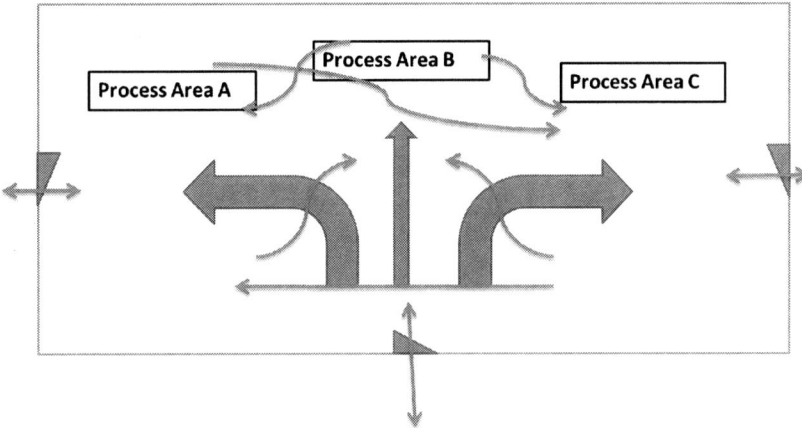

Figure 10.5a: Flow Analysis Using Block Diagramming

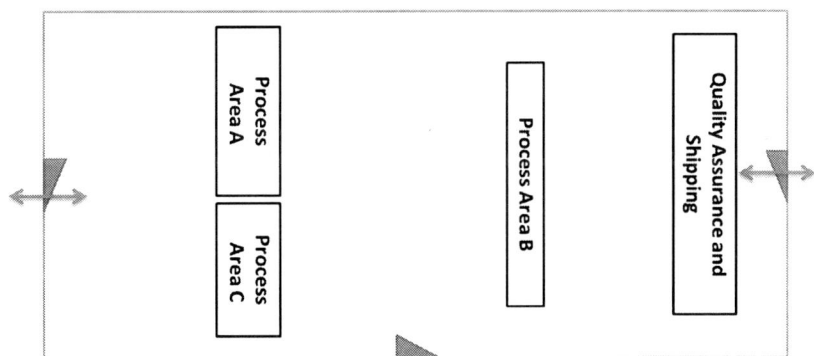

Figure 10.5b: Redesigned Facility Using Block Diagramming

ACTIVITY FROM \ ACTIVITY TO	RECEIVING	INSPECTION	AS/RS	BULK STORAGE	PALLET RACK STORAGE	RACKABLES ORDER PICKING	BINNABLES ORDER PICKING	SHIPMENT STAGING	EMPLOYEE SERVICES	DATA PROCESSING	TOTAL
RECEIVING	–	30	5	2	10						47
INSPECTION		–	15		8	3	4	3			33
AS/RS			–		7	4		9			20
BULK STORAGE				–	1			1			2
PALLET RACK STORAGE					–	6		20			26
RACKABLES ORDER PICKING						–	7	4	1	1	13
BINNABLES ORDER PICKING							–	11			11
SHIPMENT STAGING		3						–			3
EMPLOYEE SERVICES									–		0
DATA PROCESSING										–	0
TOTAL		33	20	2	26	13	11	48	1	1	155

NOTE:
    Activity units expressed as frequency factor equal to units moved
    (pallets, pounds, cu. ft. etc.) times distance per move (usually feet).

Figure 10.6: US Navy Methodology for Establishing Flow of Materials between Activities

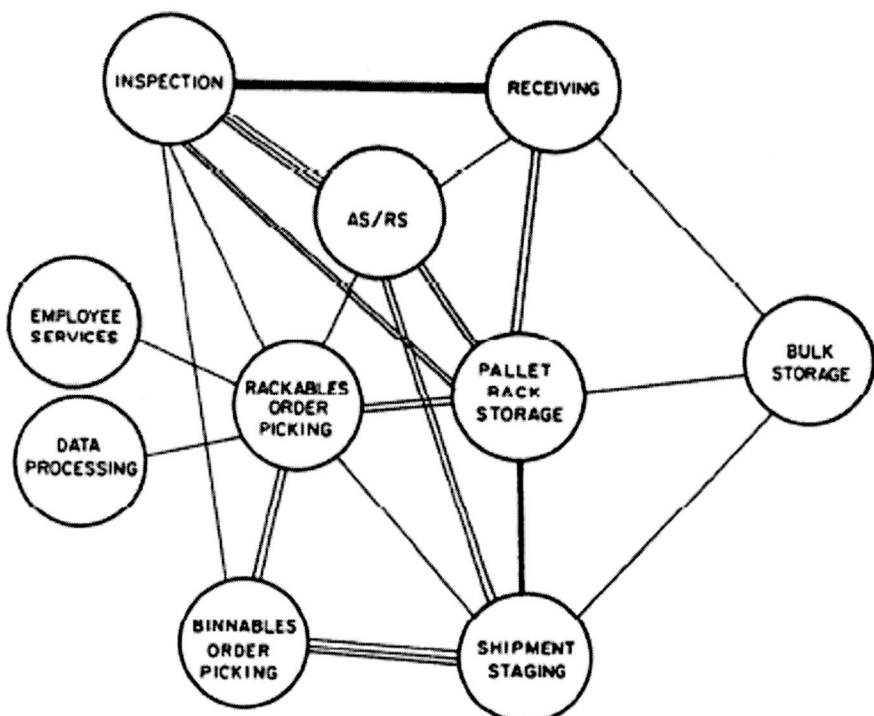

Figure 10.7: Activity Diagram

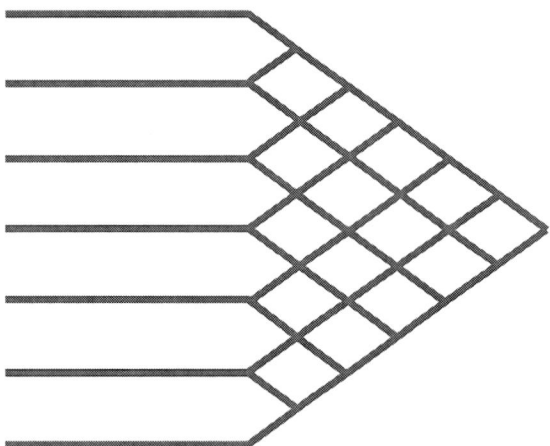

Figure 10.8: Blank Muther's Grid

Muther's work, but used the same ideas of what we thought should be close to which, when designing the new facility. The problem with a relationship diagram is that it is subjective. It is someone's opinion or best guess. A Muther's grid, when blank, looks like Figure 10.8. Notice that it looks a little like the old mileage charts on a paper map—and is read the same way. The intersection of the lines is the relationship and shows what should and should not be placed close to other activities.

Using the Muther's Grid. There are three methods of analysis using the Muther's grid to establish relationships for improving the layout design, which I have seen used. The first methodology I call is the "Vowel Method"—for obvious reasons. The relationships are shown using the following scoring system:

In Figure 10.9, the Vowel Methodology is applied to the Muther's grid. Using this grid, it is easy to see that the subjective analysis deems the relationship between the shipping department and the offices as

A   **Absolutely necessary**
E   **Especially important**
I   **Important**
O   **Okay**
U   **Unimportant**
X   **Undesirable**

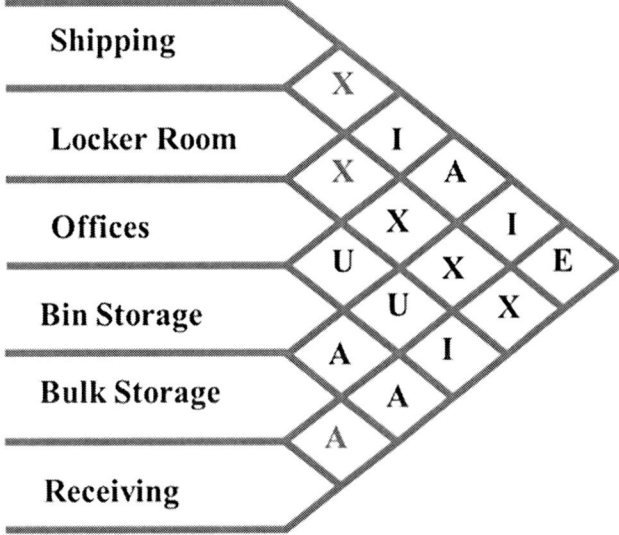

Figure 10.9: Vowel Methodology Muther's Grid

undesirable (X)—the rationale for this decision is because the need to have privacy in the offices to talk to potential employees and talk with current employees is critical to operating a business. At the same time, it is important to have privacy in the locker room to talk among the employees.

Bulk storage and receiving is deemed to be absolutely important (A) because of the desire to reduce material-handling costs and the waste of unnecessary movement. The same is true in this example for bin storage (small items) and shipping. The rationale for determining that shipping and locker rooms should not be close (undesirable—X) is to prevent the temptation to move nice-to-have items to the locker room vice the shipping dock.

Figure 10.10 shows the same rationale using the "Number Methodology." This methodology is very similar except that instead of using letters or vowels, numbers are used. The importance of using this method is to make sure the decision maker and the recommender understand the numbering system. This is why it is important to have the scale close by when looking at the grid. This is important because the decision maker needs to know the scale—is a 1—good or bad? The rating scheme of one system may have 1 as good and 6 as bad (the lower the better, like a golf score) or may have 6 as good and 1 as bad (the more points the better, like a good basketball game). The intersection between bulk storage and receiving is a 1—absolutely important to reduce movement.

Hybrid Methodology. The Hybrid Methodology comes from the US Navy's Manual for Warehousing Layout.[4] This methodology combines the two previous methods to provide a much better relationship diagram. The Hybrid Method not only shows what the recommendation is, but also the rationale of the recommender and the thought process for the recommendation. Figure 10.11 shows this methodology. Looking at Data Processing and Employees Services, the recommendation is absolutely necessary and the rationale is because they share office space.

---

[4]Navy Supply Publication 529, Warehousing Modernization and Layout Planning Guide, 1985. Although this publication is almost 30 years old, it is still the best publication available to guide a planner to design the most optimal warehouse or distribution center layout.

1   **Absolutely necessary**
2   **Especially important**
3   **Important**
4   **Okay**
5   **Unimportant**
6   **Undesirable**

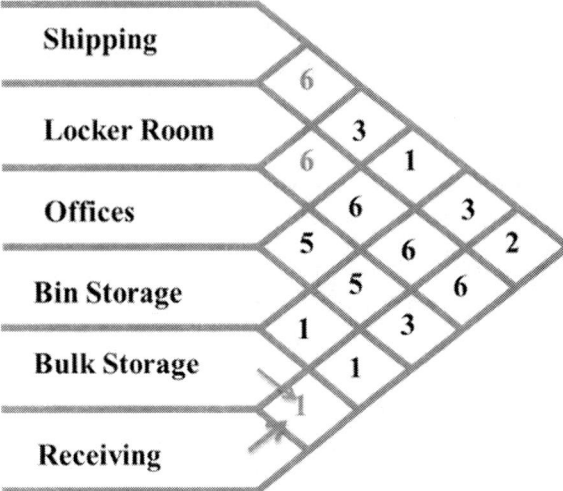

Figure 10.10: Muther's Grid Using Number Methodology

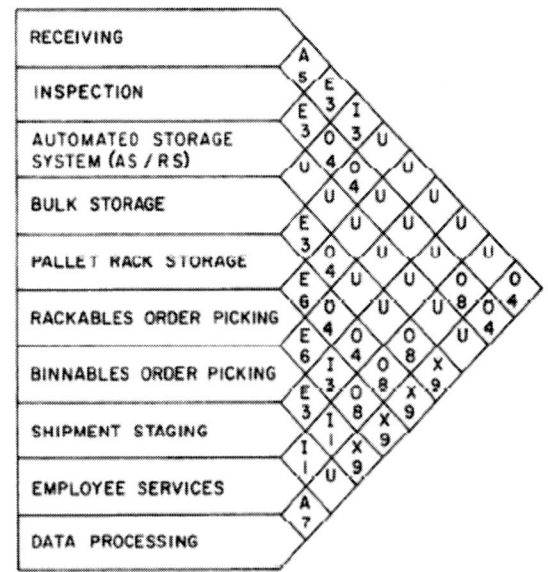

REASONS FOR IMPORTANCE

1. Supervision
2. Safety
3. Material flow
4. Work flow
5. Material control
6. Equipment proximity
7. Shared spaced
8. Employee Health and Safety
9. Security

PROXIMITY IMPORTANCE

A. Absolutely necessary
E. Especially important
I. Important
O. Ordinary closeness
U. Unimportant
X. Undesirable

Figure 10.11: Hybrid Methodology for Relationship Planning

Layout Summary. The layout of the facility may provide a competitive advantage and improve efficiency of the operations. The facility layout will determine capital expenditures and flexibility, and may constrain the capacity of the company.

Layout design is just as important in services as it is in manufacturing. If quantifiable data are available, a block diagram may be the best tool to improve the layout design and efficiency. When quantifiable data are not available, a Muther's grid or relationship diagram may be more useful to design or redesign the operations. A process walk is necessary to determine what operations precede other operations based on the walk and the process charts.

LOCATION ANALYSIS AND MODELS

Whether a company is involved in heavy manufacturing such as automobile manufacturing and high-tech manufacturing or distribution centers, there are some considerations that are common to the process and some considerations that are unique to certain industries. Land costs, utility costs, and construction costs are common to any facility.

In heavy manufacturing, decisions and considerations to be analyzed before choosing a location for a new facility include:

- What is the availability of labor in the desired area? Is there sufficient labor available and is there sufficient skilled labor to staff the facility or will the companies have to bring employees in from other locations. Although there is currently almost 10% unemployment throughout the United States, it does not mean that the skills necessary for operations will be available.
- Raw materials. Is it better for the company to locate the manufacturing facility closer to the source of the raw materials or is it better to locate the facility closer to the customers? If the raw materials have a short shelf life, it may be more advantageous for the company to have the manufacturing plant close to the source of the raw materials. If the raw materials can be delivered only by rail, the facility must be located near or on a rail siding.
- The mode of shipping the finished product may dictate the location of the facility. Certain products have to be shipped by rail; therefore, the manufacturing facility has to be located on a rail siding or rail spur. Access to transportation networks is a requirement for all facilities—the type of network, in turn, is driven by the raw materials and the finished product. Several years ago, there were sufficient potatoes in the field in Russia to feed the entire country and make all the Vodka the country could drink only to have the produce rot in the field because of a lack of sufficient transportation networks to get the produce to the factories.

In light or high-tech manufacturing, the biggest concern after the land, construction, and utilities costs is the education base of the area. There is a good reason why the Research Triangle Park (RTP) area in North Carolina is located where it is and has a large number of high-tech firms in the RTP. Within a little more than an hour of the RTP are four world-class research universities providing a well-educated workforce. North Carolina State University, Wake Forest University, Duke University, and the University of North Carolina are all nearby. The Silicon Valley area in California provides the same education-rich environment to support the high-tech needs of the industry. There are several areas that I have been stationed at during my military career that will never be high-tech hubs because of the lack of quality secondary and postsecondary education programs.

The driving factor for the location of a warehouse or distribution center should be proximity to the customer or the manufacturing facility. A decision has to be made as to whether or not it is better for the company to locate their storage facility close to the manufacturing plant or close to the customer. Wal-Mart has a good model for where to place distribution centers to support its "more than 8,446 retail units under 55 different banners in 15 countries."[5] The purpose of warehouses and distribution centers is to put the product closer to the

---

[5]http://walmartstores.com/AboutUs, accessed August 11, 2010. "We have more than 40 Regional Distribution Centers. Each one is over 1 million square feet in size. They operate 24/7 to keep our fleet of tractors and trailers rolling. Inside each DC, more than five miles of conveyor belts move over 9,000 different lines of merchandise. Each DC supports between 75 and 100 stores within a 250-mile radius."

customers and reduce the customer order cycle time. This being the case, the distribution center or warehouse should probably be placed as close to the customer base as possible. There is an exception to this rule and that is to place the distribution center close to the transportation nodes—this is why there is so much distribution center space in Ontario, CA, because of the access to the road, rail, air, and water shipping nodes.

Chicago Consulting Company provides an annual survey of warehouse locations to best meet the population base of the United States. This study is available at http://www.chicago-consulting.com/10best.shtml and updated every year. The study bases its recommendations on the road networks and the population centers of the United States. This study is based on the center-of-gravity location model. This model is based on plotting the customer locations on a grid and placing the facility as close to all of the customers as possible to reduce travel time for the customers. This model can be weighted to place the facility closer to higher priority or higher volume customers. This model can be used for retail locations or distribution centers. A center-of-gravity calculation using Excel looks like Figure 10.12. This example shows a nonweighted example. Figure 10.13 shows the same information using weights to favor the stronger customer locations.

A few years ago, *Logistics Today* Magazine ran an article on the value of locating distribution facilities in the Midwest. This analysis of the Midwest as a location for distribution centers modified the simplicity of the center-of-gravity technique by adding some other factors into the analysis. This analysis by the Midwest looked at the road infrastructure—not just the network itself like the Chicago Consulting Center of Gravity analysis, but also the quality of the road network, the congestion of the network, and the road network safety. It also looked at the access of the road networks to the major interstate highways. In addition to the road networks, the *Logistics Today* analysis looked at the rail networks and the ability to get air cargo into the area via a major airport and from the airport to the road networks. Based on this analysis, *Logistics Today* gave 5-Star ratings to Champaign/Urbana, Illinois, Chicago, Cleveland, Cincinnati, Charleston, West Virginia, and Davenport, Iowa—all of which do not appear on the Chicago Consulting Center of Gravity analysis.

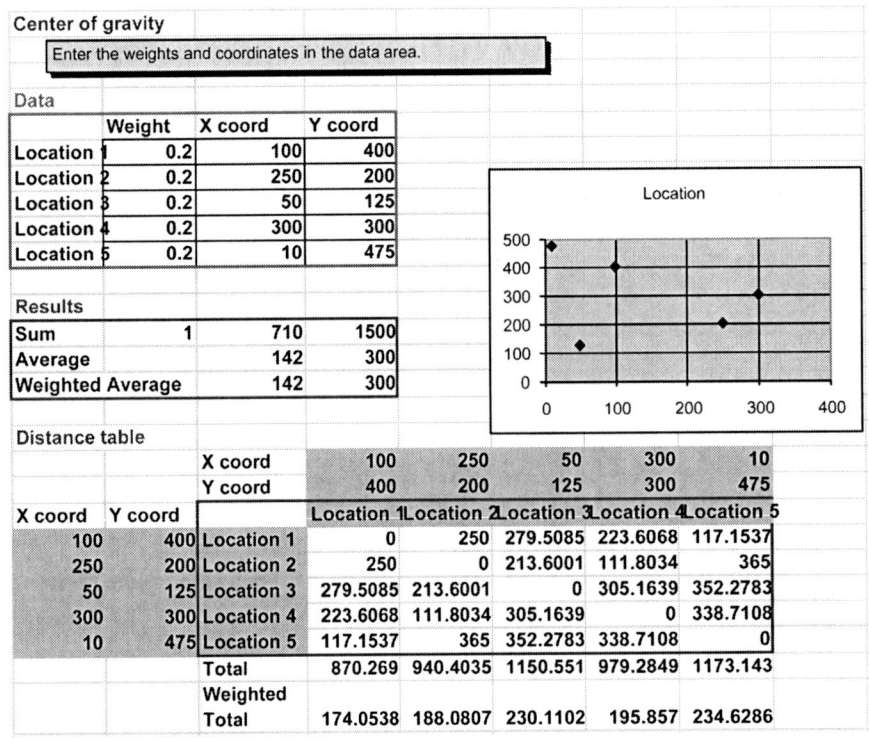

Figure 10.12: Center of Gravity Example

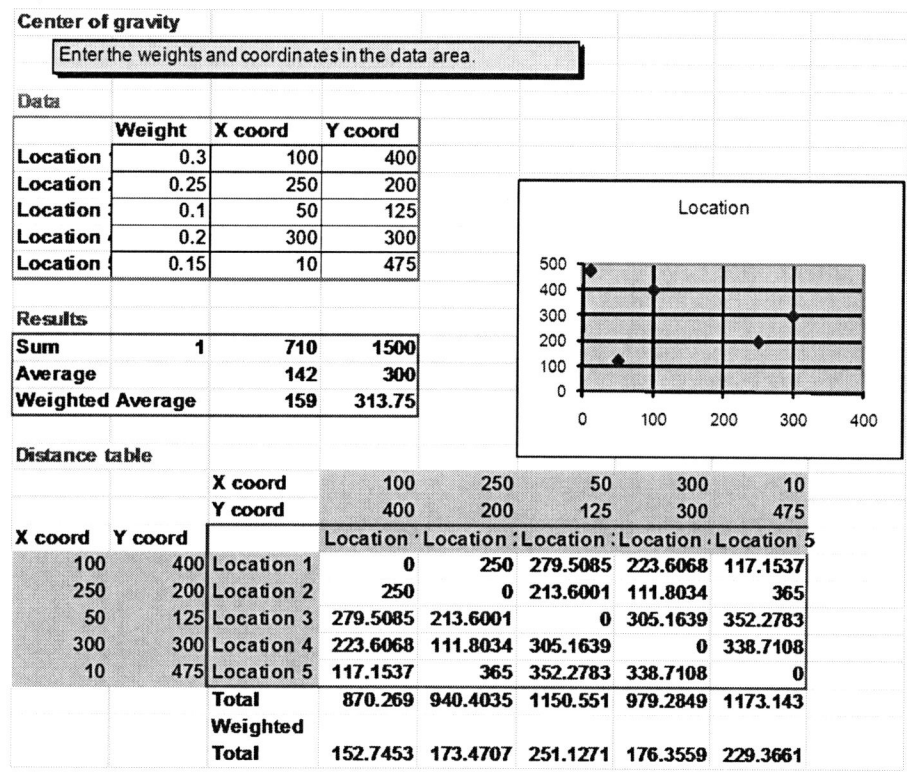

Figure 10.13: Weighted Center-of-gravity Example

DISTRIBUTION CENTER CONSIDERATIONS FOR LAYOUT AND LOCATION

The considerations for location for the distribution center have to include the location proximity to the customers besides other factors in the layout. These include:

■ **Cross-docking**—will the facility use cross-docking as a technique? Cross-docking has been discussed in greater detail under supply chain management. Cross-docking is simply planning the inbound shipments to the facility in coordination with the outbound shipments so that the items never go on the shelf, but from the inbound truck to an outbound truck within 24 to 48 hours. From a layout perspective, this requires a holding area to be designed, but may mean less shelf storage space will be needed in the design and layout.

■ **Dock doors—how many?** If moving into a current facility, this may not be a consideration; however, if the company is designing a new facility, this may be a consideration that will drive the layout. Is it possible to have inbound on one side of the facility and outbound on another side of the facility? If so, this may impact the layout as well as the traffic flow pattern.

■ **Vehicle flow**—how will the trucks come into the facility and leave the facility? This is an important consideration to the layout. The optimal solution would be to have one-way traffic flow; however, because of land constraints and security issues, this may not be always feasible.

■ **Picking techniques**—how will the items be picked in preparation to shipping to the customer? There are various picking techniques used in distribution centers to include the use of automated storage/automated retrieval (AS/AR) systems that do not have any human involvement with the put away and picking operations. Pet Foods in Topeka, Kansas uses a total AS/AR system for their state-of-the-art facility. The Defense Logistics Agency uses AS/AR systems for their small high-volume items. The type of picking technique and the analysis of fast-moving items will drive the layout of the facility.

■ **Bulk storage**—how much bulk storage will be kept and will it be kept close to the other storage areas or in a separate facility will drive the layout of the distribution center.

- **Safety/backup stocks**—safety stocks are a level of stocks above the normal stockage levels to cover variations in demand patterns. Will the company have safety stock at each location for every item or will there be a central location with the safety stocks? This will drive the layout and size of the facility needed. (We will cover safety stock in greater detail under the discussions on inventory management.)

LOCATION FACTORS

Just as there are common factors to the different industry locations, there are some common factors to the choosing the global or regional locations.

For companies considering locating overseas—whether that overseas is Asia, Europe, South America, Africa, or North America, depending on the location of the corporation—there are certain areas that need to be considered before relocating operations.

- **Culture**—obviously, or at least it should be obvious, that countries have different cultures and the norms and mores in one country are not necessarily the social norms and mores in other countries. Even Wal-Mart found this out when they tried expanding to Germany. Wal-Mart bought Wertkauf as the point of entry into Germany. Wertkauf was the German equivalent of Wal-Mart and would appear to be a good match. However, Wal-Mart discovered that there were cultural differences between the shoppers in Germany and the shoppers in the United States; now, there is no Wal-Mart in Germany and no Wertkauf either.

    Wal-Mart learned the same lesson again when they moved into China. Shoppers' behavior in China is apparently different from shoppers' behavior in other areas served by Wal-Mart. According to my students from China, they go to the store more often and buy what they need. One student reported that his family would go to Wal-Mart up to four times a day to get fresh foods. Wal-Mart also learned that the culture in China dictated that a certain percentage of the items in the stores had to come from the local area—which should not have been a problem as most of what is in the Wal-Mart stores in the United States is from China.

- **Language**—the typical American attitude is that everyone will speak English. And if they do not seem to understand English, the first time the typical American attitude is SPEAK SLOW AND SPEAK LOUD and they will understand. When I was stationed in Germany, the common attitude was: "If you speak three languages, you are tri-lingual; if you speak two languages, you are bi-lingual; and if you speak only one language, you are probably American." Companies have to ensure that employees that they are sending overseas understand the native language and can communicate in the native language.

- **Exchange rates**—how stable is the Dollar against the local currency and what is the exchange rate? Or, if a company outside the United States is looking to expand, how stable is the company's native currency against the Dollar or the Euro or other foreign currency. The wine makers in South Africa are very concerned about the stability and the exchange rate of the Rand against the Dollar. The wine makers are working hard to eliminate waste in their systems in order to compete cost-wise head-to-head with the California wineries.

- **Trade agreements or blocks**—if the company tries to expand into another country, will they have to compete against protections from trade agreements or trading blocs such as the North America Free Trade Agreement or the European Union? If so, will that include tariffs or duties for importing products or can the company take advantage of Free Trade Zones to reduce tariffs or duties? *The APICS Operations Management Body of Knowledge* defines a Free Trade Zone (or Foreign Trade Zone) as: "an area considered outside of the host country's territory but supervised by its customs department. Material may be brought in to the FTZ without paying import duty taxes and assembled or manufactured into a finished product. Duties and taxes are then paid when the finished good is moved outside the FTZ for retail sale."[6]

- **Commercial travel**—this is an area that is often overlooked when making the analysis for off-shoring operations. The cost of flying employees and management back and forth to distant locations and the time involved in the travel are critical components of the analysis that should not be overlooked.

---

[6]APICS Operations Management Body of Knowledge. (2009). *APICS The Association for Operations Management*, 2nd edition. APICS Operations Management Body of Knowledge, p. 26.

- **Supply chain/Transportation costs**—one of the critical areas that should be considered in the off-shoring analysis is the cost of moving products around the globe. For example, if a company with a primary market in North America moves operations from North Carolina to China, there is now a cost of moving the products from China back to North America. In 2009, Maersk Lines announced that they were going to save $1 billion a year in fuel costs by cutting shipping speeds in half. From a manufacturing perspective, this just doubled the shipping times and doubled the inventory in motion.

  Hilton Hotels has a goal of making the furnishings in each of its chains look the same for each room in the chain regardless of the location. For example, if a customer is a loyal Hampton Inn guest, the goal is for every Hampton Inn room to look the same, so the guest feels at home. After a very detailed analysis, Hilton determined that it was actually cheaper to buy the materials in the United States, ship them to Southeast Asia, have the furniture made, and shipped back to the United States than they could have the furniture made in the United States.

- **Labor**—unfortunately, this is the only aspect considered in too many off-shoring analyses. When the cost of oil rose to $140 a barrel in 2008, many companies started questioning the analysis that based the off-shoring on labor alone. Recent studies show that the cost of labor increases in some Asian countries coupled with fuel costs now put the difference between producing in Asia and producing in North America at approximately only 5%.

REGIONAL LOCATION CONSIDERATIONS

Many of the considerations for overseas location analysis impact regional decisions as well. However, a few other considerations must be taken into account for regional location decisions.

- **Quality of Life**—when considering other locations for operations, this must be taken into account. In 1972, Amoco Oil Company decided to move its credit card operations from Chicago. The location decided upon was Raleigh, North Carolina. The primary reason given for the selection was the quality of life in the Raleigh area, which included cost of housing, education, and cost of living in the Raleigh area. Quality of life also included better Bar-B-Que in the Raleigh area and closer proximity to the beach.

- Amoco knew when they moved into the area that they would probably move again in approximately 10 years based on their models. One of the things that Amoco did was work with the State of North Carolina on the location and **incentives** to move into the Raleigh area. Amoco received local incentives to move into the area and in exchange the State of North Carolina was promised the facility when Amoco moved in. The facility was ahead of its time with its own cooling ponds, lots of trees around the building and parking lots, and tinted windows that reflected sunlight to reduce the cooling requirements during the day, and reflected lights in at night to reduce lighting and heating requirements.

  Another example of local/regional incentives is the Wal-Mart in Kansas City, Kansas. Ten years ago, the Kansas City, Kansas area was a relatively depressed economic area and did not merit a Wal-Mart. Then, the Kansas Speedway was built, Nebraska Furniture Mart opened, Cabela's opened and quickly became the number one tourist attraction in the State of Kansas, followed by the opening of the Legends Shopping Center. All of this made the Kansas City, Kansas area the fastest growing shopping and economic district in the Midwest. However, Wyandotte County and Kansas City, Kansas had to offer tax incentives to the largest company in the world to move into the area.

- **Local/regional regulations**—are there environmental concerns or local tax concerns such as in California? The tax rates, environmental regulations, and OSHA regulations are driving companies into Nevada. More and more companies are moving operations into the Reno/Sparks, Nevada area for distribution centers. This location provides rapid response to California customers and the Interstate 80 corridor without paying California taxes or having to comply with California environmental regulations.

- **Transportation networks**—just like the previous discussion about distribution center location analysis, the availability and access to rail, air, and road networks are important to the decision of where to locate a manufacturing facility.

- **Income levels**—deciding to put a high-end retail operation such as Nordstrom will, or at least should have as part of the decision process, a consideration of the income levels of the area. In Kansas City, a high-end company called DigiKarma opened in an area that was not economically postured to support the company, and the store closed its doors less than 3 months later.

- When all else fails and relaxed government oversight or incentives are not available, you can always start your own government. This is what Disney did in Florida. They could not get incentives or full support for infrastructure improvements, so they started the Reedy Creek Development Authority and formed their own government, police, fire, sewage, and infrastructure.

SUMMARY

Location analysis is a complicated process, which enables the company's decision makers to balance costs of off-shoring, such as building a new facility and increased inventory costs, with cost savings from incentives, labor savings, and potential entry to new markets. The basics of location analysis and layout design can be used for any operation from a small gym to a large multimillion square foot distribution center.

Discussion Questions

1. Go to a retail activity and look at their layout. What is the store trying to do with their layout? Is there an obvious pattern to their layout?

2. Based on your visit to a retail facility, is there a better way to layout the facility to maximize exposure to products?

3. Visit a Home Depot or Lowe's and look at the warehouse layout that they have. Is there a pattern to their layout?

4. Create a Muther's grid to improve the layout of the Home Depot that you visit.

5. What is the difference between a product, process, and fixed facility layout?

6. What is a hybrid layout and what advantages does it provide?

7. When should you not choose to use a cellular layout?

8. Can the layout of the facility become the bottleneck for the company?

9. Why is site selection so important to the success of the company?

11 Capacity Planning and Scheduling

The Merriam-Webster Dictionary defines capacity as: "the largest amount or number that can be held or contained."[1] This does not really help when looking at capacity and capacity planning for operations management. The APICS defines capacity a couple of ways that are relevant to operations management: "(1) The capability of a system to perform its expected function. (2) The capability of a worker, machine, work center, plant, or organization to produce output per time period."[2] A simpler definition for an introduction to operations management is: the maximum amount of quality output that can be produced.

The capacity of a system is critical to the planning and production phases of products and services. Capacity is not just a production or storage concept. If you think of a restaurant as a service, the capacity of restaurant is not the maximum capacity as determined by the fire department inspection; it is the maximum amount of customers that the restaurant can service in an acceptable time. This is may explain why you may visit a restaurant and there are vacant tables, but there is still a wait time—the capacity is dictated by the number of servers and cooks, not the number of tables.

In the manufacturing sector, the first stage in capacity planning is to determine the maximum capacity of the plant or shop floor. The most commonly discussed concept for this phase is known as rough cut capacity planning (RCCP). The RCCP is defined by the APICS as: "the process of converting the master production schedule into requirements for key resources, often including labor; machinery; warehouse space; suppliers' capabilities; and in some cases, money."[3] The RCCP is a preliminary stage to determine, if all resources are available, whether the company can meet the needs for the master production schedule. The master production schedule is the anticipated build schedule based on adjusted forecasts and firm orders from customers. Often, the RCCP will indicate that a set production level is doable for the company, but when constrained by actually available resources may prove to be false.

The RCCP leads to capacity planning, which is simply determining how much capacity the company actually needs to meet the production schedule. Capacity planning includes capacity requirements planning. During this phase of the planning process, the company looks at constrained capacity to determine the actual capacity available and how to use that capacity to meet the master production schedule requirements.

Capacity requirements planning is the process of establishing the overall level of resources needed in the facility or system in order to meet the demands of the master production schedule. One of the outputs of this process may be the determination that additional capacity is needed and also when it is needed. Failure to properly conduct this phase of the planning process may impact the responsiveness of the company to the customers, which, in turn, could impact the competitiveness of the company.

Capacity planning includes a series of decisions for the company as shown in Figure 11.1. The goal is to try to maintain as level a production process as possible. Designing a facility that can be used for manufacturing more than one product is helpful in this goal.

---

[1]Merriam-Webster. (n.d.). "Capacity." *Merriam-Webster.com.* Accessed April 17, 2014. http://www.merriam-webster.com/dictionary/capacity

[2]Blackstone, John H., Jr. (2013). APICS Dictionary, Fourteenth Edition. Chicago, IL: APICS, p. 21.

[3]Ibid., p. 153.

> 1. **When do we need to add capacity?**
> 2. **How much capacity do we need to add?**
> 3. **Where is the new capacity needed?**
> 4. **What type of capacity is needed? (labor, materials, machines, etc.)**
> 5. **When do we reduce capacity? (This is not a good thing but may be necessary if demand for a product or service decreases.)**

Figure 11.1: Capacity Decisions

When do we need to add capacity? If the demand for the product or the forecasted demand for the product exceeds the company's capacity, the options are to expand the operations or outsource the additional capacity needs. If the demand increase is a short-term increase, it may be better to outsource. If it is a long-term increase in product/service demand, then the answer may be to add capacity to the firm.

This leads to the decision of how much capacity to add. The follow-on question to this is does the company add a little capacity at a time on a regular basis or one large increase in capacity and then grow into the new capacity? One distribution center in Southern California, after trying the little capacity additions, realized that they were constrained in their location and could not expand any more. Their decision was to move about 5 miles down the road, buy more than enough land for future expansion, and build a facility that was about one and one-half the size of what their immediate needs were and then grow into the facility.

The answer to the question of "where is the capacity needed?" can only be discovered by walking the process. The first place to look is at the system constraint. This leads to deciding what type of capacity increase is needed. It may be as simple as adding a machine or adding another shift or it could be as complex as designing and building a brand new facility. Temporary workers may be the answer. Department stores do this every Christmas season. They know the sales will be increased from the increase in customer traffic buying for the season and add seasonal help. Lawn and garden centers and services do the same thing with summer hires to account for the seasonal increase in demand.

The least favorable option for the company when demand exceeds capacity is to backorder the product to the customers. Backordering is not a good option as it forces the company to violate the concepts of perfect order fulfillment and means the customer will have to wait longer for the product. Since most companies do not have a monopoly on products, this may mean losing a customer or an order to a competitor.

When capacity exceeds demand for the product, there are a few options to consider. The first and most drastic is to reduce capacity. This may be in the form of plant closures or employee layoffs. The second remedy may be to reduce operational hours. Several companies went to 32-hour work weeks during the most recent recession to keep operations going and keep trained workers employed.

AGGREGATE PLANNING

Aggregate capacity planning is a long-term look at capacity needs and requirements. Usually aggregate planning looks 18 months or more into the future. Why should we be concerned that far out? The forecasted demand for the product is going to drive this long-term planning for resources. The need to look this far into to the future is based on the lead times necessary to increase capacity. This does not happen overnight. An increase in capacity may require a new facility or new equipment. The aggregate plan allows the company to start the process of creating new capacity, if needed, without waiting until the last minute, which may dictate outsourcing or product delays.

Near-term capacity planning is driven by the master production schedule. This anticipated build schedule helps to formalize the production plan and helps the company translate specific parts/components/finished products requirements into a work schedule and capacity plan. The near-term capacity plan has to extend out at least as long as the longest lead time for the components or materials for the product (this ties to the inventory concept of when to order).

SYSTEM CAPACITY VERSUS DEPARTMENT CAPACITY

When calculating a capacity for a system or facility, it is important to look at the total system as well as the capacities of individual operations. The Theory of Constraints (as discussed in Chapter 14) states that the throughput capacity of a system is the capacity at the constraint or bottleneck. Therefore, it is important to look at the total system by starting with the capacities of the component operations. Using the Theory of Constraints as a guide, the only way to increase the overall system capacity is to increase the capacity at the constraint. For example: the US Army has a system known as the fuel system supply point. Each individual system contains up to six 50,000-gallon fuel containers. However, the capacity of the system is not the total of the storage containers (up to 300,000 gallons), but the capacity of the fuel hoses that deliver the fuel from the containers to the customers' fuel trucks. The system uses a series of hoses and pumps to distribute the fuel. The constraint is the capacity of the pump, which is 350 gallons per minute.

CAPACITY UTILIZATION VERSUS CAPACITY EFFICIENCY

What is Utilization? This is a manufacturing measure of how much of a company's available capacity is actually being used. Many textbooks will make you believe that the closer a company is to 100% utilization, the better the company is managed. First, let us look at the calculation for utilization.

Equation 11.1: Utilization

$$\text{Utilization rate} = (\text{Actual output rate}/\text{Available capacity}) \times 100$$

Why is 100% or as close to 100% not always a good number? Consider the following issues. What if producing 100% utilization at one work station in the system creates a buildup of work in process inventory at the next work station because the line is not balanced or due to a constraint? What if producing at 100% results in producing more product than the customers are buying? The push for 100% utilization usually comes from the finance offices that use the justification "you wanted a new machine, we found the money and now you are not using it to peak utilization."

Another consideration for not producing at 100% utilization may be the actual hours worked compared with the hours available for work. This calculation has to take into consideration the warm-up time for machines and cool-down times for machines before and after production runs. Some machines may need to warm up to a certain operating temperature before efficient production occurs. Also, some machines may need to cool down before completely shutting down at the end of the work day. If this is not taken into consideration, their utilization rate calculation may be impacted.

Then, what is efficiency? Efficiency is the measure of how well a worker, work station, or machine produces compared with a standard output. Examples of measuring efficiency include pieces produced per hour compared with the set standard for outputs.

Equation 11.2: Efficiency

$$\text{Efficiency} = \text{Output (pieces per hour)}/\text{Standard pieces per hour}$$

Another important concept in the capacity planning process is the load. The load is the standard amount or hours assigned to a machine or facility. Balancing the load across the system is critical to help ensuring the continuous flow of operations.

DEMAND PLANNING AND BALANCING AS PART OF CAPACITY PLANNING

Remember one of the goals of facility planning is to provide for the future and flexibility in operations. One of the goals of capacity planning is to have a smooth level production rate. A methodology for accomplishing both of these goals is to try to manage the demand rate for products. This can be accomplished in a variety of ways.

The most common is to try to shift demand into slow periods. This may be the result of sales promotions or advertising campaigns to convince the customer to buy the products or services in an off-period. Disney used to do this with their Florida Resident Salute Pass. This pass allowed unlimited visits during the periods that Disney had identified as off-peak periods. This provided a win–win. Disney had guests in the park and Florida residents got to enjoy the park in less-crowded times.

Another method is to offer the product or manufacturing in off-cycle or counter-cyclic times. Burlington Coat Factory made an entire market this way. They started off by offering winter clothes in the off season and summer clothes the same way. Toro does this with their manufacturing by making lawn mowers in the winter and snow blowers in the summer on the same line. Another variation of this model is to work with customers to offer them incentives to commit to the purchase of seasonal items in the off season with guaranteed delivery in time for the seasonal sales.

SUMMARY

Capacity planning is critical to the success of the operation, whether it is a service industry or a manufacturing industry. The Theory of Constraints states the throughput capacity of the system is the capacity at the bottleneck. It is important before embarking on a capacity-planning activity to walk the process and identify any bottlenecks or constraints. The entire capacity-planning process is driven by the master production schedule and if there is an imbalance between capacity and the schedule, the planner has to make some critical decisions on how to balance the scheduled production with the necessary capacity.

Discussion Questions

1. Most textbooks state that the closer a company is to 100% utilization, the better they are in managing resources. Is this always true? Why or why not is 100% utilization important?

2. What are some of the reasons for not working at 100% utilization?

3. What are the remedies for having more capacity than demand?

4. What are the remedies for having more demand than capacity?

5. What is the difference between utilization and efficiency?

6. From your perspective, what is one example of the Theory of Constraints?

7. How does capacity planning relate to process design and product design?

12 Inventory Management

Proper and accurate inventory management is critical to the overall success of the supply chain and the operations management chain. This is one of the strongest links between operations management and accounting. Inventory management is an accounting activity. Some of the banks in Brazil are starting to see the link between finance and inventory management. These banks are starting to view automated teller machines (ATMs) as mini-warehouses and the inventory is the cash in the ATM.

The inventory manager must answer four basic questions and work closely with the forecasting to ensure that the right amount of inventory is available. Most texts only list the first three questions, but in twenty-first century supply chains, the fourth question is just as important. The four questions that must be answered by the inventory manager are:

1. What should be ordered?
2. When should it be ordered?
3. How much should be ordered?
4. Where should it be stocked?

The goal of this chapter is to help the operations manager and the inventory manager answer the first three of these questions. Question number 4 is linked to location analysis and an understanding of the customer base and customer clusters. Seeking to answer the question of where to stock an item is what has driven Amazon to go from 6 US facilities in 2000 to 230 facilities by mid-2017. Answering these questions creates a balancing act for the inventory manager. How much is enough and how much is too much?

WHAT IS INVENTORY?

Inventory is an insurance policy against stocking out and against not having what the customer wants at the time that the customer wants it. Unlike automobile insurance or home owner insurance, this form of insurance is where you want just the right amount and you want to use your insurance. Most people that pay for insurance buy the insurance with the hope that it will never be used. The insurance known as inventory is one type of insurance that you want to use every day in meeting the customers' needs because the reason for the insurance level is based on your desired customer service levels. You want your insurance to be there to prevent the customer from going to the competitor. This is where the balancing act comes in. You want enough inventory to meet the needs of the customer without having so much inventory that it goes bad, becomes obsolete, or costs the company large amounts of money to store the product while waiting for the customer to want the product.

There is another balancing act in inventory management. This balancing act is between the financial managers, the inventory managers, and the procurement/acquisition managers. Financial managers see inventory as a liability because the only good inventory to the finance managers is cash. So, finance managers want lower inventory levels and higher levels of cash. Inventory managers want high stockpiles of raw materials and finished goods to meet customer needs. The procurement/acquisition managers have to purchase the right amounts of inventories to meet the production requirements and finished goods requirements, while trying to keep the financial managers happy at the same time.

Inventory is simply the stocks maintained by a company to meet normal demand patterns. Safety stock is maintained to cover the variability in demand. The decisions made concerning inventory levels and the types of inventory maintained impact other areas of operations management and may impact positively or negatively the profitability of the company.

TYPES OF INVENTORY

There are different types of inventory that a company may have to meet the customers' needs. This list is not an exhaustive one, but it does show the primary forms of inventory.

- **Raw materials:** In any manufacturing operation, somewhere in the manufacturing chain, raw materials are needed to produce products. The operations manager has to manage the inventory levels of raw materials, especially if there is a shelf life for the raw material. The question is whether the materials spoil/rot/ deteriorate over time if more than the required amount is stocked or if the amount stocked exceeds the needs of the company.

- **Purchased parts:** If the company does not make the product from raw materials, then it will most likely stock the assemblies that will be used to assemble the product. Raw materials and purchased parts are not an either/or stockage. A company may use some raw materials for certain parts of the product and assemblies for the rest of the product.

- **Labor:** Most textbooks will tell you that this is a form of inventory. It is included in this list to show that in the real world, this should never be considered a form of inventory. The reason for this is that with the exception of professional sports, labor is not bought and sold or stored waiting for consumption like inventory. During the eighteenth and nineteenth centuries, in the United States (and continuing into this century in some countries),[1] the use of people as a commodity that was bought, sold, and traded was practiced. This practice almost destroyed the United States. The picture in Figure 12.1 is the Old Slave Mart in Charleston, South Carolina. This mart was the largest in the United States and continued to operate long after the sale of slaves was outlawed in the country. **The key with people is: you manage things and you lead people! In other words, you manage inventory and since you do not manage people, they should not be considered a category of inventory. Companies do not own their employees and although employees are the greatest asset of a company, they are led, not managed.**

Figure 12.1: The Slave Mart in Charleston, South Carolina

---

[1]One of the biggest concerns and areas of interests in 21st century supply chain is who is making the product and is the worker being forced to work in the factory or serving some form of indentured servitude or slavery while working on the products. Concerns center around knowing what is going on in a supply chain and what suppliers are doing to produce the goods at the low prices. Great Britain has new laws concerning slavery in the supply chain.

Photograph by Joe Walden

Figure 12.2: Doughnuts as Work-In-Process at Krispy Kreme

If you are ever in Charleston, SC, I highly recommend that you visit this museum to remind you of what this type of activity can do to a person and a country. The effects of this activity linger today and can be seen from a historical perspective in Kansas City, MO, at the Negro Leagues Baseball Museum.

- **Work-in-Process (WIP):** Work-In-Process inventory is simply items that are somewhere between raw materials and finished goods. WIP is partially completed products and is the only form of inventory that everyone in the company agrees is a liability. WIP has no value to anyone. It cannot be sold as a finished product and cannot be put back on the shelf for later use. Figure 12.2 shows WIP at Krispy Kreme Doughnuts. The process for producing a doughnut involves a "rising" process for the formed doughnuts and then the raw doughnut is placed in the hot oil to cook the doughnut. The doughnut is then flipped so that both sides of the doughnut get evenly cooked. Even a lover of hot Krispy Kreme doughnuts would not want a half-cooked doughnut. Sometimes the doughnut does not flip. In this case the WIP doughnut is thrown away before the product reaches the frosting water fall.

  In a manufacturing environment WIP builds up behind unbalanced work stations and may show an inventory manager where the constraints are in the process. Like the half-cooked Krispy Kreme doughnuts, the WIP in the manufacturing environment is of no value to the company or the customer.

- **Component parts:** This inventory category includes the nuts, bolts, screws, washers, and fasteners used to assemble a product. This type of inventory is not usually the high-dollar inventory items but is just as critical to the success of the manufacturing operations and should not be neglected.

- **Maintenance, Repair, and Operations (MRO):** This is an aspect of inventory that is often overlooked by most academic textbooks. According to the *APICS Operations Management Body of Knowledge*, MRO inventory is defined as: "items used to support general operations and maintenance, such as spare parts, and consumables used in the manufacturing process and supporting operations."[2] Although these parts are critical to the successful operations of a facility or manufacturing process and not the glamorous inventory items like raw materials and finished goods inventory, MRO inventory should be managed as carefully as other forms of inventory. A spare part for any of the machines or material handling equipment will bring an operation to as quick a stop as the shortage of the component parts. While managing MRO inventory it is important to remember that a $6.00 fan belt can cripple a machine as quickly as a $3,000 engine. This makes it critical to understand each item that is or may be stocked in MRO inventories.

  MRO inventory is not limited to manufacturing operations. In an office setting MRO inventory is found in the supply room as office supplies. Work in an office can come to a halt without the necessary office supplies. Can you put together a professional presentation without printer cartridges or printer paper? Of course you cannot.

---

[2]MRO, *APICS Operations Management Body of Knowledge*, 2nd edition, APICS, Chicago, IL, 2010, p. 45.

MRO supplies are also necessary in an academic environment. Imagine trying to take an exam in a large classroom without the printed exams or the scantron sheets or the "blue" essay books, or pencils?

- **Working capital:** This is the finance manager's favorite form of inventory. This form of inventory is necessary for the success of the any operation. A lack of cash flow or available cash will cripple any operation regardless of the size of the company.

- **Tools, machinery, and equipment:** In a manufacturing environment or in a distribution operation, the tools, machines, and equipment used to make the products or move the products are part of the inventory. If the proper levels of this category of inventory are not maintained, the capacity and production capabilities of the company could be significantly reduced.

  In the distribution center, a shortage of pallet jacks, pallet racks, or forklifts can impact the ability to provide a rapid response to the customers. In the classroom, the shortage of desks or chairs impacts the capacity of the school to provide quality education if it means students are sitting in folding chairs or on the floor.

- **Safety stock:** Safety stock is an additional insurance policy above and beyond the inventory used as insurance as discussed above. Safety stock is stockage above normal stock levels to help prevent a stockout due to increased demands for the product, longer-than-normal lead times for replenishment, or variability in the levels of the demand for the product.

  The US Army's manual for warehousing operations refers to safety stock as a safety level and describes the safety stock as the "quantity of stock on hand to sustain operations in the event the demand rate changes unusually or the replenishment time becomes longer than expected. It is a safety factor intended to be used while replenishment requisitions are still due in."[3]

  Safety stock does not need to be carried for every item. A company may decide to take acceptable risk with certain high-dollar items in order to have safety stock for less expensive items. After all, a smaller, less expensive repair part such as a fan belt can cripple a car just as quickly as a blown engine and probably a fan belt needs to be replaced more often than a complete engine. Therefore, a repair parts company will more likely have safety stock for fan belts and windshield wipers than automobile engines.

  Nor does the safety stock need to be kept at each location. It may be more economical for the company to maintain safety stock at a central location rather than at every distribution center or at every store. A centrally located safety stock for a retail operation with 100 stores would mean one set of safety stock rather than 100 sets of safety stock. This concept only works if the centrally located safety stock can be delivered to the needed location quickly. This may be the justification for a safety stock distribution center located near the FedEx or UPS major sorting facilities. Otherwise, the savings from the centralized stock may be negated by premium shipping charges or lost sales due to stockouts.

- **Just-in-Case:** Just-in-Case inventory is the opposite of Just-in-time Inventory. Just-in-Case stocks are kept in the inventory just in case a customer may want it. Just-in-Case inventory is not supported by any calculation or inventory model. This form of inventory may or may not be demand-supported or even productive inventory. In many cases, the Just-in-Case inventory may be reducing the inventory turns calculations because the inventory is not moving as it is there just in case someone orders it or asks for it.

  Sometimes, Just-in-Case inventory is a good thing. Some items in inventory need Just-in-Case stocks to prevent stocking out of the items. Toilet paper is a good example of stocks that should be kept as Just-in-Case, because stocking out of toilet paper is not a good thing. However, in the real world, Just-in-Case stocks manifest themselves as stock on the shelves of the stores just in case a customer may need that product again in the future. The key here is to determine that point in the life cycle of a product that the repair part should no longer be stocked or how long a product should be kept on the shelf before it is removed from the inventory.

- **Vendor Managed Inventory (VMI):** This concept was discussed in the supply chain chapter, but needs to be discussed here to complete the discussion of inventory. The VMI is inventory on the shelf, but does not count against the inventory value of the facility. The inventory on the shelf belongs to the vendor until it is sold by the store. An example of this is the tool department at The Home Depot. The tools

---

[3]Department of the Army Pamphlet 710-2-2, Supply Support Activity Supply System: Manual Procedures, Headquarters, Department of the Army, Washington, DC, 1998, p. 19.

belong to the vendors until the product is sold. The bottom line of the VMI program is that the onus is on the vendor to keep the products stocked on the shelf.

Wal-Mart and Procter & Gamble have perfected the partnership on VMI. The benefit to Procter & Gamble is information on what is being sold in order to better schedule deliveries and production. The benefit to Wal-Mart is a savings of eight man-years per store per year by not having to count the products on the shelves, place orders for the items, receive the items, and place the items on the shelves. With "8,613 retail units under 55 different banners in 15 countries,"[4] this amounts to approximately 68,000 man-years for Wal-Mart.

■ **Finished goods**: Upon completion of the manufacturing process, inventory may take the form of finished products awaiting shipment or waiting for customer orders in the case of make-to-stock items. If the forecasts are relatively accurate for the make-to-stock items, the amount of finished product held for sale will not become obsolete inventory. These finished goods may be in warehouses/distribution centers or may be in-transit inventory.

■ **In-transit inventory:** This form of inventory is finished goods that have departed the manufacturing facility *en route* to a distribution center or from a distribution center to a customer or retailer. The problem with in-transit inventory is that this inventory, if not *en route* to a customer, is not available to for sale to a customer or available for use in a manufacturing facility. The goal of all companies is to minimize in-transit inventory. In 2009, Maersk Lines announced that they would save over $1 billion (USD) by reducing shipping speeds by half. For Maersk Lines, this move produced savings from reduced fuel costs. For customers of Maersk Lines, this move doubled the in-transit times for product in-transit—more dollars tied up in inventory that is not available for sale to customers.

The bottom line is that inventory is held in all of the above forms as an addiction. Inventory is used to cure ills and inefficiencies in a company's processes or supply chains. When I was at the US Army's National Training Center the first time, I had over 120 days of inventory on hand. The average replenishment cycle was over 58 days. My customer base changed every 28 to 35 days. Simple math reveals that any item ordered by a customer that was not on my shelves probably would not arrive before the customer left. However, because I had so much inventory on the shelves, I was not worried about any possible inefficiency or inefficiencies in the supply chain. All of my supply chain ills were cured by the huge pile of inventory on my shelves.

No good discussion of inventory management is complete without some form of a "water" diagram. In Figure 12.3, the water level represents inventory levels and the boulders under the water represent the problems or ills cured by the inventory. As long as the water level remains high, the inefficiencies or boulders are not a problem.

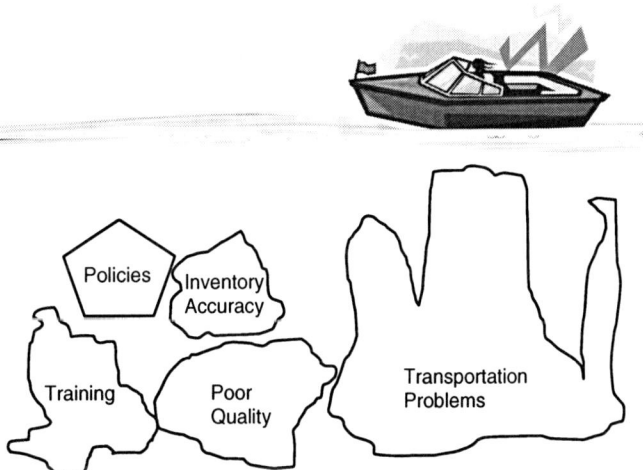

Figure 12.3: Water levels and Inventory Management

---

[4]http://walmartstores.com/AboutUs, accessed September 27, 2010.

Here is where this text and other texts disagree. Most texts recommend lowering the inventory levels to reveal the inefficiencies—or in line with the water analogy, lower the water level to reveal the boulders. The problem with this is if the water is lowered, the boat will hit the rocks or the waterway will be impassable. This technique also assumes that all inventory is productive inventory. Reducing nonproductive inventory has no impact on the operations and will not produce savings or reduce inefficiencies.

The best way to improve inventory efficiencies while reducing the inventory levels is to start by walking the process and identifying the inefficiencies protected by the excess inventory levels. Then and only then should the inventory levels be reduced.

The solution to the high levels of inventory at the National Training Center was to walk the process and identify the inefficiencies that drove the high levels of inventory. While walking the process, it was discovered that the shipping time from the supporting wholesale distribution center was taking 10 days on average. However, the driving time from the distribution center was 8 hours in a small Ford Escort.

When asking questions as to why it was taking so long for the delivery, it was discovered that the company point of view was: "We've been delivering here for almost twenty years. The first time we delivered there we had a mechanical problem and it took 10 days. No one complained, so we assumed 10 days was the standard."

Further questioning produced a new solution. The transportation manager said, "We can close the door on the truck at 8:00 p.m. tonight and deliver to your door by 8:00 a.m. tomorrow morning." By walking the process, almost 10 days was removed from the in-transit time. This improvement allowed us to reduce the inventory levels accordingly. Each subsequent process-walk revealed more inefficiency in the system. Each time any inefficiency was identified and fixed, the inventory levels were further reduced again.

Walking the process, identifying inefficiencies, and fixing them enabled us to reduce the inventory level from approximately $200 million (USD) to approximately $20 million, while reducing the replenishment times from 58 days to 4.6 days over a couple of years.

WHY HAVE INVENTORY?

Now that we have discussed the types of inventory, it is important to discuss why companies have inventory. As we saw in the previous section, companies may have inventory to cover up the inefficiencies in their supply chains—even if they do not realize that this is the reason for their high levels of inventory. Other reasons for maintaining inventory on hand include:

- The primary reason to have inventory in the supply chain is to ensure that the company covers any variations in the demand of the customers. As mentioned earlier, this form of inventory is an insurance policy against a stockout. When the company maintains inventory for this purpose, the goal is to have what the customer wants in the quantities the customer wants to improve customer service.
- Inventory may serve as a buffer to prevent stockouts in the manufacturing chain. If all of the facility is not balanced or if the demand for the products being produced varies, insurance can provide a buffer to keep the operation flowing.
- Inventory may serve as an insurance policy against price increases or to take advantage of price breaks for purchasing large quantities. There is a downside to this type of inventory management practice. A company has to conduct a good analysis of the carrying costs of having the inventory on the shelf. A price break for a large quantity of inventory that is in excess to the needs of the company is not a savings. A purchase that provides the company a hedge against inflation or against a price increase that results in so much inventory that the inventory becomes obsolete is not a deal for the company; or if the cost to keep the inventory on the shelf exceeds the "savings" from the price break or anticipated price increase, there is no benefit to the company.
- Inventory may provide a buffer for contingencies such as hurricanes, fires, or any bad weather. Rapid response supply chains should maintain certain levels of stocks to support operations during such occasions. For example, an agency or company may stockpile generators, bottled water, and staple food items to posture the supply chain to support any disaster relief operations—manmade or natural. Contingency stocks may very well include a backup stock of wine and other important items to carry one through an emergency.

REASONS AGAINST HAVING INVENTORY

Just as there are valid reasons to have inventory in the supply chain, there are also reasons against having inventory. Keeping in mind the need for customer service to remain a viable entity, these reasons may not be as valid from a holistic supply chain perspective.

The first reason against having inventory has been touched on already—using the inventory to mask inefficiencies in the supply chain. As long as large piles of inventory (sometimes called mountains of inventory) exist, companies may not become concerned with nonvalue-added processes and nonvalue-added inventory. So, the argument is that inventory must be get ridded of and the system improved. As we discussed earlier, this may not fix the problems.

One company that I worked with reduced inventory by 20% across the board based on this philosophy of getting rid of inventory to improve operations. Costs did not decrease as rapidly while the customer service levels did as a result of the decreased inventory levels. Why? These reductions also included reducing the authorized levels of the nonproductive inventory. As the nonproductive inventory items were not selling, the value of those stock keeping units (SKUs) did not decrease and the impact on inventory turns remained the same. An item that is not selling will not turn over and will lower the inventory turns for the facility or the company. In addition, the 20% reduction to the fast-moving items resulted in sales that exceeded the ability to replenish, thus producing stockouts.

Other reasons for not maintaining include not tying up precious financial resources with inventory—especially if the inventory is not moving. Large levels of inventory divert management attention from other strategic issues. More companies are discovering the value of strategic and aggregate inventory management as a cost savings and to improve efficiency and customer service.

AGGREGATE INVENTORY MANAGEMENT

"Every management mistake ends up in inventory."

—Michael C. Bergerac, Former CEO, Revlon, Inc.

Aggregate inventory management seeks to answer the questions of inventory management by answering the following questions:

1. How much do we have now? What is our on-hand inventory? Knowing how much we have on hand is important before any inventory decisions are made. If a company does not have a good idea of how much inventory is on the shelf, they may order more or find themselves unable to fill customer orders. Not knowing the amount of an item on the shelf is an indicator of poor inventory management and poor warehouse/distribution center management.
2. How much do we want? The answer to this question is based on the forecast of what the company needs to make or needs to ship to customers. To know how much inventory a company wants depends on knowing the answer to the first question.
3. What will be the output? How much product does the company need to make? This is based on the manufacturing forecast or hopefully from the master production schedule. How many products the company is going to make from the items in the inventory drives the previous questions. How many end items the company will make drives the total number of the component items the company must have in the inventory at the start of production.
4. What input must we get? In order to know how many items the company needs to order, the company needs to know how many end items need to be produced less than the on-hand balance. This produces the amount of each component or raw material that needs to be ordered to meet the production numbers.
5. When do we need to order the items? This is the final aggregate inventory question necessary to be answered to be successful in operations management. The answer to this question may be more important than knowing how much to order. Why? Because if a company knows how much to order, but does not know when the item should be ordered, the product may not arrive in time to meet the production requirements. However,

if the company knows when the product should be ordered, but does not have an exact number that needs to be ordered because of other warehouse problems, at least some of the finished product can be made to meet part of the customer orders.

Good aggregate inventory management leads to customer satisfaction and meeting the needs of the customers. Poor inventory management decisions can be identified by looking for the following symptoms:

- A large number of backorders. This is a good indicator of not having the right items on the shelves at the retail facility or distribution center to fill the orders of the customers. A similar symptom may be filling the customer orders from another distribution center in the supply chain. Backorders or passing of orders to another distribution center is a red flag that should indicate to the management that the inventory on the shelves is either too little or consists of wrong items.
- The first symptom may lead to another symptom. This symptom is customer turnover or customer churn. The inventory management problem in the previous symptom leads to this problem. If an activity does not have what the customer wants and passes the action or backorders the action, customers will leave and "shop" elsewhere. This may be evident by the number or orders that are cancelled by the customers as a result of the backorders. Customers usually only order something when they need it and they want it now!
- Poor inventory may manifest itself in an increasing investment in more and more inventory with no change in backorder levels. How can this happen? If we add more to the inventory and spend more money would it not fix any problem? This attitude leads to compounded problems. The goal is to have the right stuff on the shelf in the right quantities to meet customers' requirements. If the company adds more of the wrong inventory or adds more wrong items, the number of backorders will not decrease. A careful analysis of the inventory is necessary to know what to add and how much to add to meet the customers' needs.
- Not enough inventory and/or the wrong items in the inventory produced the previous problems; having too much inventory produces different symptoms. Having too much stuff not only leads to higher inventory costs as discussed below, but also produces a shortage of storage space and the requirement to store items outside in trailers (a very expensive form of storage) or leasing additional or contract warehouse space.

INVENTORY MANAGEMENT METHODOLOGIES

Once a company determines the answers to the four questions above, the company must decide on three basic inventory management methodologies. These three methodologies are Just-in-Time, Pull, and Push. Almost every inventory management method falls under one of these three methodologies.

- **Just-in-Time (JIT).** Although we will discuss this in detail in the next chapter, it is important to mention it here as part of inventory management. As you will see in Chapter 14, there is much more to JIT than inventory management, but many companies only see JIT as an inventory methodology. As an inventory management methodology, JIT seeks to have as little on the shelf as possible. This leaves no buffer against demand variations or lead time deviations. As the total demand for a product does not change rapidly in most cases, a company that goes to JIT as an inventory management methodology is simply passing the requirement for stockage to the next level of supply support. We will discuss this concept in detail in Chapter 14.
- **Push.** The Push methodology is based on the assumption that the folks at corporate headquarters know more about what an activity needs than the folks managing that activity. Most textbooks will tell you that the Push methodology is not efficient in the long run. The fact is **Push** is not efficient in the long run or the short run. Look at the mess in Kuwait in March 2003 as a result of the Push mindset, as shown in Figure 12.4. This same mindset provided the mountains of inventory that provided the background for LTG Gus Pagonis' book, *Moving Mountains,* from the first Gulf War.[5] The Push mindset is the reason for so many "Sales" at the end of a season—this coupled with poor forecasting. The Push formula is to send items forward in the supply chain based on what the higher corporate headquarters thinks should be in the stock mix.

---

[5]Also known as Operation Desert Shield/Desert Storm

Photograph by Joe Walden

Figure 12.4: Inventory as a Result of the Push Method of Inventory Management

- **Pull.** This methodology is similar in nature to JIT. Both methods seek to minimize unneeded inventory. Pull means that nothing is shipped to a company or location for their inventory needs until the items are asked for. This methodology is based on the premise that the retailer, customer, or facility knows better what they need than the next level up in the supply chain.

INVENTORY COSTS

The decision on what methodology is used may very well impact on the costs associated with inventory (remember, the costs of the inventory is one reason for arguments against having inventory at all). Inventory costs are driven up by poor inventory management decisions and poor inventory forecasting methodologies. An inventory cost above the value of the inventory itself includes the inventory carrying costs. Inventory carrying costs are the costs to the company to keep items on the shelf over time. The biggest percentage of inventory carrying costs is the cost of the capital tied up in inventory that could be used for other purposes in the company. This cost includes the cost of the interest that could be made if the capital is simply put in an interest bearing account.

Other costs associated with inventory carrying costs include:

- Taxes. This is one of the reasons why companies have sales at the beginning of the year. If items can be sold before the annual inventory, two benefits occur. First, there will be fewer items on the shelf to count during the inventory and the value of the total inventory is less, so taxes on the inventory value will be less. Also included in the taxes part of the carrying costs may be an allocated portion of the property taxes on the facility. Because of the difficulty in allocating property taxes on a facility to inventory, this is not a common practice.
- The cost of inventorying the products. This is not cheap. Someone has to be paid to conduct the physical count of the items on the shelf. Then someone has to reconcile the inventory count and conduct recounts, if necessary. All of this costs time and money.
- There is a cost associated with obsolescence. Obsolete, excess, dormant, or aged inventory are the same thing. Regardless of what a company calls this inventory, it is a liability on the books and costs the company money to continue holding these items or to dispose of the items. The better the inventory management decisions, the lower the obsolescence costs.
- Another aspect of inventory carrying costs is the insurance to cover any natural or manmade disaster. My first warehouse was destroyed by a hurricane force wind. A recent storm in the Memphis, Tennessee area did similar damage to a much larger distribution center. Without insurance on the inventory items, the company would face large losses. Figure 12.5 and Figure 12.6 show the outside before the storm and the inside of my facility in Hawaii after the storm passed through.

Figure 12.5: Outside the DC before the Storm

Figure 12.6: Inside of DC after the Storm Passed

- Theft and pilferage. This is also known as shrinkage cost. We will discuss this in Chapter 18 when we discuss supply chain security and supply chain preparedness. Losses to distribution centers and warehouses from theft and pilferage cost supply chains, depending on the source, a range as high as $30 billion (USD) annually in the United States alone. These costs add to the inventory carrying costs. One major home improvement company simply adds 10% to their budget and costs to cover tool theft.

All of these costs added together create a cost that is usually measured as a percentage of the inventory value. The biggest problem with inventory carrying costs is that many companies have no idea what their inventory carrying costs really are. These companies use the industry average as the figure for their carrying costs. As we will see when we discuss the economic order quantity as an ordering technique, not knowing what the real inventory carrying costs are can have a major impact on funding and ordering quantities. This creates a continual problem with more carrying costs. Benchmarking studies show that inventory carrying costs may reach as high as 40% of the value of the inventory. Remember there is a flaw to managing the averages. Someone is above the average and someone is below the average. If a company does not know what their true inventory carrying costs are, there are problems, but this may also be another symptom of inventory management problems. The other side of inventory-related costs comes from not having enough inventory on the shelf. This leads to stockout or shortage costs. The inventory manager has to find the right balance between carrying costs and shortage costs.

WHEN TO ORDER

Now that we have established the costs of having too little or too much inventory on the shelves, it is important to determine when to order the items—remember it may be more important, depending on the product, to know when to order than how much.

If a company does not have a fixed interval for ordering, a reorder point (ROP) is necessary to determine when to order. A fixed ordering interval simply states that at certain intervals the company will order enough to raise the inventory levels back to a pre-established maximum authorized stockage level—usually referred to as the stockage objective or maximum inventory level.

If a ROP is used, the calculation can be a very simple calculation as shown in Formula 12.1. This calculation will work if the lead time is in days, weeks, or hours.

Formula 12.1: Reorder Point Calculation

$$ROP = D \times LT$$
$$ROP = (D \times LT) + SS \text{ (if safety stock is used)}$$
$$D = \text{Demand during lead time}$$
$$LT = \text{Lead time to replenish}$$
$$SS = \text{Safety stock}$$

There are at least seven commonly used ROPs. Some of these ROPs are more common than the others, and one is the precursor of a commonly used Just-in-Time technique. These ROPs are used for independent demand items—those items that are not dictated by the demand for another product. The opposite of independent demand is dependent demand—the inventory level of a dependent demand item is dictated by the master production schedule.

- **Fixed ROP.** This is also known as a periodic demand. A fixed ROP dictates that at a set time or period, a replenishment order is placed. At this predetermined period, the inventory is counted and the on-hand balance is subtracted from the maximum-desired inventory level. The difference between the on-hand and maximum-desired levels is ordered.
- **Variable ROP.** Rather than ordering at a fixed time interval, an order is placed whenever the on-hand inventory reaches a set inventory level. At this point, the quantity ordered will take the on-hand inventory to the maximum stockage requirement.
- **Two Bin.** The Two Bin ROP is the precursor to the Kanban system (see Chapter 14 for more details on the Kanban system). The Two Bin system is used for smaller parts such as nuts, bolts, screws, or washers. This system of reordering uses two bins for storage of the items. The ROP occurs when the first bin is emptied. The quantity of each bin equals the demand during the replenishment lead time multiplied by the lead time (ROP = demand during lead time x lead time). When the first bin is emptied, the necessary replenishment quantity is ordered. The theory is as long as the lead time is constant, the second bin will become empty at the same time that the first bin is replenished. A variation of the Two Bin system is one bin with a line placed inside the bin. When the line is visible, it is time to reorder.
- **Card.** The card ROP is a visible card to tell the company or store that it is time to reorder. Bookstores use the card system for books and the small carousels of book markers at the checkout line. When a bookmark is removed from the carousel, the card is visible to the clerk and a reorder or restock is made. In the books on the shelves, a card signals the checkout clerk to key in the reorder. Figure 12.7 is an example of a card ROP.
- **Judgmental.** This form of ROP is based on someone's judgment or experience. This form of ROP is not common except in smaller operations. For this form of reordering to be successful, there has to be a good level of experience and knowledge of the products and the sales of those products. At the US Army's National Training Center, different units would use repair parts at different levels depending on their equipment mix. The repair parts distribution center used a variable ROP. However, when certain units were scheduled to train, judgmental increases to the stockage levels helped to prevent stockouts.

Figure 12.7: Card Reorder System

- **Projected Shortfall.** Like the judgmental reorder, this form of reorder is dependent on someone's experience and knowledge of the products. If forecasts show a projected shortfall using the normal ROP, an additional replenishment order may be placed.
- **Min–Max.** This is the newest ROP methodology. However, like many "new" ideas, Min–Max is just a variation of the traditional ROP. When on-hand inventory hits the acceptable minimum level, an order is placed to take the inventory back to the maximum-desired inventory level.

ECONOMIC ORDER QUANTITY

Just as the ROP and reorder quantity may tell a company how much to order, the real purpose of the ROP is to tell the company when to order. The economic order quantity calculation helps the company determine how much to order. The goal of the economic order quantity is to balance ordering costs and inventory carrying costs.

Formula 12.2: Economic Order Quantity Calculation

$$EOQ = \sqrt{2ACo/I}$$
A = Annual Demand
Co = Cost of Ordering
I = Inventory Carrying Costs

The economic order quantity (EOQ) calculation depends on five basic assumptions in order to be useful as a tool for determining how much to order. Not all of these assumptions may be valid in today's business environment. These assumptions are:

1. The demand rate is constant and known. Demand is not always constant in today's businesses. Customers have the option of buying via the Internet and buy when they need a product. When the EOQ formula was developed, the majority of orders were placed by stores at set quantities. If demand is not constant, this assumption is not valid and, therefore, the EOQ calculation may not be the best methodology for a company to use.
2. There are no quantity discounts for products. Any good corporate buyer is going to try to get a discount for quantity buys. If the buyer gets the discount, this EOQ assumption is not valid and again the calculation may be flawed.

3. The entire order is delivered complete. This means no split shipments, no substitutions, and no backorders. Is this valid in today's environment? Substitutions and split shipments are commonplace in today's business. Sometimes, the split shipment is by design because the company only needs part of the product now and part of the order later. Split shipments and backorders also occur when demand is not constant and the supplier has a stockout. This is reality.
4. The ordering costs and the carrying costs are known. Every company should know these costs. As long as the company knows these costs, this is a valid assumption.
5. Stockouts are not allowed as demand is constant. Look at assumption number 1; if that assumption is not valid due to variable demand patterns, then this assumption may not be valid either.

Even when all five assumptions are valid, there are some times when the EOQ is not needed as a replenishment calculation. If a company receives a fixed order quantity from a customer for a product and the EOQ quantity is different from the customer order quantity, then the customer order quantity should drive the company's order. If there is a limit on the size of an order such as a fixed lot size, then the lot size or multiples of the lot size should be ordered. A third exception to the EOQ is when there is a limitation on the tool/machinery life or the shelf life of the raw materials. For example, if the EOQ calculation determines that 4,000 lb of a raw material should be the order quantity, but the material has a limited shelf life that is shorter than the forecasted usage period, then the order quantity may be less than the EOQ.

Example 12.1 EOQ Calculation

Annual demand (A) = 45,000 units
Ordering costs (Co) = $50 per order
Carrying costs (I) = 30%

$$Q = \sqrt{2(45,000)(50)/.3}$$
$$= 3872.98 = 3873 \text{ (have to round up to a whole number)}$$

With the EOQ, a company can forecast the number of orders that it will make each year. Example 12.2 shows the calculation to estimate the number of orders. Knowing the forecasted number of orders for a year enables a company to more accurately forecast ordering expenses for the year and when all orders are summed up, it may allow the company to forecast how many purchasing employees should be employed for the next year.

Example 12.2 Calculating the Number of Orders per Year

\# ORDERS/YEAR = A/Q
$$= 45,000/3,873$$
$$= 11.6 \sim 12 \text{ orders a year}$$

SAFETY STOCK

Safety stock is an additional insurance policy to back up the primary insurance policy known as inventory. This is simply a level of stockage above the normally calculated inventory levels to prevent against increased demands or lead times, longer-than-normal replenishment times, or variability in demands for a product. Normal inventory levels are set to meet customer demands, while safety stock insures against stockouts from variations in demand or lead times. Safety stock is also maintained in some companies as a buffer to protect the manufacturing company against forecasting errors.

Safety stock may as well be called sacred stock in most organizations. The reason for this is that many companies do not want to touch their safety stocks. One particular company actually preferred to backorder customer requests than use their safety stock and go to a stockout position to meet the customers' orders. Their rationale was that they reported SKUs that were stocked out to their Vice President and CEO, but their reports did not include backorders.

Safety stock adds costs to every location that maintains a safety stock without necessarily adding value to the ability of the inventory to support the customers. A company may better serve the customers by consolidating the safety stock for the entire distribution network at one central location. Safety stock is usually set as either a set days of supply above the normal stockage level or a percentage of the lead time demand.

Safety stock can be set in a number of ways.

- A set number. The company decides that they will add 5 to the stockage level for every item as safety stock.
- A set percentage. In this case, the company decides to add a 1% safety stock level to every item. The advantage of this over the set number is that the safety stock will be set for each item based on its sales levels.
- A set days of supply. For example, the company decides that it wants a safety stock level of 1 day of supply or sales for each item. If the item demand is 10 per day, the company would then add 10 to that item's stocks as safety stocks.
- Customer service levels. In this case, the company will set the safety stock level based on a desired customer service level. To do this, the company will need to know the average demand for the product and the standard deviation for the demand pattern. The z table from statistics books is necessary for this calculation. The formula for safety stock is:

Equation 12.3: Safety Stock Formula

$$\text{Safety stock} = z \times \sigma$$
$$= \text{Customer service level} \times \text{Standard deviation}$$

For a safety stock level to equal a 99% customer service level ($z = 2.58$) and a standard deviation of 5, the safety stock calculation would be:

Example 12.3 Safety Stock with Customer Service Level

$$\text{Safety stock} = z \times \sigma$$
$$= \text{customer service level} \times \text{standard deviation}$$
$$z = 2.58$$
$$\sigma = 5$$
$$\text{Safety stock} = 2.58 \times 5 = 12.9 \sim 13$$

INVENTORY TURNS

The most misunderstood metric for distribution centers is the measure of inventory turns. Inventory turns is a simple calculation as shown in Formula 12.4. Inventory turns provides a benchmark for companies within their industries. Comparing inventory turns calculations between different industries only creates confusion and frustration. Comparing the turns for a dairy product with a hardware store will not produce a good benchmark. For years, everyone wanted to benchmark against Dell Computers even if they were not in the computer industry.

Formula 12.4: Inventory Turnover Rate Calculation

$$\text{Inventory turnover} =$$
$$(\text{Annual Cost of Goods Sold (COGS)})/$$
$$(\text{Average inventory value})$$

Theoretically, the following issues are associated with inventory turns. Remember, all things change when you go from the abstract to the concrete.

- Low inventory turns equates to high carrying costs and very low stockout costs. In actuality, low turns may show that there is too much inventory on the shelf, which would indeed equal low or no stockout costs. However, it could also mean that there are too many of the wrong items on the shelf. If a company is stocking the wrong items on the shelf, the turns will be low, but the stockouts or backorders will still be high. One company with multiple distribution centers was experiencing very low turns (less than four a year), but was also backordering a very large percentage of customer orders because the items the customers wanted were not stocked in the right distribution center.
- High inventory turns should mean lower inventory carrying costs, but high stockout costs. However, if the inventory is the right size, replenishment times are stable, and the forecasts for sales are relatively accurate, a high level of turns can be achieved while keeping stockout costs to a minimum.

OTHER PERFORMANCE MEASURES

- Average inventory investment: The average inventory investment is calculated for the year in most cases. Comparing average inventory levels is not an effective method to benchmark between companies. This is a necessary financial metric to help companies determine how they are doing compared with previous years.
- Days of inventory (days of sales): This metric is related to inventory turns. This measure looks at how many days of sales can be supported from the on-hand inventory. In theory, the lower the days of inventory, the more efficient the inventory is performing.

Formula 12.5: Days of Inventory Calculation

$$\text{Days of Inventory} = \text{Average Inventory Investment}/\text{Annual Cost of Goods Sold (COGS)}$$

INVENTORY ANALYSIS USING ABC STRATIFICATION

The ABC analysis has nothing to do with activity-based costing. The ABC analysis is based on Pareto's Law—also known as the 80/20 rule. Pareto postulated that 80% of the wealth was in the hands of 20% of the population. This rule also applies to distribution centers and inventories. The application of this principle to inventories states that 80% of the inventory value is tied up in 20% of the inventory items. By applying the 80/20 rule, inventory items can be stratified into A items (20% by value and volume), B items (25%–30% of the items), and C items (50%).

The ABC analysis using this methodology can dictate inventory management and inventory control measures. "A" items are those high-value items that should be more stringently controlled and inventoried as often as once a week or once a month. "B" items can be inventoried a little less frequently—perhaps quarterly. "C" items include the small dollar items that fill up distribution centers. These items can be inventoried once a year.

There is another application of ABC—the organization of the distribution center by volume. The A items in this application are the very fast-moving items and should be placed closest to the shipping area to reduce movement and improve picking times for the fastest moving items. Further analysis may determine that in lieu of placing these items close to the shipping area, the items may be candidates for cross-docking. The C items are the slow-moving items. These items may be candidates for elimination from the stocks altogether or placed in the farthest locations from the shipping docks.

The ABC analysis also applies to customers. Just as the inventory is stratified to better manage the distribution center, customers can be stratified to make sure the better customers or largest customers get better service or have priority for low volume or constrained stocks.

INVENTORY CONTROLS

Inventory control is the physical counting of the items and the security of the items in the distribution center. Inventory control sounds easy on paper—what comes in should be counted and what is in the center should be accounted for, and what goes out should be carefully counted and checked. Remember Clausewitz? This is another way that things change when moving from the abstract to the concrete. If inventory control was as easy as it sounds, everyone would have perfect inventory control. And, no one would have a shrinkage problem with their inventory.

Proper inventory control starts at the receiving dock. A proper count is necessary when the items come into the distribution center, warehouse, or store. After counting the items, they must be put in the proper location. While in the location, the items must be counted, and when the items are picked for shipping, the items need to be counted again. If an item is stored in more than one location, this information should not be a secret. Every location has to be recorded to make sure an accurate count is possible.

There are four basic inventory-counting techniques in use today. Most companies use an annual wall-to-wall inventory count, a cyclic count, a periodic count, and may also use a sensitive item inventory count. Usually, a tolerance is set for the count. As long as the physical count is within the set tolerance, the count is accepted. If the count does not match the inventory record or is out of tolerance, research is necessary to determine why there is a discrepancy and when the discrepancy may have occurred.

The wall-to-wall count is the preferred method of the finance officials. This count happens once a year and every item in the facility is counted and matched against the inventory record system within the warehouse management system. The problem with an annual wall-to-wall inventory is that the facility is usually closed down for the duration of the count. If the counts do not match, this closure could last for up to a week. This impacts customer service if orders are not being picked during the count. One facility in South Los Angeles has a 50% employee turnover rate each year. This means that half of the employees that may have made an inventory mistake or picking error in February will not be there to help solve the problems next January when the wall-to-wall inventory is conducted. This may impact the ability to solve the problems.

The best alternative to annual wall-to-wall counts is the cyclic inventory. Cycle counting counts each of the items at least annually, but does not require shutting down a facility to do the count. A cycle count may be conducted in conjunction with routine order picking. A worker may be told to go to a location to pick an item and then count what is left and record it. Like the wall-to-wall count, this count will be matched against the inventory record for accountability. If a cycle count is properly organized, each item in the inventory will be counted at least once a year and some items may be counted more often. Cycle counting does not require closing the facility to do the count, and, as it is done more frequently, finding the cause of problems may be faster and much easier to identify. To prevent any complications with cycle counts, in one facility, we established a third shift that did nothing, but cycle counts. This facility went from 84% inventory accuracy to 99% accuracy within 3 months of adding this new counting shift.

A periodic inventory is an adaptation of the cycle count concept. This methodology states that a certain percentage of the items are counted each period—week, month, or quarter. The goal of this program is to count every item at least once every year.

A sensitive item inventory is another adaptation of the cycle count concept. A company that normally does annual inventory counts may choose to conduct more frequent counts of high-dollar or highly pilferable items to ensure that these items do not walk out of the facility. This type of inventory count makes the insurance folks happy and helps to keep facility managers feel more comfortable about the safety of the inventory.

The ABC analysis can be applied to the inventory count methodology. The A items, those expensive or fast-moving items, may be counted monthly. The B items may be counted semiannually and those low-cost and/or slow-moving items may only be counted annually or when a stockout occurs.

SPECIAL CONCERNS IN INVENTORY MANAGEMENT

Inventory management is critical to the operational success and financial success of a company. There are some very real concerns that impact on the quality of a company's inventory management efforts.

The first major concern is the proliferation of stock keeping units (SKUs) in the inventory. This is a two-part problem. The first part of the problem is how a SKU number is assigned. Some companies assign a different SKU for the same item stocked in a different store or warehouse. This causes confusion. An SKU should be a unique item identifier for an item throughout a supply chain. The second part of this problem is the increase in SKUs across supply chains. The AMR research recently revealed a 15% increase in the amount of products in supply chains over the past several years. Consumer pressure to produce new products contributes to this problem. The more the items that a supply chain can stock contribute to the accuracy problems and the pilferage problems.

Dead/obsolete inventory is a concern for inventory managers. This is inventory that is of no value. This inventory is driven partially by the pressure to increase the number of products and the shelf life of those products. This inventory is also partially driven by forecasting inaccuracies. Dead or obsolete inventory not only takes up space and contributes to higher inventory carrying costs, but it also contributes to lower inventory turns rates while reducing profitability for companies.

Substitute and complementary items cause inventory problems. When the primary item is an out-of-stock item, does the company have another item that can be substituted that is acceptable to the customer? The Department of Defense Logistics Agency maintains and publishes a listing of interchangeable and substitution items. Complementary items also create a problem if the forecasting effort does not link the items together. These items may be used at the same time such as oil and oil filters that can be placed in a kit or may be like the shirts stocked by L.L. Bean that are usually ordered together. In the fashion world, complementary items may be the matching shoes and bag or suits and ties. Keeping complementary items in stock together may create challenges for inventory managers, but helps to improve customer service levels.

Repair parts and replacement parts create problems for inventory managers. Why? If everybody has repair parts, how can this be a problem? Remember the discussion of independent versus dependent demand items under the forecasting discussions? Repair parts are independent demand items and, therefore, much harder to forecast since end items breakdown at different rates. These items reinforce the need to have good forecasting techniques for repair parts and replacement parts in the supply chain.

Items going backward create issues and problems for inventory managers. Reverse logistics is discussed in detail in a later chapter, but is important enough to mention here as one of the areas of concern in inventory management. Any resaleable item that comes backward adds to the on-hand inventory and adds to the inventory value, inventory carrying costs, and inventory turns calculations.

SUMMARY

In this chapter, we have looked at why have inventory. Inventory is needed to cover the normal customer demands for products. Inventory is an insurance policy to prevent against stockouts from normal demand. On top of the inventory is another level of inventory called safety stock that prevents stockouts from variations in demand or variations in replenishment lead times. The long-running argument between operations managers and finance managers centers on the utility of inventory. Operations managers believe that much of the inventory is an asset, while finance managers believe any inventory that is not cash is a liability. Both camps do agree that WIP inventory and obsolete inventory are indeed liabilities.

Inventory management seeks to answer four questions. We looked at three of these questions in detail in this chapter. The first question is what to order. This is driven by the master production plan in a manufacturing facility. The second question is how much to order which is driven by the EOQ, which seeks to balance ordering costs and carrying costs. The third question may be the most important question of all—when to order. This is driven by the ROP calculation. The ROP uses demand during the replenishment time and the length of the replenishment time to prevent stockouts and determine when to order. The fourth question ties to supply chain management and location analysis: where should the product be stocked to meet the needs of the customer?

Having the right inventory on the shelf in the right quantities drives the calculation for inventory turns. Although this calculation is widely misunderstood, it is a good metric for the inventory levels necessary to support customers.

Inventory management is critical to successful operations and important for meeting the needs of customers. Poor inventory management produces lost sales, excess stocks on the shelves, and higher inventory carrying costs. Good inventory management is important for customer service and profitability.

Discussion Questions

1. Why do companies have inventory?

2. Is inventory an asset or a liability? Can it be both? Explain your answer.

3. How can an inventory item that is an asset become a liability? Give an example.

4. A company has an average inventory value of $450,000,000 and their cost of goods sold for the year is $4,500,000,000. What is their inventory turn? Is this good or bad?

5. A company decides to add safety stock to its distribution centers. The company has 15 distribution centers throughout the United States. Would the company be better served to have safety stock at each location or should they consolidate the safety stock at one location? Justify your answer.

6. If JW, Inc. has a fixed lead time for replenishment of its Widget B of 10 days and an average demand of 12 Widget Bs per day, where should JW Inc. set their ROP? Would this change if JW, Inc. decides to add safety stock of 20?

7. KW Industries has analyzed their inventory and come up with the following data:
   Inventory carrying costs = 15%
   The cost of placing an order = $45/order
   Annual sales of Product X = 3,000,000
   Calculate KW's EOQ for Product X

8. Using the information from Question 7, how many orders will KW place in the next year?

9. Using the data from Question 7, what happens to the EOQ if the ordering costs increase to $65/order?

10. What are the types of inventory a company may have?

11. What is safety stock and why would a company have safety stock?

12. When is the EOQ not necessary?

13. Is the EOQ calculation still valid in today's business environment when applying the assumptions of the EOQ? Explain your answer.

14. If a company wants to set safety stock at 99% and has a standard deviation of 8, what would be the safety stock level?

13 Logistics/Warehousing/Distribution Management

Chapter 5 set the foundation for a detailed discussion of the supply chain functions of logistics, warehousing, and distribution center management. Each of these critical functions is important to the success of any supply chain and any operations management chain.

The 14th edition of the APICS Dictionary defines distribution as: "The activities associated with the movement of material, usually finished goods or service parts, from the manufacturer to the customer. These activities encompass the functions of transportation, warehousing, inventory control, material handling, order administration, site and location analysis, industrial packaging, data processing, and the communications network necessary for effective management."[1]

According to the Warehousing Education and Research Council's WERCipedia (WERC's online dictionary), a warehouse is a "Place for receiving, storing and shipping material and merchandise and making changes to their packaging or configuration."[2] A distribution center is defined as "a building, structure or group of units used to store goods and merchandise that are to be delivered to various places on an as-needed basis."[3] The WERC also provides a definition of logistics as: "Logistics plans, implements, and controls the efficient, effective forward and reverse flow and storage of goods, services, and related information between the point of origin and the point of consumption in order to meet customers' requirements."[4] Logistics is the historical term for what most companies call distribution today—getting products or people from one location to another. Distribution centers and warehouses are part of this logistics network.

Warehouses and distribution centers are commonly used interchangeably. This is erroneous. Although both facilities have the same basic functions as we will discuss in this chapter, a distribution center focuses on getting products in and out quickly; whereas a warehouse may store products for an extended period of time. For this reason, when we discuss inventory turns later in the chapter, remember that because of the length of storage, a distribution center should have much higher inventory turns numbers than a warehouse. The changing face of supply chain management and the increase in smaller/individual orders and the processing of returns have also had an impact on the size and layout of distribution centers.

WAREHOUSING

The introduction to the US Navy's publication on warehousing design lays out the reason for warehousing and distribution channels. "Because of the pattern of logistics management and the technical nature of many supply functions, consolidation of operations on the basis of material handling configuration is inhibited. Although a carton of wrenches, hammers, or pliers might have the same handling characteristics as a unit of avionics

---

[1]"Distribution." APICS Dictionary, 14th edition, APICS, Chicago, IL, 2013, p. 40.
[2]"Warehouse." WERCipedia, Warehousing Education and Research Council, www.werc.org, accessed, August 30, 2010.
[3]"Distribution Center." http://www.wisegeek.com/what-is-a-distribution-center.htm, accessed April 21, 2010.
[4]"Logistics." WERCipedia, Warehousing Education and Research Council, www.werc.org, accessed August 30, 2010.

or a pilot's crash helmet, these items generally flow through different distribution paths in their paths in their movement between the supplier and the ultimate user."[5]

Because of the differences between the various forms of materials and goods moving through the supply chain, warehouses are a necessary part of the supply chain. Warehouses exist to provide storage of the items moving through the supply chain; they provide this storage at a location that is in close proximity to the customer. In general, the design of a general supply warehouse must be based on the characteristics of the material being handled and stored (shape, environment, stackability, etc.), the volume and flow pattern through the facility (transaction and cube movement rate profile), and the inventory pattern (item count, item cube, quantity mix, and inventory turnover patterns).

Types of Warehouses

- **Cold storage.** Cold storage warehouses are used for the storage of food items that require temperature-controlled storage. Cold storage warehouses can be a standalone facility that is capable of storing either climate-controlled storage (i.e., fresh fruits, meats, or vegetables) or frozen storage. One of the critical considerations for operating a cold storage facility is the compatibility of the material handling equipment used with the items being stored and the lower temperatures associated with cold storage facilities. A cold storage facility may be collocated with a dry food storage facility.

- **Dry food storage warehouse.** A dry food storage warehouse stores staple items such as canned goods and other food items that do not require a "cold" temperature for long-term storage. Just as there are considerations for the equipment to facilitate the operation of a cold storage facility, the equipment used to move dry storage food items require compatibility with the food items being stored. For example, electric or propane forklifts are better for a dry food facility than gas-powered forklifts.

- **General supplies warehouse.** A general supplies warehouse is a facility that can handle almost any type of supply or material. The limit to what can be stored in a general supply warehouse is the square footage of the facility, the material handling equipment available, the size of the materials being stored, and the compatibility of the items being stored.

- **Warehouse in a warehouse.** A "warehouse in a warehouse" is a concept for organizing warehouses to be more efficient. This concept involves organizing the products being stored in a facility. A typical Home Depot store is a good example of a warehouse in a warehouse. A Home Depot store is organized to place like items in zones or "warehouses" within the overall warehouse. Look at the paint department or the flooring department. Each of these departments is a miniwarehouse in the Home Depot Warehouse. In a repair parts warehouse, items may be stored together by vehicle type or vehicle model to enable ease of finding the right product.

- **Climate-controlled facility.** This type of facility differs from a cold storage facility in that it is not designed or certified to store food items. In the Kansas City area, there are a number of caves used for climate-controlled storage of items as diverse as old Hollywood movie props to old vintage films and film canisters. The purpose of this type of facility is to provide protection for the items in the warehouse that may deteriorate if stored at "room temperature" or in changing climatic conditions.

- **Other Miscellaneous Warehouses and Distribution Facilities**:
  - **Local warehouse**—the purpose of a local warehouse is to provision the stocks and materials closer to the customer thus reducing the transit time for resupply of retailers or shorter transit time to the customer.
  - **Fulfillment center**—a fulfillment center is designed to receive/pick/pack/ship smaller orders. A fulfillment center may be part of a larger distribution center or may be a standalone operation. A fulfillment center is normally a distribution center that only deals with online sales or e-commerce.
  - **Value-added/service center**—the purpose of a value-added services center is to provide services not normally associated with the warehouse or distribution center. These services may be the type discussed in Chapter 5 as part of the distribution center. The value-added center may be collocated with the

---

[5]Warehouse Modernization and Layout Planning Guide, Department of the Navy, Naval Supply Systems Command, NAVSUP Publication 590, March, 1985, p. 1.

distribution center or warehouse in order to provide overnight shipping coordination. In this case, the shipping company such as UPS or FeDex may collocate in the shipping area of the facility to speed the shipment of overnight deliveries or parcel shipping.

WAREHOUSING HISTORY

Warehousing is one of the oldest professions known to man. Once early man discovered fire, it became a mission to "store" the fire to keep it burning. Hunters throughout history have stored meat during the winter to ensure food throughout the winter season.

In Biblical times, Joseph, after being sold into slavery by his brothers, made history in Egypt running the grain warehouses for the Pharaoh. This led to the migration of the Israelites to Egypt during the famines and the eventual exodus of the Israelites from Egypt. The mass migration led to eventual problems that seem to be continuing today between Egypt and Israel.

Alexander the Great learned the importance of warehousing to supply his Macedonian Army as the army moved across the Asian continent. He also learned the expense of warehousing and was one of the first operations leaders to decide that warehousing was not a core competency of his army and "outsourced" his warehousing by foraging from the local country side to support his army.

Venice became the crossroads and warehouse location for all of the East–West trade. The warehousing industry helped to support the goods coming to and going to China and the rest of Europe.

In the United States, the military outposts west of the Mississippi served as warehouses of supplies, ammunition, and other goods to support the movement of settlers and civilization across the country. A study of the expansion of the United States is not complete without considering the purpose of these storage outposts and the contribution of these warehouse outposts to the success of the country's expansion.

The forklift first appeared in the 1940s and changed the face of warehousing and distribution forever.

Warehousing/Distribution Challenges

- **Proliferation of stock keeping units (SKUs).** According to AMR Research released in early 2010, the number of SKUs in the commercial supply chains has increased by 15% over the past 3 years. Each of these items must pass through a warehouse or distribution center *en route* to the ultimate customer.

- **Instant customer service requirements.** As a result of the ability to order on the Internet, more direct-to-customer shipments are occurring each day from warehouses and distribution centers. This has several impacts on the facilities. The first is that the distribution center that used to have pallet storage, case storage, and bulk storage areas in the facility now have to also have an individual item picking and storage area in the facility. This also impacts packing and shipping requirements and, in many facilities, creates the need for a cross-docking area.[6]

- **Pressures to make inventories smaller, yet more responsive.** Financial pressures to lower inventory levels puts pressure on the warehouse manager/distribution center manager. The typical act is to cut inventory levels across the board. The problem with this approach is that reducing inventory levels for nonproductive inventory or inactive inventory will not produce cost savings. The typical method for reducing the stockage levels is to reduce the level through attrition of the product and not replenishing to the previous levels. However, if the inventory is not moving, the opportunity to reduce the stocks through attrition is not available. The result from this technique is usually frustration and no visible improvements in the inventory values.

  The more productive technique to improve the responsiveness of the inventory while reducing the inventory value is to do an analysis of the inventory activity. If an item is no longer moving, it may be time

---

[6]Cross-docking according to the APICS Operations Management Body of Knowledge is "a distribution technique in which items are brought into a distribution center for immediate dispatch. Instead of being received and stored away, these items are loaded into the distribution center's sorting system or are taken directly to shipping for sorting and dispatch." *APICS Operations Body of Knowledge*, 2010, p. 22.

to completely eliminate the product from the stocks. Then after the nonproductive inventory is removed, the active stocks can be reduced to improve the inventory turns and responsiveness to the needs of the customers.[7]

- **Pull philosophy.** The pull philosophy is an outgrowth of Just-in-Time. The details of Just-in-Time and the pull philosophy or pull methodology are discussed in Chapter 11. The fundamentals of pull state are that an item will not be moved or shipped until someone has ordered or requested the item. The impact on the warehouse or distribution center is that the product has to be on-hand in order to be available when the customer asks for it. This concept is counter to the previously discussed pressure to reduce inventory levels.

- **Smaller transactions.** This has already been discussed in other areas. The number of smaller transactions requires more space in the facility to handle the individual item picking and packing. This also requires additional personnel in the facility.

- **Value-added services.** We have already discussed the use of value-added services in the distribution centers. The pressure to add these services impacts on the space utilization in the facility and the number of personnel required to add these services to the offerings of the facility to improve customer satisfaction.

- **English as a second language.** The biggest complaint in the distribution business today is that the number of workers that do not speak English or speak English as a second language. This is primarily because there are certain jobs that some Americans will not do anymore. Driving a forklift 8 hours a day fits into this category. However, this is not a new complaint. In 1945, the biggest complaint in the warehousing industry was that the workers did not speak English. This was a result of so many men deployed to Europe or the Pacific Theater to fight in World War II. This problem is not going to go away. The solution is that management has to learn another language. One facility that I worked with in Southern California had a predominant number of Spanish-speaking workers and very few Spanish-speaking managers. This facility complained that productivity was not good and even bragged about being "the worst distribution center in the country." Their issue was a language problem. Only one manager spoke Spanish and only a few of the workers spoke English. The answer was to enroll managers in Spanish classes and workers in English as a second language classes.

- **Complicated warehouse management system (WMS) and proliferation of systems.** Every week, a new advertisement hits my e-mail box about a new WMS or new/updated enterprise resource planning program. Not only do these systems continue to expand and change, but they also continue to become more and more complicated. These systems require additional training and systems analysts to keep the chains strong.

- **Integration of online and brick-and-mortar operations.** Traditional operations were always brick-and-mortar operations. The traditional stores had a traditional way of doing business. These stores received shipments from the distribution center or warehouse and sold the products to customers in the brick-and-mortar stores. With the advent of the Internet, stores had to change their strategies and were forced to incorporate sales through the Internet to customers that may never walk through the door of the brick-and-mortar store. This change in customer support strategy also impacted the way items were stored in distribution centers and warehouses.

- **Smaller orders.** The trickledown effect from the change in customer support requirements was the realization that customers ordering over the Internet were ordering smaller quantities of products. These smaller quantities required new picking techniques and new picking areas to support individual item orders rather than the traditional case lot or pallet load shipments from the warehouse or distribution center to the stores.

- **Returns.** In Chapter 16, we will discuss the returns and reverse logistics problems and processes in great detail. The reverse logistics problem is nothing new, but the increase in the number of items coming backward from the intended customer has created a whole new industry. In addition, the increase in returns and the focus on returns as a way to capture costs from the system have created a requirement for distribution centers and warehouses to have an area for returns processing and the need to store the returned products until the products are back on a store shelf or disposed of properly.

---

[7]One particular distribution center called their inactive stocks as "dormant" stocks to avoid calling the stock nonproductive. This particular facility had over $63 billion dollars in "dormant" stocks. Their definition of dormant was no orders for the item in the past two years and no replenishment actions in the past year.

- **The appearance of 3PL providers.** A 3PL provider is a third-party logistics support provider. Once companies realized that doing logistics and distribution was not a core competency, 3PL companies started appearing around the world. These companies provide the services, warehousing, logistics, and transportation that have been outsourced by companies. There are now over 1,000 companies in the United States alone that perform these functions as a core competency that other companies have determined are not core competencies, but are still critical to the success of the company.

WAREHOUSING MANAGEMENT

Warehousing focuses on the storage of products, whereas distribution centers focus on the short-term storage and rapid movement of products through the distribution center and out to the customer. Warehouses are concerned about storage times and holding times, while distribution centers are concerned about throughput rates. The throughput is the amount of products flowing in the receiving door and out of the shipping door. The use of cross-docking helps to improve throughput rates. Cross-docking is a methodology for managing the flow of products by managing the inbound products and synching these products with the outbound flow of products. This method increases the throughput through the facility because the items being cross-docked never go into a storage facility. These products come in one day and are out of the facility within 48 hours or less. Most major distribution centers have created a cross-docking area to hold products until the products are loaded on an outbound truck. This concept not only increases throughput and reduces inventory investment levels, it also increases the speed of the product to the customer.

WAREHOUSING FUNCTIONS

- **Receive:** This is the function of unloading the inbound freight. The accuracy of the performance of this function sets the stage for the success of the overall operations. If the receiving function is not properly performed, the product and product quantities will not match what should be on the shelves, and the ability to properly support the customer will be impacted.
- **Putaway:** Once the products have been received at the warehouse or distribution center, they have to be put on a shelf if the products are going into storage locations or moved to the cross-docking area, if the products are identified for cross-docking. The importance of accurate and proper putaway is critical to the overall success of the facility. If the items coming into the facility are properly identified at the receiving docks and put in the proper location, then the right item will be in the right location in the right quantity when a customer orders that item.

    Putaway also involves housekeeping in the facility. When items are placed on the shelves or in a storage location, the items must be placed neatly in the location. This helps to make sure the warehouse/distribution center worker can properly identify the items when performing the picking function discussed below.
- **Store:** This function is relatively self-explanatory. This is the warehouse/distribution center function of keeping items on the shelf or in the facility. This is the focus of warehouses.
- **Prepackaging—kitting:** This function of distribution centers is the concept of putting items of similar use together to create a "kit" that can be shipped as one item. A prepackaged oil change kit is an example of this. The distribution center may kit the oil, filter, and filter wrench into one kit with a new stock number that will be sold as one item rather than three separate items. Some repair parts facilities not only kit the items together, but by also storing items by vehicle type in the distribution center create a warehouse in a warehouse similar to the concept discussed earlier.
- **Order entry:** Order entry may be automated and linked to the WMS or could be a manual entry "fat-fingered" in by someone in the warehouse or distribution center. This is another critical function to the success of customer service operations. If the wrong stock number or SKU is entered into the system, the wrong item will be picked by the warehouse/distribution center worker and if an audit of the shipment does not catch this error, the customer will get the wrong product or the wrong quantity of the right product.
- **Picking:** This is the physical function of getting the items off the shelf and ready for shipping. Picking may be accomplished by sending workers to various zones or sections of the warehouse/distribution center and then consolidating the items into one shipment or the picking may be accomplished as an order where one worker travels through the facility picking all the items for the order before moving to another order.

Picking may be done from a printed pick list with SKUs, storage locations, and quantities. Picking may be accomplished with a manual pick list. More modern distribution centers are using either "pick to light" where the worker stops at the next location with a light and either uses an accompanying pick list or the location will have an LED with the number to be picked; or the picking may be performed using voice picking, which is relatively new compared with the other picking techniques.

With voice picking, the worker has a headset linked to the WMS that directs the worker to the next location and tells the worker how many to pick from that location. Before the voice picking system will allow the worker to move to another location, the worker must confirm the location and the quantity picked. This system frees up both hands to pick the items and move the tote or cart to the next location and is a more accurate system for picking items in the facility.

The more accurate the picking process runs, the more accurate the items and quantities in the shipment to the customer will be and the more satisfied the customer will be. This has two benefits. The first benefit is that the customer will most likely buy again, if satisfied, and the second benefit is that the proper shipments help reduce returns, thereby, saving money for the company.

- **Packing—includes checking for completeness, labeling, weighing, loading:** This is the function of preparing the items for safe shipping. If the items are properly packed, they should arrive undamaged when delivered to the customer. Packing the item is more than just putting it in a box or envelop. The packing department has to know what size package to use, if additional packaging is needed to protect the item. Packing also includes ensuring the address is correct and that the item is properly labeled, weighed, and prepared for loading to the outbound movement. The checks of the packing department help to ensure that the packages are delivered to the right customer.

  An example of the checks at the packing department comes from a distribution center in Kentucky that was experiencing a large number of discrepant shipments. The packing department was not checking the accuracy of zip codes and addresses. For example, shipments to Missouri had zip codes for Massachusetts. The result was delays in shipping to the customer and a decrease in customer satisfaction. A simple matching of addresses and zip codes in the packing department significantly reduced the number of delayed shipments.

- **Shipping:** This is the last function under the control of the distribution center or warehouse. Accurate shipping is critical to customer satisfaction. As discussed earlier, some of the shipments via FedEx and UPS may be managed by the shipping company at the distribution center to facilitate accuracy and speed. Some shipping companies will actually plan the shipping manifest and loading to facilitate more efficient shipping from distribution centers to customers or transshipment sites.

All of these functions feed:

- **Perfect order fulfillment.** Perfect order fulfillment is a metric of warehouse effectiveness and efficiency. Perfect order fulfillment is a measure of how well you are meeting the needs of the customer. This metric looks at the ability of getting the right item to the right place, at the right time, in the right quantity, in the proper condition, and with the proper billing. The calculation for perfect order fulfillment is shown in Equation 13.1.

Equation 13.1: Perfect Order Fulfillment

Right Item % × Right Quantity % × Right Place % × Right Condition % × On-Time Delivery % × Correct Billing %

Example:
Right Item % = 99%
Right Quantity % = 99%
Right Place % = 99%
Right Condition % = 100%
On Time Delivery % = 99%
Correct Billing/Invoicing % = 99%
Perfect Order Fulfillment = .99 × .99 × .99 × 1.00 × .99 × .99 = 95.09%

- **Carrying costs.** As we had seen when we discussed inventory management and the economic order quantity in Chapter 11, the carrying costs for a distribution center's inventory include the opportunity cost of the money used for the inventory, the insurance for the inventory, the overhead allocated to the inventory items, the cost of the labor to count, pick, pack, and ship the items, and the costs of loss or obsolescence. A properly managed distribution center or warehouse will have lower than the industry average for carrying costs.

- **Loss.** This could be loss of inventory as a result of misshipment, theft inside the supply chain, or employee theft. The distribution center management must be involved in the security of the inventory to prevent pilferage by the employees and theft from outside the distribution center. The distribution center management must also be engaged and constantly monitoring the housekeeping of the center. Proper housekeeping will prevent the internal misshipment and items placed in the wrong locations that give the illusion of losses.

- **Damage.** Damage in the warehouse or distribution center is inevitable. When things are moved or sit for long periods of time as they do in warehouses, things get damaged. The goal of the distribution center management or the warehouse management team is to minimize this damage. Some of the damage can be eliminated by changing the metrics for productivity in the facility. In one facility that I had the opportunity to do some work with, this was the case. The metric for productivity in most facilities is items or orders picked per hour—a measure of how many different items are taken off the shelf to prepare for shipment to the customers each hour. In this particular facility, no attention was given to the condition of the items or the techniques used to pick the items. What was happening in this facility was that the workers had "cracked the code" for productivity. They realized that the key to higher productivity was not to take the time to take the items off the top pallet in a stack of three high, but to simply pull a can or two out of the middle pallet. This saved time and improved their items per hour metric. However, what it created was a lot of pallet stacks that were leaning like the Tower of Pisa by the end of the day. The other result was that cans in the middle pallet were bent and damaged from the shift in weight placed on them. This problem was preventable with management oversight and training.

- **Misshipment.** This is the problem of items going to the wrong customer. This problem is fixable and preventable with proper supervision and training. I am not an advocate of 100% inspection of every shipment to prevent this, but regular spot-check sampling and proper training coupled with good housekeeping in the facility help to ensure that the right product goes to the right customer.

- **Frustrated cargo.** This is really a misnomer. The cargo is not frustrated. The one that is frustrated is the warehouse manager. Frustrated cargo is a distribution term that describes cargo or shipments that are either not deliverable or the customer cannot be located. Frustrated cargo can be a huge problem for distribution centers and warehouses. Frustrated cargo represents materials that have been prepped for shipment, represents money tied up in products that are not available to other customers, and may end up as "lost" products. In one distribution center, a couple of years ago, there was a pallet of frustrated cargo that sat in the same place for so long that it became invisible to the workers and became lost even though every worker had to pass the pallet almost every day and some of them multiple times a day.

  In Kuwait in 2003, we had an area we called the miscellaneous line. The miscellaneous line was two pallet positions wide and about 100 yards long. These pallets were technically frustrated cargo, but we renamed it miscellaneous cargo. The miscellaneous cargo was cargo that the customer unit could not be identified because of the loss of shipping labels or unknown customers such as the Defense Intelligence Agency and the Embassy.

  Frustrated cargo is not necessarily an indicator of poor facility management. But, the handling of the frustrated cargo may be an indicator of poor management. A good facility manager will dedicate resources to research the frustrated cargo and the causes of the frustrated cargo in order to better serve the customers.

FACTORS INFLUENCING DISTRIBUTION OPERATIONS

Time is critical in today's distribution operations. The most successful distribution and warehousing operations are those that focus on reducing every aspect of the distribution operations. This is accomplished by walking the process and identifying areas that can be improved and getting rid of the nonvalue-adding, time-consuming processes that are impacting customer responsiveness of the facility.

Figure 13.1: Unsafe Pallet Storage in Panama

Just as time is critical to the customers of the distribution systems, quality is also important to the customers. This is not just the quality of the product; it is also the quality of the distribution system from the suppliers' suppliers to the customers' customers. This includes error-free delivery. If you buy a new washer and dryer from a store, you expect the delivered products to match what you picked out in the store. If the delivery workers drop the dryer off the back of the truck, the quality of the system is jeopardized. If a company outsources the delivery, this should not change the expectations for quality in the distribution system.

The workforce mix is a challenge as distribution systems continue to try to provide quality support to their customers. This workforce mix is a combination of cultures and generations. The challenge for leaders of distribution centers is to get the most out of their employees. The challenge is to first understand what motivates each individual employee and to understand the language and culture of the employees. The leader must motivate the workers to want to provide quality support to the customers. Without an understanding of the language and/or the background or culture of an employee, a leader cannot motivate the worker.

Safety is another aspect that impacts operations in the warehouse or distribution center. The Occupational Safety and Health Administration (OSHA) provides very strict safety guidelines for facilities in the United States. These guidelines sometimes appear to be hand-cuffing the management of the facility to improve operations, but are provided to prevent worker injuries. In the warehouse, forklifts pose a great threat to safety, if these OSHA guidelines are not adhered to. Here is an example of an unsafe practice in a facility outside the United States.

TYPES OF FACILITIES: PRIVATE VERSUS PUBLIC

Most facilities fall into either categorization of a private warehouse/distribution center or a public facility.

A private warehouse/distribution center is wholly owned or wholly leased by one company and stores only the products of that one company. This form of storage provides control to the owner or lessee of the facility. This control comes in the form of what products are stored and control of the management of the facility. If the facility is occupied by the owner, there may be tax advantages for owning the facility and the possible advantage of an increase in value for the facility and the land that it sits on. The downside of private facilities is the fixed costs and overhead for owning the facility. There is also an assumption that there will be enough sales and stocks to make the ownership of the facility profitable. At the same time, there is an intangible benefit of having your own facility.

A public warehouse/distribution center can store products for multiple companies in the same facility. The advantage for the companies using this facility is that they do not have to own the facility to use it and only pay for the area that is used. This may be to meet peak requirements or abnormal demand requirements. Another advantage of using a public facility is the ability to store products in a facility operated by a company whose core competency is running a distribution facility. Because the company running the public facility has this as a core competency, the exact costs of the storage and distribution operation will be known by the companies using the facility.

One downside of the public facility is that the needed space may not be available for peak periods. Another potential downside is that if a company has a specialized storage requirement, the expertise may not be available in a public facility that would be available in a privately owned facility. One more major drawback of the public facility is the compatibility of WMSs. Not all WMSs are the same and may require either manual intervention or middle ware to translate information from a company's system to the public facility's automated systems.

WAREHOUSE/DISTRIBUTION CENTER LAYOUT AND DESIGN

The design of the facility will enhance the profitability of the warehouse or distribution center. The primary goals of the distribution center or warehouse design are the maximization of space utilization (both square footage and cube footage) while minimizing the movement of products in the facility. These goals may be accomplished by using cross-docking or by analyzing the velocity of the products. The other goals discussed while dealing with the facility layout and design also are applicable for warehouse and distribution centers.

Figure 13.2 shows a layout option for consolidating shipments at a transshipment facility to produce full truckloads to customers. This diagram from the US Navy Supply Publication 590 shows the flow of products in a transshipment distribution center.

Figure 13.3, shows a typical flow pattern for distribution centers. This flow shows a logical flow of products through a facility to minimize movement and maximize space utilization in the facility.

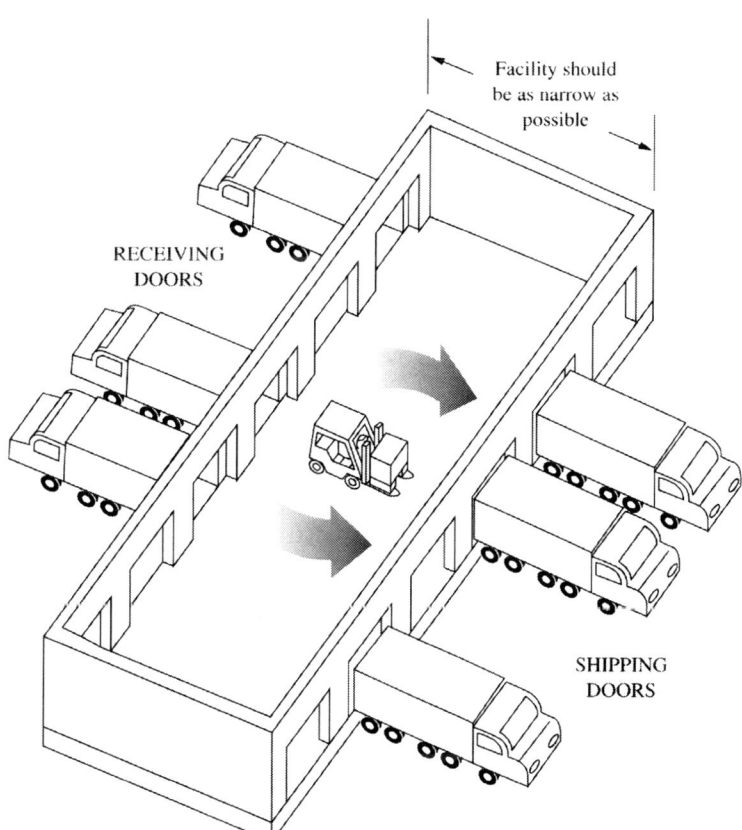

Figure 13.2: Ideal Facility for Pure Supplier Consolidation (Full Pallet Movement)

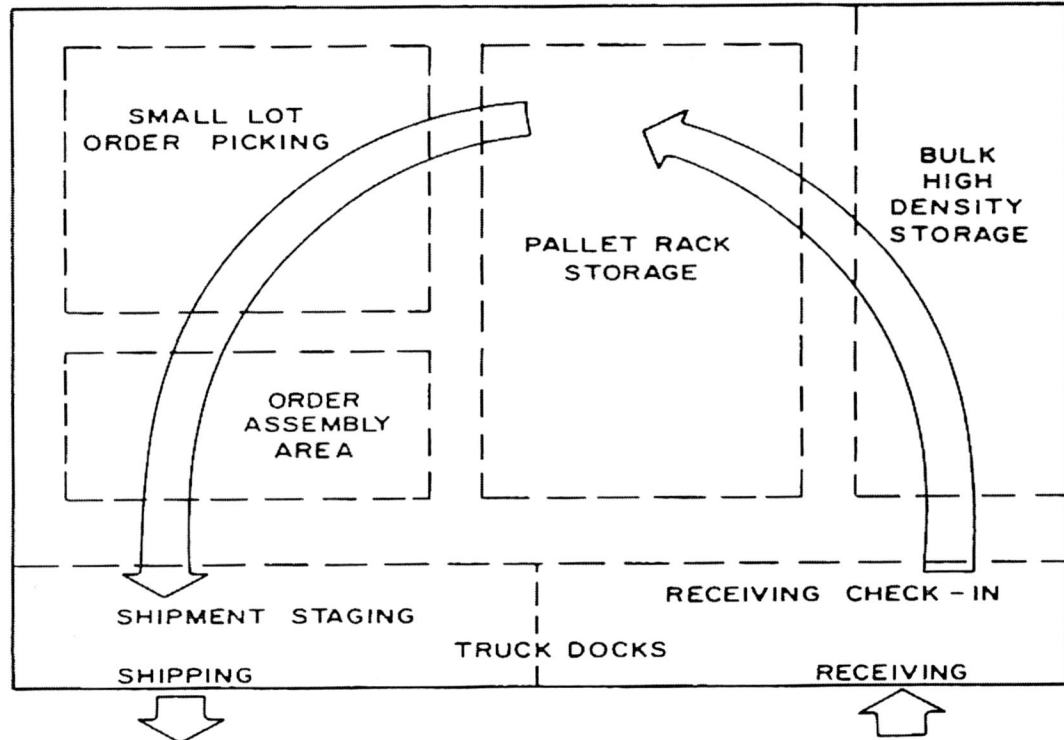

Figure 13.3: Logical Flow Pattern in a Distribution Center

CROSS-DOCKING

As discussed in Chapters 5 and 12, cross-docking is a methodology to reduce inventory value (thus increasing turns) while decreasing the time that the product is in the distribution center (also impacting turns). Cross-docking is nothing new. It is a methodology of knowing what is coming in and synchronizing the inbound shipments with the outbound shipments. For example, in Figure 13.3, the product would go from the receiving area to a holding area to the shipping area. The goal of cross-docking is to have the product in and out of the facility in less than 48 hours. This is not that different from the operations of the Pony Express that ran from St. Joseph, Missouri to points west. The packages came in and went out in the same day. Wal-Mart executives have claimed that they invented cross-docking. They did not invent it, but Wal-Mart has worked hard to perfect cross-docking. Cross-docking is not easy to accomplish, but once implemented, can reduce costs and improve distribution metrics to include inventory turns and customer responsiveness.

Cross-docking success depends on several key factors. The primary factor is world-class communications. Communications is necessary to ensure that the facility knows what is coming in so the outbound shipments can be planned. Communications is also critical to achieve synchronization between the facility's inbound and outbound transportation partners. This synchronization is also a product of good transportation planning and reliable forecasts of product demands.

ATTRIBUTES OF WORLD-CLASS WAREHOUSES AND DISTRIBUTION CENTERS

- **100% inventory accuracy.** This is a must. A facility has to have 100% accuracy in their inventory counts and inventory accountability. Proper storage techniques, proper employee training, and good housekeeping will contribute to this metric. Anything less than 100% is not acceptable. This means that something is not being done right in the facility and the automated system does not match the physical count of the products. Anything less than 100% means lost profits and lost time researching why the inventory levels do not match the automated books.

- **Perfect order fulfillment.** Although we have already discussed this in detail, it is important to mention it again as a measure of world-class warehousing/distribution. Customers have access to inventory and shipment data online and expect delivery when promised.

- **Value-added services.** Although there is no metric for this attribute, providing these value-added services or postponement services is important to attract and keep customers, who have a choice of service providers.

- **Cleanliness.** There is no metric for this attribute either; however, the cleanliness and housekeeping of the facility will contribute to the perfect order fulfillment, inventory accuracy, and on-time deliveries by being able to find the right product when needed.

- **Time definite delivery (TDD).** This attribute is tied to transportation planning and synchronization. TDD tells the customer exactly when the vehicle will be at their facility. The opposite of TDD is the cable companies that tell you they will be there sometime between 8:00 and 12:00 forcing the customer to sit around and wait. With TDD, the customer can plan his/her workforce around the time that the truck will arrive in order to quickly off-load the vehicle.

- **On-time deliveries.** This attribute is related to TDD. This metric is measured from the perspective of the customer. How often does the shipment arrive when promised? One company was allowing their contracted trucking company to measure this for them. Amazingly, every month the company was very close to perfection. But when measured by polling customers, the on-time delivery percentage was much lower. To be world class, a company has to be as close to 100% on-time delivery as possible.

- **Employee education programs.** The Toyota North American Parts Distribution Center has a requirement for over 80 hours a year in mandatory training programs for every employee. Keeping employees up to date on new technologies or old methods for standardization is important to get distribution centers or warehouses to world class or to maintain world-class levels of performance.

- **Safety.** This is important for any operation, but for warehouses and distribution centers, this must be considered and enforced. No matter how good a distribution center thinks they are, a safety problem will negate any other activity.

- **Obsolete stocks.** A well-run facility will have the right items on the shelves in the right quantities to support their customers. The amount of stocks that are obsolete drive up costs and reduce the value of the inventory. In addition, if stocks become obsolete, these stocks must be disposed of. This adds more costs to the operation.

- **Turns.** Inventory turns is a measure of how fast the inventory on the shelves is replenished. As mentioned earlier, this is a very misunderstood metric. Not because of the calculation of cost of goods sold divided by the average value of the inventory, but because of the interpretation that what is good for one facility is the right number for another facility. To compare turns, the benchmarking must be between like facilities or industries. There is no one-size turns metric.

- **Processing times.** A world-class facility is measuring their processing times in minutes. How many minutes does it take to clear the floor or load a truck?

- **Cross-docking.** A world-class facility employs the concept of cross-docking discussed earlier. This not only improves inventory turns, but also reduces the average processing times by not having to place the items that are cross-docked on the shelves and later having to pick these items.

SUMMARY

Distribution centers and warehouses are different in nature in that warehouses focus on longer storage times. However, the metrics and tools to improve facility operations are similar. The goal of every facility manager is to ensure that his/her facility is not the weakest link in the supply chain.

Discussion Questions

1. Why is perfect order fulfillment so critical to successful operations?

2. If a company is at 95% across the board for the entities of perfect order fulfillment, what is their perfect order fulfillment rate? Is this good?

3. What are the attributes of world-class distribution systems?

4. Why is cross-docking important to reducing customer response times?

5. A company has calculated their inventory turns at 12. Is this good or bad? Explain your answer.

6. A company has calculated their cost of goods sold at $25,000,000 and their average inventory as $12,500,000. What is their inventory turns rate? Is this good or bad?

7. A company has 14 inventory turns a year. The average turns calculation for their industry is 28. What should the company do to improve their turns?

8. Why is a flow important to the success of a facility?

9. What is TDD? Why is it important from the customer perspective?

10. From what perspective should on-time delivery be measured?

14 Just-in-Time/Lean/ The Theory of Constraints/ Six Sigma

Just-in-Time, Lean, the Theory of Constraints, and Six Sigma are all related methodologies. All four of these methodologies are continuous process improvement programs designed to improve a company's operations management chain and the quality of the outputs of the processes. A strong argument could be made that all four programs are basically the same program, but with a different name. This would not be unusual in the business world to change the names of programs just to make more money out of books and consulting fees. Although all the four programs have similarities in their results, the approaches of these programs, with the exception of JIT and Lean, are different. The goal of addressing these four programs in the same chapter is to provide the operations management student with alternatives for improving a process or system.

Regardless of the program used to bring about improvements to a process, the first step is to walk the process to identify the nonvalue-added activities or subprocesses and those processes that are working well and may not necessarily need changing. As mentioned before, it is important to remember two important points about improving operations. The first is that all processes add cost, but not all processes add value to an operation. The programs in this chapter will help the operations management student identify those nonvalue-adding processes as candidates for improvement or elimination. The second important point is to remember that all improvements are a change, but not all change is an improvement. A promise of "change you can believe in" should really be "improvements you can believe in."

JUST-IN-TIME (JIT)

This may very well be the most misunderstood and inappropriately implemented program in operations management. The JIT has its roots in the rebuilding of the Japanese economy after the defeat of Japan in World War II. Taiichi Ohno gets the credit for developing what became known as the Toyota Production System in the 1950s. This system grew out of the teachings of Dr. W. Edwards Deming, the American statistician, who went to Japan after the war to help the Japanese businesses recover.

The JIT made its way to the United States and the rest of the world in the 1970s as a result of the growth of the quality of Japanese products, in general, and the Japanese automobiles, in particular. In the 1960s, the words "Made in Japan" on a product almost assured the buyer that the quality was suspect at best. Then, the quality revolution in Japan started the flow of high-quality products into the marketplace. By the mid-1970s, those same words, "Made in Japan," symbolized the highest levels of quality worldwide.

As this new wave of quality rolled across the globe, everyone wanted to know how the Japanese firms were achieving lower costs and higher quality products. The answer was JIT. The problem was that the applications of JIT got lost in translation. Instead of *Lean* as Ohno called it, the JIT program became zero inventories. This spawned a series of the "Zero Inventory Papers" published by what was at the time known as the American Production and Inventory Control Society.[1] Now, APICS defines Just-in-Time as: "A philosophy of manufacturing based on planned elimination of all wastes and on continuous improvement of productivity."[2]

---

[1]The American Production and Inventory Control Society is now known as APICS—The Association for Operations Management.
[2]*APICS Dictionary*, 14th edition, 2013, p. 88. Chicago, IL: APICS.

Just-in-Time is both an inventory methodology as well as a continuous process improvement program. Much has been written about both. As a continuous process improvement program, JIT has a mantra to eliminate all waste. You may recall the discussions on positioning the firm that to be successful if competing on cost must eliminate all waste. As an inventory management philosophy, JIT is interpreted to have just enough on the shelf to meet the needs of the customer. Many companies have realized that JIT, as a pure inventory methodology, may not be the best method available.

For example, in the United States in 2001, all forms of transportation came to a halt after the attacks of September 11. Those companies that had moved to JIT inventories had problems meeting deliveries after transportation starting moving again. Hewlett-Packard missed deliveries as a result, while Dell was able to meet almost all of their deliveries.[3] The delays in transportation created stockouts and forced companies to re-evaluate their JIT policies. Those companies that did not change after 9/11 got another wakeup call in 2002, when the dock workers went on strike on the West Coast. The strike delayed the shipment of items on approximately 300 to 500 ships depending on which report is most accurate. The 9/11 delays and the dock strike forced many companies to move from JIT to Just–in-Case inventories.

As a process improvement program, JIT has great applications to all companies. Reducing waste is important to any company that wants to remain competitive. So, let us look at the goals of JIT. The goal is to eliminate waste. Here are the wastes as identified by the Toyota Production System that has become known as JIT.

- **Overproduction:** The JIT seeks to eliminate the waste of producing too much. This includes too much of the right stuff and eliminating the production of items that do not sell at all. This is one area that causes conflicts between accountants and operations management managers. The age-old philosophy from the accounting side of the house is that a machine should operate at 100% utilization. However, if 100% utilization of an operation produces more product than the customers want, then waste is the result. The JIT mandates only producing what is needed and nothing more.

- **Waiting:** The waste of waiting always reminds me of the *I Love Lucy* episode, where Lucy was working in the candy factory and spent time waiting for the candy to show up, and then the candy started coming faster than Lucy could keep up with it. The waste of waiting comes from not balancing the manufacturing line and having machines in the line that produce faster than other machines in the line. If the line is not balanced, there will be waiting at some machines and overproduction at other machines in the line. Balancing the manufacturing line will eliminate the waste of waiting.

  This could also be the waste of watching a machine run. If the machine works well without any human intervention, there is no need to have someone standing there watching the machine just in case it breaks down.

- **Unnecessary handling:** Every time an item is handled, there is a chance of damaging, misrouting, or misplacing the item. Eliminating the waste of unnecessary handling prevents this damage or loss of the product. A good facility layout will eliminate unnecessary handling of the product.

- **Nonvalue-adding processing:** This has been discussed earlier in the text. Every process adds cost, but not every process adds value to an operation. Walking the process, documenting each activity, and then preparing a process map will help companies identify nonvalue-adding processes. Eliminating nonvalue-adding processes helps companies reduce costs and, thereby, makes the company more competitive and profitable.

- **Inventory in excess of immediate needs:** This waste is very close in nature to the first waste of overproduction. Careful and accurate forecasting coupled with knowing what the customers need and want will help the company eliminate this waste. This is the waste that led to the misconception of zero inventories. Managing this waste does not mean zero inventories; it does mean reducing nonproductive inventory.

- **Inessential motion:** Moving for the sake of moving or moving products to multiple intermediate locations is the waste of movement. In some distribution centers, there is the process of re-warehousing

---

[3]Dell was reportedly a JIT company at the time of the September 11 attacks. However, Dell mandated that its suppliers keep 6–8 weeks of supply in the Dell Supplier Center across the street from their Texas assembly plant. This may be a case of semantics. Technically, the Dell Assembly Facility was using JIT with deliveries every 4 hours and the supplies in the Dell–owned Supplier Center were indeed owned by the suppliers—but, if Dell mandates the stockage levels of the Supplier Center, is that really pure JIT?

monthly or quarterly. This results in products moving from one location to another. Like the waste of unnecessary handling, this produces lost, damaged, or misplaced items. One of the beauties of radio frequency identification tags is the ability to see stuff move around a storage yard for the sake of movement.

One facility that I worked with several years ago had a large quantity of shipping boxes prepped for shipment out of the facility for disposal. Instead of loading the boxes for outbound shipment, when the managers were notified of the boxes, the boxes were moved to another location in the yard that was out of sight. Unbeknownst to the managers, I had put my initials and date on the boxes, while inspecting their yard. A month later, the boxes were discovered again during a walk through the yard. This time, the manager tried to tell me that this was a new set of boxes being prepped for outbound shipment. However, the manager was a bit embarrassed when I showed him the dates and initials. This was not only a breach of honesty, but a classic example of movement for the sake of movement.

- **Rework of defects:** This is a serious waste of assets, time, and money. As discussed in Chapter 4, quality initiatives will reduce the amount of rework required to fix defects before shipping to customers or fixing warranty work necessitated by allowing defective products to get in the hands of the customer. The discussion of reverse logistics in Chapter 16 will look at some of the additional costs companies incur from the waste of reworking defects.

- There is another waste that is not a part of the seven wastes of the Toyota Production System. This waste is the waste of meetings. Too many companies have meetings for the sake of meeting with nothing decided in the meeting, but to have another meeting. How many times have you sat through a meeting only to wonder what the meeting was about and when it was finished, and feel like you just wasted a couple of hours of your life?

JIT Elements

In addition to the wastes of JIT, there are some basic elements associated with JIT. Some of these basic elements of JIT are also just plain common sense.

- Flexible resources. This was the basis for the cellular structure previously discussed. This is also what drives the layouts of fast-food restaurants. In a hamburger fast-food restaurant, there is one "cell" where the burger is microwaved, another "cell" where the burger is assembled, still another "cell" taking the order, and still another "cell" operating the fry cooker. There are no specialists in this arrangement. Each of the workers is trained to work in all of the "cells."
- Pull production system. As discussed earlier, the pull system only produces a product when there is a demand for it. This concept helps to eliminate the waste of overproduction and excess inventory.
- Kanban production control. Kanban literally translates as "card." A Kanban card alerts the producer to make more of the product. A Kanban could be a signal such as a light to alert the previous operation to make more products or a square on the floor that, when emptied, alerts the previous operation to make more products. As mentioned in the previous chapter, this concept is derived from the two-bin inventory reorder point concept. Here are some common examples of Kanbans:
  - **Bin Kanban**—When the bin is empty, it is the signal to replenish the bin (much like the two-bin system).
  - **Kanban Square**—This is a marked area on the floor or assembly line that is designed to hold a certain quantity of material. When the square is empty, it is time to replenish.
  - **Signal Kanban**—This may be as simple as an Andon light to signal the previous operation to move more products forward or a triangular sign or a flag that is raised to alert the previous operation to move product forward.
  - **Calculating the number of Kanbans needed**—If a company is going to use the Kanban methodology, it is necessary to calculate the number of Kanbans necessary to support the operations. When using the formula shown in Formula 14.1, if a company wants to force more efficiency in the system, the calculation is rounded down and if the company wants to allow a little slack in the system, the company will round the calculation up (see Example 14.1).

Formula 14.1: Kanban Calculation

$$\text{\# of Kanbans} = \frac{\text{Average Demand During Lead Time} + \text{Safety Stock}}{\text{Container Size}}$$

Example 14.1 Kanban Calculation

> a. demand = 300 widgets per hour
> b. lead time = 1 hour
> c. safety stock is set at 10% of the demand during the lead time
> d. container size = 75 widgets
>
> $$K = \frac{(300)(1) + 30}{75}$$
> $$= 4.4 \text{ Containers}$$

In Example 14.1, if the company wants to force efficiency in the system, the company will round up the number of containers in the system to 4. However, if the company wants a little slack in the system, it can round up the number of containers to 5.

- Quick setups. Anything that can be done to reduce the setup times falls under this concept. For example, NASCAR teams use guides to make the pit stop tire changing go faster. There is a notch and a mark for the jack man to hit in order to speed up the setup for the tire changing as shown in Figures 14.1 and 14.2. Figure 14.3 shows another example of quick setups in NASCAR. In order to reduce setup time for the tire changers, each lug nut is glued to the tire and then the tires are arranged in the proper order of use and marked to prevent placing the wrong tires on the car.

The JIT concept of reducing setup times is often referred to as single minute exchange of dies (SMED). This concept forces a company to take a look at their operations and determine if a quicker setup is possible. In the automobile industry, it used to take weeks to retool a plant to produce a new line or model of an automobile. This is lost productivity time and lost revenue. If an operation can be analyzed and the steps and setups reduced to internal and external operations, the process can be streamlined and improved. This concept is the driver for setting up the tires and lug nuts prior to use as shown in Figure 14.3. This analysis may actually eliminate some setup steps altogether or at least allow for some steps to be accomplished simultaneously external to the operation.

Photograph by Joe Walden

Figure 14.1: Tire Jack Mark for NASCAR Pit Crews for Quicker Setup Times

Figure 14.2: Another View of the Jack Setup Mark on the US Army NASCAR Car

Figure 14.3: Tires Readied for Use on a Sprint Cup Car

Other examples of quick setups include the use of:

- Preset buttons or settings such as the quick set buttons on the car stereos. I know it is hard to believe, but there was a time when finding a radio station on the car radio (there were no stereos then) involved the use of the tuning knob for every station.
- Locator pins or guides provide quicker setups. The Indy Racing League uses a setup pin/guide to assist in getting the tires properly set on the cars prior to fastening the one "lug" nut.
- Using standardized operations helps to reduce setup times and remove wasted time from operations.
- Uniform production levels. This is the goal of every production facility regardless of whether or not JIT is adopted. If a facility can produce at a constant level, there will be less turbulence in the workforce and more predictability.

    Uniform production helps to smooth the manufacturing operations, while improving the quality of the information being shared by supply chain partners, and adds some level of predictability to the supply chain. One method of achieving uniform production is through the use of mixed model assembly operations or being able to make more than one product or model on the same assembly line. At the Harley–Davidson Plant in Kansas City, Missouri, although each of the three main lines is dedicated to a particular line of motorcycles, each line is in fact a mixed model assembly line. On the same line, the company makes V-Rods for the United States, Japan, Australia, and Europe. Each of these "models" requires different braking systems, safety features, and emission systems. Having a mixed model assembly line allows the company to balance production, while meeting the needs of the customer and keeping the employees working.

- Supplier networks with fewer suppliers. The JIT emphasizes on fewer suppliers and more long-term relationships with suppliers. Long-term relationships with suppliers are usually a good practice as this leads to better cooperation and the sharing of information between customers and suppliers. This is an adaptation of the single sourcing concept discussed earlier. There is an upside to using fewer suppliers. This fosters a better understanding of what customers need. The downside of fewer suppliers is the loss of supply if one of your suppliers has financial problems or goes out of business.

- Quality at the Source. This is important regardless of whether a company uses JIT or not. Some of the Japanese terms and ideas have migrated to other countries as part of this aspect of JIT. One of these concepts is the idea of Jidoka. This is simply empowering the employee to stop the assembly line if the employee discovers a quality issue with the parts or the assembly itself. Another concept that has found its way into both JIT and Six Sigma is the concept of "poka-yoke." This is simply idiot proofing the operation, so a mistake cannot be made.

KAIZEN

The 14th edition of the APICS Dictionary defines Kaizen as: "The Japanese term for improvement; continuing improvement involving everyone—managers and workers. In manufacturing, Kaizen relates to finding and eliminating waste in machinery, labor, or production methods" (John Blackstone, 2014). Kaizen is a continuous process improvement program; however, it sounds so much sexier and important to call it a Kaizen rather than a common continuous process improvement program. Kaizen is literally for the greater good of everyone. An excellent continuous process improvement program is for the good of everyone in the program. Just because JIT came from Japan and Kaizen sounds so much more impressive, do not get wrapped around doing a Kaizen program and waste time developing a Kaizen when everyone understands continuous process improvement.

JIT SUMMARY

As a continuous process improvement program, JIT can be used by anyone, as an inventory management program, it may not be applicable to your operations. Eliminating waste is important even if your company is not positioned on competing on cost. Getting rid of nonvalue-adding operations or processes can make a company more competitive and more profitable. Getting rid of inventory for the sake of JIT may make a company go out of business because of the inability to support customers. If the demand remains constant in the supply chain, someone has to have the product somewhere to meet customer needs.

THE THEORY OF CONSTRAINTS

> *"Focusing on everything is synonymous with not focusing on anything. Can we condense all of TOC into one single sentence? I think it is possible to condense it to a single word—focus."*
>
> —Dr. Eli Goldratt[4]

The Theory of Constraints (TOC) grew from the business novel, *The Goal*,[5] by Eli Goldratt, a physicist from Israel. According to the APICS Dictionary, the Theory of Constraints is "A holistic management philosophy developed by Dr. Eliyahu M. Goldratt that is based on the principle that complex systems exhibit inherent simplicity."[6] Despite this inherent simplicity, every system has at least one variable or constraint that limits the throughput of the system. Any increase in the capacity of the system anywhere except for the constraint does

---

[4]J. Cox, III, and J. G. Schleier, Jr., eds. (2010). *The Theory of Constraints Handbook.* New York, NY: McGraw-Hill, p. 3.
[5]*The Goal* was released in 1984; the term theory of constraints did not appear until 1987.
[6]APICS Dictionary, 14th edition, 2010, p. 142.

not increase the capacity of the system. A constraint is a bottleneck that restricts the flow of materials in the system much like the bottleneck of a Coke bottle that limits the amount of Coke that can flow out of the mouth of the bottle. This is exactly why Mickey's went with the wide-mouth bottle—more liquid can pass through the wider mouth and the bottleneck is changed. It is important to remember that just because a process is not the constraint that does not mean that the process is not important.

The TOC, like JIT, is a continuous process improvement program that seeks to produce a process of ongoing process improvement or POOGI. The TOC improvement process has a series of five focusing steps. The first step is to simply identify the constraint in the system. In TOC terminology, an hour lost at a bottleneck or constraint is an hour lost in the entire system. This bottleneck must be modified or eliminated.

Once the constraint is identified, a decision is necessary on how to modify or exploit the constraint. The third step is to subordinate all of the nonconstraint operations to the bottleneck. The fourth step is to remove the constraint or modify the operation to increase flow through the constraint. The fifth step is the continuous process improvement step—go back to step one and look for a new constraint and repeat the process, while not allowing inertia or short-term satisfaction to prevent the POOGI.

The TOC works on a system known as Drum–Buffer–Rope to make an operation work. The drum is the constraint. The constraint provides the drum beat that the rest of the operation should be moving to. Just as the drum beat sets the cadence for a marching unit, the constraint provides the cadence for the operation. The buffer is the amount of product positioned in front of an operation to prevent work stoppage. The rope is the flow of material that links the drum to the rest of the operation or the release of materials to the consumption at the bottleneck.

SIX SIGMA

We looked at Six Sigma during the discussions on quality as a methodology of reducing variability through the use of the Define–Measure–Analyze–Improve–Control (DMAIC) methodology developed by Motorola.

- **Define**—define who the customer is; what the customer wants; and how our company can do it better than the competition.
- **Measure**—in this step, the process is walked and documented and a detailed process map with date and time stamps is produced.
- **Analyze**—look at the data from the measure activity and determine how the process can be performed better with less variability and develop this new process.
- **Improve**—put the new process into place.
- **Control**—put controls in place to institutionalize the process and ensure that it works as designed.

Just like JIT and TOC, Six Sigma is a continuous process improvement program. The key to the success of Six Sigma is the continuous aspect. Too many companies complete the DMAIC steps and then find that Six Sigma did not work for them because they did not go back to the define step and make sure the new process actually worked and worked better than the original process.

Six Sigma originated as a manufacturing process control, but has applications to other aspects of the operations management chain. Six Sigma can be applied to warehousing and distribution operations as well as service industry. Granted, in service industries, a company may not have one million opportunities, but the ability to apply the Six Sigma methodology to reduce variation and improve the quality of the service is available to all companies in the operations management chain.

SUMMARY

Just-in-Time, the Theory of Constraints, and Six Sigma provide tools for operations managers to improve their operations. Although each of these approaches is different, the success from them comes from the continuous process improvement aspects of the programs.

Discussion Questions

1. Is Just-in-Time an inventory management technique or a continuous process improvement program? Justify your answer.

2. Does every system have a constraint? If so, describe the methodology to improve the constraint or eliminate the constraint.

3. How do JIT, Six Sigma, and the Theory of Constraints compare and contrast?

4. Are JIT, Six Sigma, and TOC the same?

5. What is the goal of Six Sigma?

6. What are the seven wastes of the Toyota Production System? Give examples of each.

7. If a company increases the capacity of their system at a non-bottleneck process, what is the impact on the system?

8. Does nonconstraint also mean nonimportant? Explain.

9. What is "Zero Inventory" and how does it relate to JIT?

10. Describe the concept of the Drum–Buffer–Rope.

11. Can Six Sigma be applied to services?

12. What is Kaizen? How does it apply to JIT?

13. The JY Company wants to move to Kanbans to move its supplies forward in the supply chain. If the lead time is 2 days, the demand during the lead time is 400, and the company is using a container that holds 50 items, how many Kanbans will the company need?

14. The JY Company wants to improve the efficiency of the company and its Kanbans; what will that do to the calculation in question 14?

15. How can quick setups improve operations?

15 Forecasting

"Flu Vaccine Shortage Sparks Worries Amid Surge In Cases"[1]

The above headline is an example of a forecasting faux pas. The shortage of flu vaccine supplies in 2018 was a result of forecasting errors coupled with the loss of manufacturing capabilities as a result of Hurricane Irma. This is a very serious forecasting error. This is not the only forecasting error in business. But, it does show the need to have a good forecast—especially important in forecasting the need or demand for perishable items such as the swine flu vaccine. This is not the first forecasting error related to flu vaccines. Over forecasting has serious implications as well resulting in excess inventory levels. According to reports on the 2009/2010 swine flu vaccine, approximately 43% of the vaccines will be destroyed.

The story of the swine flu vaccine was the subject of business case studies for the ability to react, forecast, and produce the vaccines. The Food and Drug Administration, the Center for Disease Control, and the manufacturers will now become the subject of case studies for the inability to forecast properly and get the product to the market in time to be used by the consumers.

Forecasting has impacts on multiple areas of the operations management chain. Take a look at some of the key areas of the chain impacted by forecasting: (The impacts on each of these areas will be clear by the end of the chapter.)

- Sales—a forecast of what the company will sale.
- Production—a forecast of what should be made to meet the sales forecast.
- Inventory—a forecast of how much the company should have in finished goods to meet normal demands and to cover fluctuations in demand.
- Facilities—a forecast of how large the facility should be and where should the facility be.
- Raw materials—a forecast of how much should the company have in raw materials to meet the production forecast.
- People—a forecast of how many people are required to support the customer and to make the products necessary to support the production forecast.
- Profits—a forecast of how much profits the company will make based on the other forecasts.
- Products—a forecast of what products the company should make now and in the future, as well as a forecast of what products should be retired or eliminated as they reach their planned end of life.

Forecasting may be accomplished using a number of different models and techniques. We could spend the entire semester on forecasting models and techniques. The goal of this chapter is to provide the operations manager with the tools necessary to make educated forecasts in order to support decision making and the requirements placed on the managers by their bosses.

Forecasts can be presented in graphs, tables, and spreadsheets, and can even be used in "what-if" analyses to improve operations for the company. Regardless of how the forecast is used and presented, regardless of what technique or formula is used, the key is to use a presentation technique that the boss understands and

---

[1]CBSNewYork. Flu Vaccine Shortage Sparks Worries Amid Surge In Cases, January 31, 2018 . http://newyork.cbslocal. com/2018/01/31/flu-vaccine-shortage

that you understand and can be explained in plain language to the boss and his/her advisors. Regardless of the value of the forecast, if you cannot explain how the forecast was derived, it will be of no value to you, the boss, or the company.

EXAMPLES OF USING THE WRONG FORECASTING MODEL

- **Iraq rebuilding.** The original forecast for the rebuilding of Iraq was based on the intelligence provided at the time. This proves that a forecast with flawed information will be a flawed forecast. The forecast was for a very short occupation and a very quick rebuild of the infrastructure. Obviously, the infrastructure was in worse shape than the intelligence reported and the strength of the insurgency was stronger than the intelligence reported.
- **Overstock.com/Big lots.** These two corporations have made a business out of other people's forecasting errors based on flawed forecasting models.
- **End-of-season sales.** These sales are obviously a result of flawed forecasts either by the store or the corporation coupled with a push strategy.
- **Going out-of-business sales.** A good forecasting model should prevent this type of sale. Of course, sometimes this type of sale comes from the owners just getting tired of the business or the owner passes away and the children are not interested in keeping the family business. However, most going out-of-business sales are the result of bad forecasting on what should be stocked, how much should be stocked, and when the stocks should turnover.[2]
- **Empty shelves in the store.** Empty shelves are a result of a supply chain shortfall by the supplier or the customer. Usually this is a forecasting error at one of the nodes in the supply chain.

WHAT IS FORECASTING?

Forecasting is simply a prediction of a future event. Most common forecasts involve what will happen with the weather tomorrow or for the weekend. In operations management, we are still concerned with forecasts. Depending on the where we are in the operations management chain, the weather forecast may be important. However, we are really concerned with how much we need to have, make, stock, ship, or return. In the operations management chain, the true benefits of forecasting will be the amount of inventory remaining at the end of the season or the ability to meet the need of the customer. Forecasting based on historical data makes the assumption that the events of history will repeat themselves. If demand patterns change the company may find themselves with too much inventory as was discussed earlier with the swine flu vaccine or not enough inventory resulting in empty shelves as shown in Figure 15.1.

Figure 15.1: Example of Forecasting Error Results

---

[2]We will discuss the concept of inventory turnover during the discussions of inventory management.

PRINCIPLES OF FORECASTING

- The first and most important principle of forecasting is that forecasts are usually wrong. In fact, forecasts are always wrong. There are lots of models and techniques for forecasting, but there is no way to accurately forecast the future.

- Every forecast should include an estimate of error. Actually, every good forecast should and usually does have an estimate of error. The estimates that are made every election year based on the polls have a margin of error. This margin of error tells the user of the forecast as to how accurate the forecaster believes the forecast to be.

- Forecasts are more accurate for families or groups. This is the rule of aggregation. The forecast for the product family should always be more accurate than the forecast for the individual models or colors. Automobile manufacturers can more accurately forecast the number of a particular car model that will be sold than they can forecast the number of red ones, blue ones, or yellow ones that will be demanded by the customer. A printer of college T-shirts should be able to better forecast how many of a particular slogan shirt will sell than they will be able to forecast the colors and sizes that will be demanded by the customers.

- Forecasts are more accurate for nearer periods. The closer the event is, the more accurate the forecast should be. Even in the weather forecasting business, it is easier to forecast tomorrow's weather than to forecast next week's weather. It is easier to forecast the sales for this week than the sales for next year. One company that I recently worked with had a series of forecasts. They forecasted sales eleven weeks out with an accuracy of 69% (there was no reason for a forecast that far out except, "We've always done it that way!" I am guessing somewhere in the past this corresponded to their replenishment times). They also forecasted 4 weeks out with an accuracy of about 90% (this actually was tied to their current replenishment cycle time). And, they had a forecast for next week's sales that was about 95% accurate. This company's forecasts help to prove the theory that the closer to the event, the more accurate the forecast. The most amazing thing about this company was that the only forecast that they reported to their corporate management was the 11-week forecast (because they had always reported that forecast).

THE IMPORTANCE OF FORECASTING

The ability to forecast as accurately as possible may very well impact the profitability of the company and the stock of the company. In addition, the ability to improve demand forecasting for customer demands and then sharing that information downstream will allow more efficient scheduling and inventory management throughout the entire operations management chain.

In 1997, Boeing wrote off $2.6 billion as a result of forecasting errors by themselves and their suppliers. They deemed these shortages as not only raw material shortfalls (read that to be a forecasting error), but also internal shortfalls and supplier shortages as well. Each of these shortfalls, internal and external, were the result of forecasting errors, very expensive forecasting errors. Interestingly, Boeing used the same excuse 15 years later to explain the delay in the building of the 787 Dreamliner. The issue here really boils down to communications. In order for the suppliers to know what is needed, someone has to communicate a forecast to them.

A few years earlier in 1993, US Surgical suffered from forecasting errors that resulted in excess supplies that ended up costing the company approximately $22 million, representing a 25% decrease in sales. This forecasting mistake came from not knowing what their customers had in stock at the hospitals. Knowing the customer and the customers' requirements is essential to accurate forecasts.

In 1994, the Aetna computer was unveiled by IBM. This was supposed to be the "greatest" new personal computer on the market. The problem was that IBM underforecasted the demand for the computer resulting in a potential "cost in millions in lost sales" according to the *Wall Street Journal*. As we will see, forecasting for new products is much more difficult than forecasting for the demand for an existing product. IBM learned this lesson the hard way.

In 2010, a leading sporting goods retailer sent out a flyer for a sale on a Saturday morning. This particular flyer contained an ad for a fly fishing rod and reel combination. This company had this fly rod for sale for a

4-hour period and thought that they had forecasted enough rods to last the entire 4-hour period of the special sale. Unfortunately for this retailer, the forecast was only off by about 2 hours. The result was having to place another more expensive rod on sale to meet the demands of customers that came from several states to shop the specials.

In 2013, the National Football League changed the rules for what women could carry into football stadiums. The options were a small clutch handbag/wallet, a one-gallon plastic bag, or a plastic shoulder bag sold in each stadium with the team's logo on the bag. This change was made in the name of security as a knee jerk reaction to the 2013 Boston Marathon bombing. The League as a whole did not forecast the proper numbers of bags needed at each stadium (maybe they were assuming that women would prefer carrying one-gallon freezer bags—now that's classy). The result in Kansas City was that the bags sold out hours before the first preseason game, which was only attended by about half of the regular season crowd. They sold out again at the second preseason game and it was not until the second regular season game before this bag was stocked in sufficient quantities to meet demand.

Forecasting is essential for smooth operations of business organizations. Forecasting provides the company with estimates of the occurrence, timing, or magnitude of uncertain future events. Forecasting is not free—there are costs associated with forecasting future demand or future events for the company. These costs to provide a smooth operation include the costs of lost revenues from forecasting wrong as we saw with IBM when forecasting on the short side. On the other side of the forecast are the costs of having too many people or too few employees on the job or in the factory/store; excess materials or material shortages; or having to expedite shipments and paying for expedited freight to meet customer due dates.

If forecasting is so important to the company and the operations management chains, how do you ensure that you get the right data in order to improve the forecasts? The first tip is to capture the data in the same way that you will be using the data. If the forecast is for a monthly period, the data capture has to be in monthly time buckets. If your forecast is for daily demand or daily production, monthly data will not work. One company wanted to take daily data and extrapolate hourly production from the daily data. What the company wanted to do was take 8 hours of demand data and average them over the day. The problem with this technique is that in actuality none of the hours had the average demand. If there are certain circumstances that may skew the data if not taken into consideration, these should be recorded. An example of this is the impact on building materials after Hurricane Katrina hit New Orleans in 2005. Building material demand actually increased the cost of materials by almost 10% as far away as Kansas.

Another area that may impact the ability to more accurately forecast demand or production may be to separate customers into different demand groupings. This is basically what General Motors used to do with the Chevrolet (the working man's car), Pontiac, Oldsmobile, Buick, and Cadillac. If customers are segmented for marketing purposes, their demands and resultant forecasts should also be segmented.

Forecasting inaccuracies (forecasting errors—more on this later in the chapter) can increase the total cost of ownership for the company for products being produced or stored. These increased costs come in the form of:

- Increased inventory carrying costs as a result of forecasting the production of more quantity than the customer is buying.
- Obsolete inventory (although this may be considered part of carrying costs) as a result of grossly overforecasting to the point that there is so much stuff on the shelf that it becomes obsolete before it can be sold. This is common in the electronics industry where items become obsolete about 90 days after production and also in the fresh foods industry.
- Not forecasting for sufficient quantities of raw materials to meet production levels and having to expedite more materials in or worse less-acceptance-than quality materials to make up for the shortfall in the forecast. This particular problem results in the potential of producing substandard quality because of the substandard materials substituted for the forecasting shortfalls.
- The cost of expediting finished products to the customer to meet customer due dates or required delivery dates as a result of the forecasting shortfalls. Because the product is not ready in time to meet normal delivery methods, the company may be forced to ship via expedited delivery in order to keep customers satisfied.

THE ROLE OF FORECASTING IN OPERATIONS MANAGEMENT

In supply chain management, forecasting, as we saw in Chapter 5, is critical to the overall success of the supply chain. In the short term, the forecast is critical to the production of products. This includes the forecasting of the raw materials, components, assemblies, and subassemblies, the forecasting of the personnel necessary to make the supply chain operate effectively, and the forecasting of where the finished goods should be stored based on demand forecasts. In the long term, forecasts are necessary to predict the requirements and demand for new products and how many of the new products should be stocked and where they should be stocked. The processes and facilities necessary for the production and storage of new products are part of the long-term supply chain forecast.

As the goal of the operations management chain is to satisfy customer demand, a forecast is necessary to meet the production, distribution, and quality requirements of the customers' demands. The forecast has to be robust enough to ensure an uninterrupted flow of products and/or services for the customers. The strategic plan of the company has to include some form of forecasting in order to plan where the company needs to be in the future and what capacity the company will have to have in order to meet these forecasts.

This strategic plan and the ability to meet the forecasts in the strategic plan for publicly held companies are very closely watched by Wall Street. Sometimes, companies play games with their forecasts and production to meet the forecasts.

Krispy Kreme Doughnuts tried to do this. Several years ago, Krispy Kreme tried to pump up their production and shipment numbers and the resulting forecasts for future production. Seems Krispy Kreme was not actually selling and shipping the numbers of doughnuts that they were reporting. The company was actually shipping the doughnuts to their retail customers (grocery stores and convenience stores) at the end of reporting periods with the understanding that the retailers would not be charged for the extra amount of doughnuts shipped.

After the reporting period was closed out, Krispy Kreme would have the retailers ship the excess doughnuts back. The quantity shipped and not the actual sales quantity was reported thus skewing the forecasts for future sales and drove the stock price through the roof. When this deceptive practice was discovered, the price went from approximately $40 per share to $4 per share almost overnight. The darling of Wall Street crashed and 7 years later, the stock price is still depressed.

FORECASTING TECHNIQUES

There are basically two commonly used techniques (not methods) for forecasting or predicting future events/demand/production.

- Extrinsic Forecasting Technique. With extrinsic forecasting, the forecast for the future is based on external indicators that are related to the product being forecasted. For example, a distributor of refrigerators may use the extrinsic technique to forecast sales of refrigerators based on the historical correlation between the sales of new homes and the sales of refrigerators. Another example: every summer, approximately 800 midgrade US Army Officers move to Fort Leavenworth, Kansas for a year-long Intermediate Level Education program. These officers and their families transfer in to Fort Leavenworth from all over the world and include foreign officers attending the education program. Extrinsic forecasting techniques would allow local merchants to base their stocks of household products on the number of families moving into the area and the historical correlation between families moving into the area and the number of household products such as blinds, cleaning supplies, and rugs that are sold.
- Intrinsic uses straight historical data to forecast future demand or production. These techniques are more common and will be discussed in greater detail by looking at the different methods of forecasting used under the intrinsic forecasting umbrella.

INTRINSIC FORECASTING

Intrinsic forecasting basically falls into two categories of methodologies. These methodologies are qualitative and quantitative methods. Qualitative forecasting is based on subjective methods when quantitative data is not available. Conversely, quantitative forecasting is based on mathematical models and formulas.

Qualitative Forecasting. Qualitative forecasting is subjective in nature. It is based on best guesses, opinions, and judgment. A qualitative forecast may be used for marketing, production, or purchasing decisions. The problem with opinion-based forecasts or expertise-based forecasts is that it is critical to have a well-experienced person making the forecast. Anyone can make a forecast based on an opinion, but if the opinion is not based on experience in that particular area, the forecast may not be of any value.

Another qualitative technique used in academia frequently is the Delphi method of forecasting. The Delphi method uses a panel of "experts" to come to a consensus to make forecasts or predictions for the future.

The Delphi methodology takes its name from the Oracles of Delphi in Greek Mythology. This technique's validity is obviously dependent on picking the right "experts" for the panel.

Several years ago, I had the opportunity to participate in a Delphi panel looking at the future trends that would affect supply chains into the future. The panel submitted a list of potential trends. These lists were consolidated and redistributed to the panel members for rank ordering of the trends. The top 25 trends were sent out again to the panel with the goal to get the top 10 trends that would impact supply chain management in the future. We were fairly accurate; however, the panel of "experts" did not forecast the increase in fuel/crude oil prices that hit supply chains in 2008 or the recession that followed closely in late 2008/early 2009. Had we possessed the "expertise" to foresee these issues, we would all probably be retired now from shorting the stock market and placing the timely puts and calls on oil futures.

Quantitative Methods. Quantitative methods for forecasting employ the use of mathematical formulas and calculations to predict the future. These models and calculations make the assumption that what happened in the past will happen in some form in the future. Qualitative methods may take the form of a linear trend line, a regression analysis, an average, a moving average, a weighted average, or another more complicated method.

Each of these methods looks at the trends, cycles, seasons, and random events that may impact the forecast and indices from business that may also impact the forecast. In 2005, the Fortune Business Council conducted a survey on what indices companies used to shape their forecasts. Some of these indices are still used very frequently today and some of them have greater importance now than they did in 2005. The Consumer Price Index is still frequently used; the price of a barrel of oil is much more prominent in shaping forecasts today than it was in 2005 after the $140 a barrel price in 2008. As a result of the recession of 2008 to 2010, everyone is aware of the unemployment rates and considers these rates as part of the forecasting process.

A **Trend** is a gradual up or down movement in the demand of the product. A trend can be used to predict what will happen in the future. It is important for a firm to know where they are in the trend in order to accurately forecast the future. The ability to spot a trend, up or down, is critical to the forecaster and his/her company. Figure 15.2 and Figure 15.3 show trend lines.

A **Cycle** is usually tied to a business cycle. A cycle is a repetitive upward and downward movement of the production or demand for a product. Just like the trend, it is important for the forecaster to know where in the

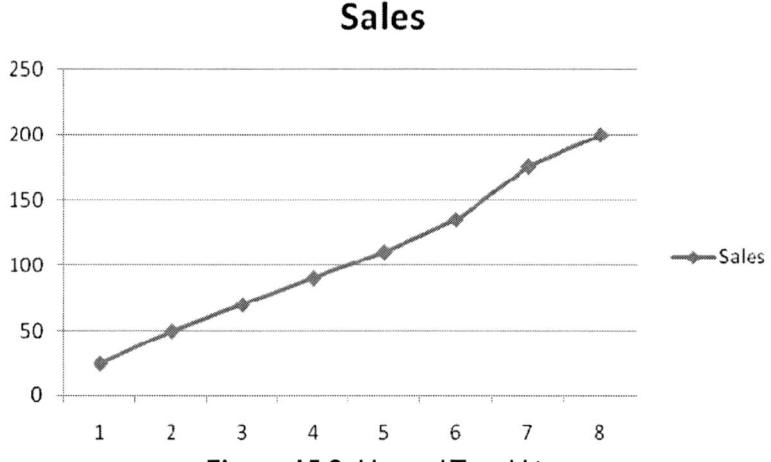

Figure 15.2: Upward Trend Line

Sales

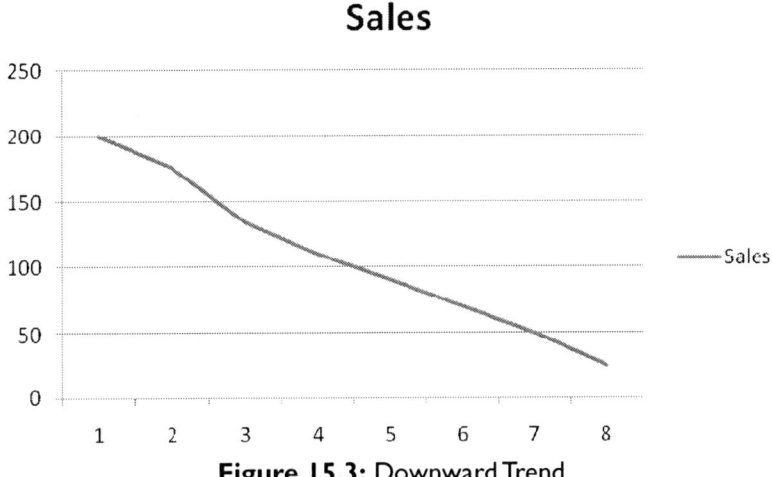

Figure 15.3: Downward Trend

Sales

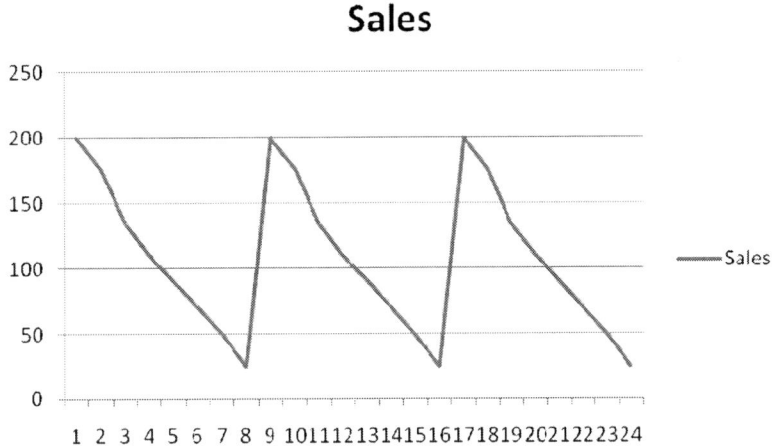

Figure 15.4: Example of a Cycle

cycle his or her product or company is at the time of the forecasted period. Not knowing where they were in the cycle is what helped to deepen and lengthen the recession of 2008 to 2010. Companies that did not identify where they were in the business cycle continued to produce products based on the previous trend and not the new business cycle that was spiraling downward. Figure 15.4 shows a cycle for the sales of a product.

A **Seasonal** pattern could possibly be a trend line with spikes during certain seasons. Or, the seasonal pattern may be more obvious as shown in Figure 15.5. Seasonal items show a propensity to be sold in certain periods of the year. In Kansas, the sale of snow shovels is, thankfully, a seasonal item. Swimsuits in most parts of the country are seasonal items. Winter coats are also seasonal items. The sale of turkeys is seasonal in nature. The majority of turkeys sold in the United States are sold in the fourth quarter—the largest demand for turkeys come around Thanksgiving and the Christmas holidays. After the holidays, the demand for turkeys falls off dramatically.

Time Series Quantitative Methods. Time series methods are statistical methods that use historical data with the assumption that the historical patterns will repeat themselves in the future. For the application of these techniques to operations management and supply chain management forecasting, we will focus on moving averages, weighted moving averages, exponential smoothing, and seasonal forecasting. However, a discussion of forecasting would not be complete without a discussion of the simplest technique of all—the **Naïve Forecast**. The Naïve Forecast is very easy to use. It simply assumes that whatever happened last period will repeat itself exactly in the next period. In Figure 15.6, the use of the Naïve Forecast can be seen. Whatever was demanded in the previous month is forecasted for the next month.

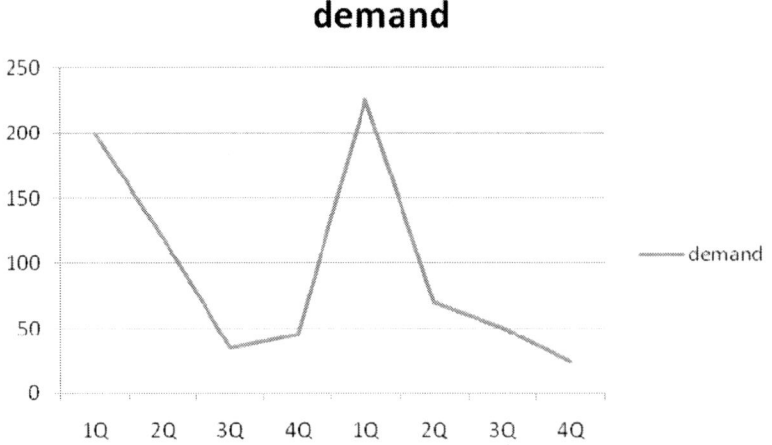

Figure 15.5: Example of a Seasonal Pattern

	Actual Demand	Forecasted Demand
January	75	
February	90	75
March	125	90
April	130	125
May	150	130
June	175	150
July	185	175
August	125	185

Figure 15.6: Naïve Forecasting

The **Simple Moving Average Forecast** is also a simple methodology to use to forecast future demand, production, or shipments. Stock market analysis usually starts with a moving average to show the trend line for the markets. With this technique, all the forecaster does is to average the demand/sales/production for previous periods. Formula 15.1 is the formula for calculating the moving average:

Formula 15.1: Simple Moving Average

$$\text{Moving Average} = \frac{\text{Sum of Periods' Data}}{\text{Number of Periods}}$$

Using the same data as in Figure 15.6, Figure 15.7 shows the forecast using a 3-month and 5-month moving average. Which one is better? That depends on some historical analysis of the forecasts. We will discuss forecast error and compare the techniques in another section. For example purposes to understand the calculations, Figure 15.6 shows the decimal places in the forecast; as we move from the academic calculation to the concrete forecast for the business, we need to round to the next whole number. The rationale for this is that we cannot

	Actual Demand	3-Month Moving Average Forecasted Demand	Calculation	5-Month Moving Average Forecasted Demand
January	75			
February	90			
March	125			
April	130	96.666667	(75 + 90 + 125)/3	
May	150	115	(90 + 125 + 130)/3	
June	175	135	(125 + 130 + 150)/3	114
July	185	151.66667	(130 + 150 + 175)/3	134
August	125	170	(150 + 175 + 185)/3	153

Figure 15.7: Simple Moving Average Forecast

make a 0.666667 of a product; therefore, in the example below, the forecast for April using the 3-month moving average should be rounded to 97. The moving average is a good technique when forecasting for products that are in a trend and have relatively stable demand patterns.

The Weighted Moving Average. The **weighted moving average** method sometimes creates confusion with students the first time they encounter forecasting. The weighted moving average method does not involve any division as in the simple moving average method. This method is called weighted moving average because weights are assigned to the data. The weights are usually provided by the forecasting team, the marketing department based on the validity of the data, or the manufacturing department based on their assessment of the data. The weights may be subjectively assigned that may reduce the value of the forecast. The weights can be used to place more emphasis on the most recent data by placing a higher weight on the most recent data or can be used to place more importance and value on the older data by weighting that data more heavily. All of the weights must add up to 1. The weights are multiplied by the corresponding data and all of the products of the multiplication are added together to get the forecast. The goal of this method is to take into account data fluctuation. The formula for the weighted moving average method is shown in Formula 15.2, while Figure 15.8 shows the forecast using our previous data:

Formula 15.2: Weighted Moving Average

$$(\text{Weight } 1 \times \text{Data } 1) + (\text{Weight } 2 \times \text{Data } 2) + (\text{Weight } 3 \times \text{Data } 3)$$

So far, we have forecasted August's demand to be 170 using a 3-month simple moving average, 153 using a 5-month simple moving average, and 177 (176.5) using a 3-month weighted moving average. Which one is best? That will depend on the forecasting error calculation we will look at soon.

Exponential Smoothing Forecasting. The **exponential smoothing** method is widely used in business to help shape a more accurate forecast. Like the **weighted moving average** method, this method also uses weights to smooth the forecast. And like the weighted moving average, the weights have to add up to 1. This method uses a smoothing factor alpha ($\acute{\alpha}$). The smoothing factor has to be between 0 and 1:

$$(0 \le \acute{\alpha} \ge 1)$$

	Actual Demand	3-Month Weighted Moving Average Forecast	Weight	
January	75			
February	90			
March	125			
April	130			
May	150		0.15	22.5
June	175		0.3	52.5
July	185		0.55	101.75
August	125	176.75		
		(.15×150) + (.3×175) + (.55×185)		176.75

Figure 15.8: Weighted Moving Average Example

The closer the smoothing factor is to 1, the emphasis is being placed on the most recent data; consequently, the closer the smoothing factor is to 0, the more emphasis that is being placed on the older data. There are four basic steps to applying the exponential smoothing method to create a forecast:

1. The **first period** that will be forecasted using this method will be the **Naïve Forecast**—the actual demand/ production/sales from the previous period.
2. The next period forecasted will use **Formula 15.3**, exponential smoothing forecast by taking the ACTUAL DEMAND from the PREVIOUS PERIOD multiplied by the smoothing factor.

Formula 15.3: Exponential Smoothing Forecast

$$\text{Forecast} = (\text{Actual Demand Previous Period} \times \acute{\alpha}) + (\text{Previous Demand} \times (1 - \acute{\alpha}))$$

3. Using **Formula 15.3,** multiply the FORECAST (this is the only forecasting calculation that uses the previous forecast) from the PREVIOUS PERIOD by (1 − the smoothing factor)
4. ADD the results from step 2 to the results from step 3 to get the next period's forecast. Always remembering to round up on the forecast.

Figures 15.9a and 15.9b show an example of the exponential smoothing forecasting using the same data that we have used for the other forecasting methods.

SEASONAL ADJUSTMENTS TO THE FORECAST

In some cases, a **seasonal adjustment** may be necessary to provide a more accurate forecast for a period. The seasonal adjustment is designed to do just that. A seasonal forecast and forecast factor are necessary when there is a repetitive increase or decrease in the demand tied to a particular set of periods. The sale of winter sports apparel is seasonal by design, but becomes even more seasonal in nature every 4 years after the Winter Olympics. As discussed earlier, the sale of turkeys is seasonal. When a seasonal spike is noticed, then the seasonal factor can be computed and a seasonal adjustment made to the forecast. Computing the seasonal factor is done using Formula 15.4.

Formula 15.4: Seasonal Factor Computation

$$\text{Seasonal Factor} = \frac{\text{Demand During Period}}{\text{Total Demand}}$$

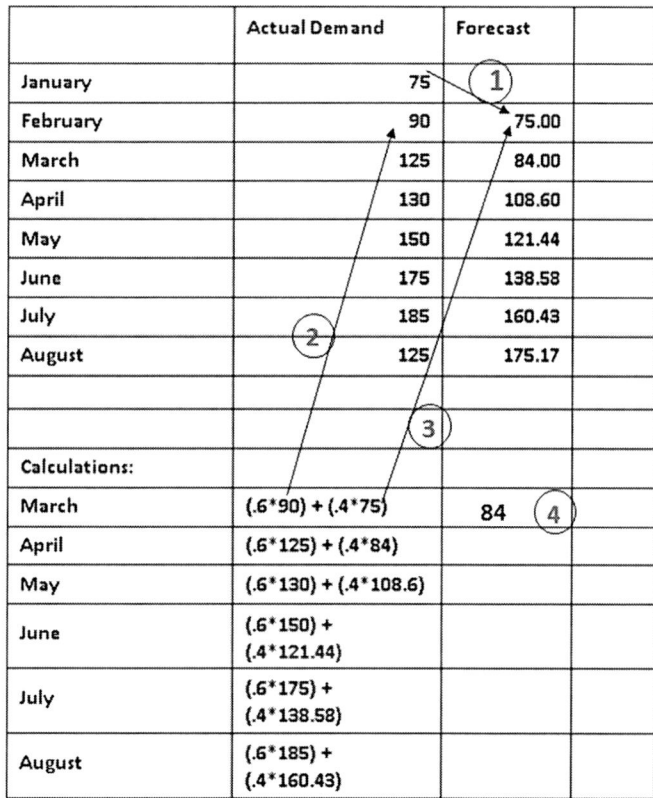

	Actual Demand	Forecast	
January	75 ①		
February	90	75.00	
March	125	84.00	
April	130	108.60	
May	150	121.44	
June	175	138.58	
July	185	160.43	
August	125	175.17	
		③	
Calculations:			
March	(.6*90) + (.4*75)	84 ④	
April	(.6*125) + (.4*84)		
May	(.6*130) + (.4*108.6)		
June	(.6*150) + (.4*121.44)		
July	(.6*175) + (.4*138.58)		
August	(.6*185) + (.4*160.43)		

Figure 15.9a: Exponential Smoothing Forecasting with .6 Smoothing Factor

	Actual Demand	Forecast	
January	75 ①		
February	90	75.00	
March	125	85.50	
April	130	113.15	
May	150	124.95	
June	175	142.48	
July	185	165.25	
August	125	179.07	
		③	
Smoothing Factor = .7			
Calculations:			
March	(.7*90) + (.3*75)	85.5 ④	
April	(.7*125) + (.3*84)		
May	(.7*130) + (.3*108.6)		
June	(.7*150) + (.3*121.44)		
July	(.7*175) + (.3*138.58)		
August	(.7*185) + (.3*160.43)		

Figure 15.9b: Exponential Smoothing Forecasting with .7 Smoothing Factor

Let us look at an example to make this concept clearer

	Sales Per Quarter				
Year	1	2	3	4	Annual
2007	172	26	3	125	326
2008	191	23	5	102	720
2009	213	56	1	226	735

- Sales for 1Q = 172 + 191 + 213 = 576
- Sales for 2Q = 26 + 23 + 56 = 105
- Sales for 3Q = 3 + 5 + 1 = 9
- Sales for 4Q = 125 + 102 + 226 = 453
- Total Sales for all 3 years = 1,143
- Factor for 1Q = 576/1143 = .503—this tells us the ~ 50.3% of all the sales for this product over the past 3 years came in the first quarter of the year.
- The next step is to compute the simple moving average to forecast 2010 sales = 1143/3 = 381 as the forecast for total sales in 2010
- To get the seasonal adjusted forecast: multiply 381 (total annual forecast) by .503 (seasonal factor) = 191.64 = 192 as the forecast for sales in the first quarter of 2010

FORECASTING ACCURACY

So far, we have looked at methods and variations of methods to produce a forecast of future demand, production, sales, or shipments. The purpose of looking at various methods is to allow some "what-if" analysis to find the most accurate method for our company and our products. Just because one method worked at your last company does not mean that it will work at your new company.

Forecast error is a very simple calculation as shown in **Formula 15.5**. Forecasting accuracy is simply the actual sales/demand/production minus the forecast. Figure 15.10 shows the forecast error using our original example with the 3-month and 5-month simple moving averages.

Formula 15.5: Forecast Accuracy

Forecast Error = Actual Demand—Forecasted Demand

Note that in some months, the forecast was over and, in some months, the forecast was under. Simply adding up the forecasting errors will give a distorted picture of the impact of the forecasting error. Therefore, in order to get a more accurate picture of the magnitude of the forecasting error over time, the mean absolute deviation is used to measure the accuracy of the forecast. Figure 15.11 shows the original forecasting example for the 3-month simple moving average and the calculation of the mean absolute deviation. This will tell us, on average, how much our forecast deviated from the actual sales of our product. It is important to remember that this is an average and you will note that at no point did our forecast actually deviate by 38. This calculation does give us a mark on the wall as to how well we are forecasting.

1. The first step is to convert all of the forecast errors to their absolute values. This simply means removing the negative signs in front of the forecast errors when the forecast was short.
2. Sum up all of the absolute values.
3. Divide the sum from step 2 by the number of periods that were forecast and you have the mean absolute deviation.

	Actual Demand	**3-Month Moving Average Forecasted Demand**	**Forecast Error**	**5-Month Moving Average Forecasted Demand**	**Forecast Error**
January	75				
February	90				
March	125				
April	130	97			
May	150	115	35		
June	175	135	40	114	61
July	185	152	33	134	51
August	125	170	−45	153	−28

Figure 15.10: Forecasting Error

	Actual Demand	**3-Month Moving Average Forecasted Demand**	**Forecast Error**	**Absolute Error**
January	75			
February	90			
March	125			
April	130	97		
May	150	115	35	35
June	175	135	40	40
July	185	152	33	33
August	125	170	−45	45

Sum of Absolute Errors   153
Mean Absolute Deviation   38.25

Figure 15.11: Mean Absolute Deviation Example

Another method of measuring or gauging the forecast accuracy is called a **tracking signal.** A tracking signal is used to alert the forecaster of when a forecast is out of tolerance. Remember all forecasts are wrong and a good forecast has a margin of error. The tracking signal provides an indicator of when the forecast is not within acceptable limits. One rule of thumb states that band of ± 3 mean absolute deviations (MAD) is an acceptable tracking signal. This is also tied to the law of large numbers—the larger the numbers, the more accurate the forecast. In our example above, if the ± 3 MADs is the standard, then the forecast is not out of tolerance. However, if you are running a small company with forecasts for smaller numbers, ± 3 MADs may not be an acceptable tracking signal. In that case, a tolerance level based on a certain number of units may be used as the tracking signal. Whatever the technique used to establish a tracking signal, it is important to note that the larger the number, the more the forecast is out of tolerance.

FORECAST CONTROL

Some events are out of the control of the forecaster or the company, but still may impact the accuracy of the forecast. Research is necessary to determine why a forecast is out of tolerance or out of whack. Any number of things can impact the demand for your product and, therefore, impact the accuracy of the forecast. The following is a short list of potential impacts to the forecast accuracy:

- Politics and political change. In 2008, the United States made history with the election of the first Hawaiian-born President and the first surfing President. This caused ripples across the hunting and gun-owning world as there was a fear (based on transition and campaign rhetoric) that the sale of weapons and ammunition would be severely controlled or banned. This created a "run" on the sale of hand guns, rifles, shot guns, and ammunition. Such a run that Cabela's had a record quarter based on the 6 weeks of sales after the November election. This had a serious impact on their forecasting for that quarter as well as the forecasts for future quarters to show progress.

- The appearance of an unexpected business cycle. This is exactly what happened worldwide in 2008. A new and unexpected business cycle appeared. This cycle is now called the Great Recession. Forecasts drove manufacturing and retail stocks based on a continued growth trend. This drove the recession farther down as a result of increased inventories coupled with severely decreased sales. And, when no one is buying basically no one is selling and the forecasts, based on historical data, become skewed and out of tolerance.

- Changes in the weather. After a hurricane, the demand for building and rebuilding supplies goes through the roof, no pun intended. The same phenomenon is seen after a major flood. These weather changes impact the accuracy of forecasts that did not include these events and could very well impact future forecasts for demand, if the abnormal demand from the weather change is not backed out of the forecast.

- The appearance of a new competitor. When Lowe's and Best Buy went into the major appliance business it impacted, or should have impacted, the forecasts of Circuit City. Apparently, since Circuit City is no longer in business and Lowe's and Best Buy are in the top three sellers of major appliances, Circuit City should have altered their forecasts to take into account the new competition.

- Not seeing trends. In the 1970s and 1980s, there was a clothier named Merry-go-Round. This chain of stores carried the latest in fashions for the high school, college age, and young professionals. It was the darling of Wall Street and consistently outperformed the competition. Then in the early 1990s, Merry-go-Round did not see a new trend in clothing coming and forecasted the wrong merchandise—a critical and fatal mistake in the fashion industry. As a result of not seeing a trend coming, this company, like Circuit City, is no longer in business.

SUMMARY

Forecasting has the capability to impact positively or negatively the success or failure of a company. Although forecasts are almost always wrong and a good forecast should have a margin of error, forecasting remains critical to smoothing production, getting the right product on the shelf in the right quantities to meet the customers' needs. Because everyone admits that forecasts are almost always wrong, we discussed multiple ways to create a forecast. The different methods of forecasting allow companies to conduct "what-if" analyses to tweak the forecast and get the best method to minimize forecasting error.

Discussion Questions

1. A _____ is an up-and-down repetitive movement over a long period of time.
2. _____ methods of forecasting are based on best guesses, past experience, and other subjective methods.
3. What impacts does forecasting have on the operations management chain?
4. Look at the newspaper or an online article or an Annual Report for a company and see if forecasting is a problem for that particular company.

5. Calculate the 3- and 5-month simple moving average for the following data:

	Actual Demand	3-Month Moving Average Forecasted Demand	5-Month Moving Average Forecasted Demand	Forecast Error
2002	275			
2003	195			
2004	250			
2005	275			
2006	325			
2007	400			
2008	225			
2009	275			

6. Using the data above, calculate the mean absolute deviation for the forecast error for both the 3- and 5-month calculations.

7. Using the table below and the following weights, calculate the weighted moving average starting in 2005. Most recent data $=.45$; next previous data $-.35$; next previous data $= .2$

	Actual Demand	Weighted Moving Average
2002	275	
2003	195	
2004	250	
2005	275	
2006	325	
2007	400	
2008	225	
2009	275	

8. Using a smoothing factor of $\alpha = .75$, calculate the forecast for the following sales data:

	Actual Demand	Forecast
January	1100	
February	1125	
March	1125	
April	1300	
May	950	

(Continued)

	Actual Demand	Forecast
June	2000	
July	2100	
August	2500	
September		
Smoothing Factor = .75		

9. Using the data above, calculate the forecast through September using a smoothing factor of .45.

10. Which of these forecasting calculations provides the company with the most accurate forecast?

11. Think of a situation, politically or otherwise, where the actions may have impacted the forecast.

16 Reverse Logistics

"In an ideal world, reverse logistics would not exist."[1]
"1.9 million Dishwashers recalled."
"Chrysler issues recall."
"Cadmium prompts new recall. 12 million of the McDonald's collectibles affected."[2]
"GM Recalls 1.5 million vehicles"

These are just a few of the recent headlines that have impacts on reverse logistics operations. As Jim Whelan stated in his article, "In through the out door," in March 2001, if we lived in a perfect world, we would not have to worry about the reverse logistics operations. Obviously, as the above recent headlines show, we do not live in an ideal world. Because we do not live in an ideal world, as operations managers and supply chain leaders, we need to be concerned about stuff in the supply chain going backward. This chapter looks at reverse logistics and its impacts on operations management and supply chain management.

The Chrysler recall noted above involved over 35,000 cars. This is small in comparison with the early 2010 recall for Toyota, which involved an estimated 4 million vehicles worldwide or the 1.5 million General Motors vehicles recalled in 2014. The above-referenced McDonald's recall of Shrek collectible glasses involved over "12 million" glasses that contained cadmium, a toxic metal known to cause cancer. "In all, the Wall Street Journal reports, 51.26 million vehicles were recalled in 2015, just slightly more than the 50.99 million officially recalled in 2014."[3]

Each of these recalls requires collecting the recalled items and shipping them backward through the reverse logistics pipeline and possibly impacting the forward flow of materials and supplies through the forward supply chain as we will see in this chapter. In this chapter, we will look at reverse logistics and attempt to answer the following question: Is reverse logistics a problem, an irritant, or an opportunity?

WHAT IS REVERSE LOGISTICS?

The APICS Dictionary defines reverse logistics as: "A complete supply chain dedicated to the reverse flow of products and materials for the purpose of returns, repair, remanufacture, and/or recycling."[4] Another commonly used commercial definition of reverse logistics is: the process of moving products from their typical final destination to another point, for the purpose of capturing value otherwise unavailable, or for the proper disposal of the products.

The Reverse Logistics Association defines reverse logistics as: "as all activity associated with a product/service *after* the point of sale, the ultimate goal to optimize or make more efficient aftermarket activity, thus saving money and environmental resources."[5] According to Gailen Vick, President of the Reverse Logistics

---

[1]Jim Whalen. (2001). "In Through the Out Door." *Warehousing Management*, March 2001.
[2]*The Kansas City Star*, Justin Pritchard. (2010). The Associated Press, June 5, 2010, p. 2.
[3]https://consumerist.com/2016/01/22/2015-was-another-record-year-for-vehicle-recalls, accessed September 12, 2016.
[4]Reverse Logistics, APICS Dictionary, 14th Edition, 2013, APICS—The Association for Operations Management.
[5]Reverse Logistics, Reverse Logistics Association, http://www.reverselogisticstrends.com/reverse-logistics.php, accessed June 5, 2010.

Association, "In other words, anytime money is taken from a company's Warranty Reserve or Service Logistics budget that is a Reverse Logistics operation."

"Over the past dozen years or so, an increasing number of businesses have recognized the need to ramp up their reverse logistics operations to a global capability. . . . .

The areas of Logistics and Reverse Logistics probably represent the greatest opportunities for cost savings and are, therefore, among any organization's most important functions."[6]

The attention to reverse logistics is relatively new in the history of logistics and supply chain management. The US Army did their first study of reverse logistics operations in 1998.[7] The first commercial study of reverse logistics was conducted the same year by Dr. Dale Rogers and Dr. Ron Lembke. This study by the Reverse Logistics Executive Council was published as *Going Backwards: Reverse Logistics Trends and Practices.*[8] This study is still the most comprehensive commercial study on reverse logistics.

Prior to the Army's study and the study by Drs. Rogers and Lembke, many companies did not want to even admit that they had reverse logistics problems or processes. For many years, reverse logistics and returns was a lot like many families' crazy uncle or aunt. Everyone knew that returns and reverse logistics were taking place, but no one wanted to admit it. In fact, some companies viewed returns and the resultant reverse logistics as the seedy side of the company and refused to discuss it. The study by Rogers and Lembke put a new light on returns and reverse logistics and opened the door for others to start looking at the processes. The authors of *Going Backwards* wrote, "Reverse logistics is a new and emerging area, and as such, only a limited amount of information has been published to date."[9]

In 2003, The Reverse Logistics Association was formed as an industry association to focus on returns, recycling of materials, and ways to turn the reverse logistics processes from money pit to profit center. The first annual conference for the Reverse Logistics Association was held in Las Vegas in February 2004. This conference had about 100 attendees and about 20 vendors that focused on reverse operations. The 2012 conference had over 1,500 companies represented and over 150 vendors that focus on returns and reverse logistics. An example that more companies are becoming aware of the need to focus on reverse logistics.

In 2006, reverse logistics was reported as a $100 billion industry in the United States alone. This was up from the $35 billion estimated in *Going Backwards* just 8 years earlier. The problem of returns and reverse logistics is becoming an international problem, but is a problem created in the United States, and the liberal returns policy of most retailers and suppliers have created a "try it before you buy it" mindset. This mindset is partially what drives the reverse logistics processes. The other driver is overproduction and excess.

If liberal returns policies help drive the reverse logistics problems, why do companies continue to offer these liberal returns policies? The biggest reasons for these policies are customer service and to provide a competitive advantage or at least provide the company with an order qualifier to keep them in the game. If all of the competition is offering liberal returns programs, a company has to do the same to remain competitive.

REVERSE LOGISTICS IN HISTORY

Although it would appear that the problem of reverse logistics is a late twentieth century/early twenty-first century problem, it is far from a new problem. Let us take a look at some of the earlier examples of reverse logistics:

- After the end of the American Civil War in 1865, North Carolina lore has it that as General William Sherman was heading north to link up with General Ulysses Grant after the surrender of General Joseph E. Johnston

---

[6]Pollock, William K. (2008). "The Globalization of Reverse Logistics Operations." *Reverse Logistics* Magazine. May/June 2008, pp. 16–19.

[7]The US Army defined reverse logistics as: "The return of *serviceable* supplies that are surplus to the needs of the unit or are *unserviceable* and in need of rebuild or remanufacturing to return the item to a serviceable status." The study by the US Army revealed that over 50% of every item ordered and 50% of the dollar value of all orders were being returned for whatever reason.

[8]The book *Going Backwards: Reverse Logistics Trends and Practices* is available as a free download at http://rlec.org/reverse.pdf

[9]Rogers, Dale, and Tibben-Lembke, Ron, *Going Backwards: Reverse Logistics Trends and Practices*, Reverse Logistics Executive Council, 1998, University of Nevada-Reno, p. xix.

in North Carolina, he encountered a problem. This problem was that the spring rains in North Carolina caused the Neuse River to rise well above normal levels. Rather than take all of the now unnecessary supplies north over the swollen river, General Sherman's logisticians decided to dump the supplies on the south side of the Neuse River north of Raleigh. The idea of dumping excess/obsolete items carried well into the twentieth century as a method of "dealing" with unwanted stuff.

- In 1894, Montgomery Ward started what is now a major driver of the reverse logistics operations. Montgomery Ward was the first retailer to offer a 100% guarantee with the promise of a full refund if you were not satisfied with the product. This is somewhat ironic that the company that started the returns problem is no longer in business.

- As a result of the critical shortages of materials such as metals and rubber during the 1940s as a consequence of the need to support the war efforts for World War II, the recycling of materials and the advent of remanufacturing were born. This new business practice continues today. A large proportion of the starters, alternators, and generators in the automobile repair parts industry today are remanufactured or rebuilt.

- At the end World War II in Europe, there was over 77,000,000 square feet of storage locations holding materials and supplies that were excess to the needs of the United States Army. As the United States moved from a combat force to an occupation Army, items shipped to Europe for combat were no longer needed. The value of these items scattered across the European continent was approximately $6.3 billion in 1945 dollars. All of these items had to be disposed of, donated, or returned to the United States.

- On the other side of the war in the Pacific Theater, reuse and recycling had a different theme. Because of the extremely long order cycle times to get resupplied in the South Pacific, Armed Forces units started "recycling" and salvaging clothes and shoes of Soldiers and Marines being shipped home. The shoes were resoled and the clothes were repaired and reissued to counter the long replenishment lead times.

- In 1982, McNeil Labs and Johnson and Johnson provide us with a more modern example of a need to conduct reverse logistics. In Chicago, Tylenol laced with cyanide was discovered. All of the Tylenol across the United States was pulled off the shelves and returned to McNeil Labs facilities. The result of the reverse operations produced tamper-resistant containers and was handled in such a manner that customer confidence was not shaken. This also provided Johnson and Johnson and McNeil Labs with a blueprint for similar recalls in 2010 as a result of contaminated raw materials used to produce Tylenol. The problem in 2010 and 2011 was that instead of following the blueprint for success, they denied the problem was theirs and the result was another issue with Tylenol a year later. In 2010, Johnson and Johnson tried to blame the wood pallets for a "musty" smell that was making customers sick. It was later discovered that one manufacturing plant had some bad materials and this was the cause, not the pallets.

- European concerns about the environment led to recycling initiatives and packaging concerns that have spread across the ocean to the United States. The Europeans as a whole have been concerned about the environment long before it became a Nobel Prize winning concern in the United States. Items that were being recycled in Germany in 1995 are still not recycled in the United States. In Wiesbaden, Germany, there was a city official who had the sole responsibility of going through the trash dumpsters in the US Military housing areas to make sure the Americans were not throwing away items that should be recycled. Why is this important in a discussion of reverse logistics? Because, items that are recycled have to go backward in the supply chain. A 1991 Ordinance in Germany put teeth into recycling, thus impacting the reverse pipeline.

- Legislation in the United Kingdom in 1996 concerning the size and waste in packaging and shipping was followed by legislation by the European Union in 2001 that added goals for the reduction of packaging materials. The size of packages and the requirement to recycle or return packaging materials impact the reverse logistics pipeline. These legislations put the onus on the shippers and producers to minimize package sizes and forces the shippers to bring back the packing materials. Reducing the package size also contributes to a reduction in the energy and natural resources necessary to produce the packages.

MILITARY AND COMMERCIAL PERSPECTIVES OF REVERSE LOGISTICS

As we mentioned earlier, the first real study of reverse logistics in the commercial sector was published in 1998 by the Reverse Logistics Executive Council about the same time that the US Army was analyzing their reverse logistics operations. So, let us take a look at the operations from both perspectives.

Reverse Logistics from the Military Perspective

"The Army's reverse logistics pipeline processes are relatively slow and variable . . . for reference, we define improving the flow in the reverse logistics pipeline to mean timely movement to minimize the amount of inventory investment. In other words, the objective is to make the most cost-effective use of existing inventories."[10]

When the US Army conducted research in 1999 on reverse logistics, they found out that at one point in 1999, the value of the items going backward actually exceeded the value of the items going forward. This is no way to run a business.

In 2002 to 2003, the US Army moved the equivalent of 150 Wal-Mart SuperCenters from the United States and Europe into Kuwait in anticipation and preparation for the eventual invasion of Iraq to topple the Saddam Hussein Regime. Any time that much stuff is moved, there is bound to be excess or the wrong stuff sent. In 1997, the US Army went into Bosnia to provide humanitarian support. Within 48 hours, excess items started coming backward in the supply chain. The same situation was seen when in 1992, the Army went into Somalia to provide humanitarian assistance. Within a few days of US forces arriving in Somalia, items started going backward in the supply chain.

The movement of supplies and equipment in 2002 to 2003 created excess and the steady flow of personnel, supplies, and equipment into and out of the country complicated the situation by adding some fog and complexity to the supply chains. In August of 2003, the US General Accounting Office did an audit of supplies in Kuwait and Iraq. The result was a renewed focus on reverse logistics. The evacuation of American Soldiers and Marines from Iraq at the conclusion of hostilities created a huge reverse logistics operation that involved over 30,000 vehicles alone that had to be processed and returned to the United States.

Part of the problem with the excess supplies was that soldiers were sent to their staging areas prior to entry into Iraq from Kuwait. Prior to moving to the staging areas, the soldiers had recreation activities and fitness centers in Kuwait; however, while awaiting the invasion, these soldiers had nothing to do in their free time. When the soldiers got bored, they ordered stuff to see if it would really come in. General George S. Patton, Jr. stated, "In battle, troops get temperamental and ask for things which they really do not need. However, where humanly possible, their requests, no matter how unreasonable, should be answered." Based on that attitude, whatever was ordered was shipped. The result according to *Jane's Defence Weekly* was an area approximately 100 acres (*Jane's Defence Weekly* stated it was an area about 40 hectares) filled with stuff waiting to be returned to the United States. Some of this can be seen in Figures 16.1 and 16.2 from the GAO report.

Photograph by Joe Walden

Figure 16.1: Items Waiting Return from Kuwait According to the General Accounting Office

---

[10]Diener, David, et. al., "Getting Value from the Reverse Logistics Pipeline," Rand Arroyo Center, 2000, p. xiii.

Photograph by Joe Walden

Figure 16.2: Items Waiting Return from Kuwait According to the General Accounting Office[11]

For every item ordered that was not really needed or that for whatever reason did not reach its intended customer, the reverse logistics problem grew. As the US Armed Forces start the withdrawal from Iraq and Kuwait, perhaps the largest reverse logistics operation in history will occur.

The Commercial Perspective

"Life is like a box of chocolates, you never know what you are going to get."[12]

Reverse logistics is very similar. Even when a company knows what should be coming back based on the returns merchandise authorizations, there is no guarantee that that is all that will show up at the distribution center. Experience shows that when you open the door to the truck, you never know what may be in the boxes of stuff coming backward.

In 2003, the Reverse Logistics Trade Association[13] was formed to focus companies on reverse logistics operations and assist companies in harvesting dollars from what was previously a little discussed problem for companies. The Reverse Logistics Trade Association defines reverse logistics as, "as all activity associated with a product/service *after* the point of sale, the ultimate goal to optimize or make more efficient aftermarket activity, thus saving money and environmental resources."[14]

Work with large and small companies has revealed that many companies still do not know the rate of their returns. Companies often quote "industry averages." The problem with averages is that half of the companies are above the average rate and half of the companies are below the average rate. If a company does not know its true rate of returns, there is no way the company can get a handle on the problem—profit from the opportunity that the returns offer. In addition, companies do not seem to know what it costs to process a return. Again, this can create a problem for companies. A third problem for many companies is that they do not know how long it takes to get the resalable/serviceable product back on the shelf and ready for resale.

Regardless of the situation, rates of returns, and time to get back on the shelf, there are costs to reverse logistics above and beyond the cost of the item itself. Figure 16.3 shows some of these costs.

When an item comes back from the customer—for whatever reason, whether that customer is another distribution center, a retail activity, or the ultimate end user—the cost of the item being returned is only a part of the reverse logistics equation. Someone in the reverse supply chain has to process the merchandise credits

---

[11]*"Defense Logistics: Preliminary Observations on the Effectiveness of Logistics Activities during Operation Iraqi Freedom."* General Accounting Office, 2003.

[12]*Forrest Gump*, Paramount Pictures, Robert Zemickis, 1994.

[13]For more information on the Reverse Logistics Association click on the link above or click here: http://www .reverselogistics.org

[14]Reverse Logistics Association. http://www.reverselogisticstrends.com/reverse-logistics.php, accessed February 6, 2010.

```
-  Merchandise credits to the customers
-  The transportation costs of moving the items from the
   retail stores to the central returns DC
-  The repackaging of the serviceable items for resale
-  The cost of warehousing the items awaiting disposition
-  The cost of disposing of items that are unserviceable,
   damaged or obsolete
```

Figure 16.3: Typical Costs of Reverse Logistics above the Cost of the Item

or payment to the returning party. Even if this is an automated process, someone has to process the request for reimbursement and the Returns Merchandise Authorization.

Once the item has been returned to the store by the customer, the item has to be transported to a distribution center—either corporate owned or a third party logistics provider such as GENCO.[15] Either way, there will be transportation costs to get the returned item back to determine if the item can be resold as is, repackaged, repaired, rebuilt, remanufactured, or disposed of. Until their purchase of ATC a few years ago, GENCO focused solely on reverse logistics activities.

If the item is still serviceable or complete without damage—which means it can still be resold as new, it may need to be repackaged. As all parents know, children do not always carefully take products out of the package when opening gifts. Too often, children will receive more than one of the same gift thus creating a need to take one of the gifts back to the store for exchange. If the package has been destroyed in the process of opening the gift, this item will require repackaging before it can go back on the shelf.

Once the item has been repackaged, rebuilt, repaired, or remanufactured for resale, it is usually stored somewhere in the supply chain awaiting return to a store or shipping after an online purchase. This storage, even if only for a short time, is still a part of the company's carrying costs and can, therefore, detract from the bottom line for the company. In addition, there is another unplanned transportation expense to get the item back to a store or shipped to a customer, if purchased online.

If the returned item is not able to be resold, rebuilt, or remanufactured, then the item must be disposed of. If hazardous materials are involved in the operation of the product or the manufacturing of the product, additional disposal costs are involved. Disposal costs are incurred for items that may still be in a resalable condition, but for whatever reason are now obsolete due to changes in trends or having been replaced by an updated product while the original product was moving backward in the system.

There is another cost of processing returns that sometimes gets lost in the system. This is the cost of lost sales because an item is bought bringing the inventory to a stockout situation or as the Army calls it a "zero balance" situation. If a customer buys a product with the intent of using it for a day or two and taking it back, a lost sale may ensue when another customer really wants that product that is not on the shelf. This may sound farfetched, but let me give you an example. When I was in college, a fraternity brother in charge of "Pledge Recruitment" bought a film projector to show films of the fraternity in action the previous year.[16] This fraternity brother did not own a projector so he "bought" one and took it back the next day for a full refund. Assuming this was the last projector on the shelf, if a customer that really wanted to buy and keep a projector came in after the fraternity brother and found an empty shelf, a sale would be lost and possibly a true customer would be lost for good. A more modern example was the Palm One Company. This company experienced about a 25% return rate on its hand-held computers and personal digital assistants. The majority of these items returned show no defects or no faults noted. This means that any given day, there is a large number of salable items going backward and not available for sales to customers.

Another example of lost sales during the Christmas sales and post-Christmas sales is Wal-Mart. The returns after the Christmas season across Wal-Mart represents approximately 4 days of sales for Wal-Mart according to

---
[15]For more on GENCO go to: http://www.genco.com/Reverse-Logistics/reverse-logistics.php

[16]This was a Military Fraternity with a competitive drill team that competed in National Championships and also performed in local and national parades and had a Bicentennial Drill Team that served as the official representative for the Governor of North Carolina at official Bicentennial activities.

Wal-Mart officials.[17] To give you a feel of the size of 4 days of sales for Wal-Mart, Wal-Mart makes approximately $52 million an hour every hour of the day. By comparison, the sales of Wal-Mart for the 3 days after Thanksgiving in the United States (Black Friday, Saturday, and Sunday) exceeds the Gross Domestic Product for South Africa for an entire year.

Other examples from commercial industry that demonstrate the costs of returns to the companies include:

- One major small home appliance company disposes of over $40 million annually of their returned products rather than refurbish the items because the company is concerned about degrading the value of their new items. This is money lost to the system completely.
- Many companies do not really know the cost of processing a return and continue to process and refurbish items that are really cost prohibitive. A manufacturer of video recorders was spending approximately $85 to process and repair a device that only sold for $50. After discovering this problem, the company started shipping a new device to customers under warranty and having the customer dispose of the old product. Sure this opened them up for some customer fraud, but was still cheaper than the original system.
- In 2001, Corporate America processed over $60 billion in returns. Of this, it cost approximately $40 billion to process these returns and, once processed, they discovered that almost $52 billion worth of products were in excess to the systems that accepted the returns and, therefore, provided little value to the company. This is why reverse logistics and the returns process started getting corporate attention.
- One major distribution company conducted an auction for items that were in excess to their operations and sold most of the items at about half price.
- A major West Coast discount company was in the practice of returning seasonal items to a central distribution center. In fact, this company leased a 300,000 square foot distribution center for the sole purpose of storing seasonal items that were returned by its stores. The problem was that a large percentage of the seasonal items for the Christmas season arrived back at the distribution center slightly damaged or were damaged during the year before they could be sold or shipped to the stores for possible sale. The consulting company working with this company recommended donating the seasonal products to local schools for arts and crafts and taking a write off rather than experience multiple handling and damage during the returns and storage processes. This brought the company reduced costs and more "good will" in the local communities.

REVERSE LOGISTICS AND UNCERTAINTY

Because of the uncertainty in the reverse logistics system, the time to process returns is considerably longer than the time to process items in the forward supply chain. One particular major distribution center took an average of 1.1 days to completely process the expected and known inbound shipments. However, it took this distribution center approximately 8.5 days to process returns to the distribution center. This additional processing time included identifying the item, identifying the condition, and serviceability of the item (which included testing for electronic items) and then disposing of the item, repackaging it for restock, or sending the item out for refurbishment or rebuild for future sales.

Another distribution center had nonvalue-adding operations in its returns process for items that had been rebuilt or refurbished. These items coming back into the distribution center for the third time (the first time was as a brand new item; the second time as returned item; and the third time as a rebuilt or refurbished item) were unpacked, inspected, and then the batteries for the items were taken out and separated from the end item. When a refurbished or rebuilt item was ordered on the company's Web site, the end item and the battery were reconnected at another station before shipping to the customer. This appeared a bit strange and the only explanation I could get was that the company had "always done it this way."

---

[17]According to one Wal-Mart representative, the returns after the 2003 Christmas season equated to approximately two thousand (2,000) 20 ft Equivalent Units (TEUs) (a TEU is a standard 8×8×20 foot shipping container).

My original thought was maybe there was some OSHA regulation prompting this action. There was no OSHA requirement, but it was only an outdated way of doing business adding additional costs and handling requirements to the returns process. When asked why again, I was told that sometimes customers ordered just the battery or just the end item. How often? This revealed that it was very rare when the battery or end item was ordered separately.

Other examples of waste in the reverse logistics chain include:

- Estimates show that returns immediately following the holiday seasons in 2004 and 2005 were approximately $16.2 billion (USD) each year or about 25% of everything sold during the holiday season came back for whatever reason. It could be that a child received more than one of the same gift item; you bought your aunt a new sweater size 16, but she insists that she is still a size 8; the sweater was the wrong color; or you just did not like the gift. This is one of the reasons that retailers like gift cards. Not only do gift cards not come back as returns, but the other reason that retailers like gift cards is that they are hoping that the recipient does not use the entire value of the card or even loses the card.

  If this same percentage of items bought during the holiday season continues, when the data for 2016 are released, the value of returns for the most recent holiday season will exceed the 2001 value of all returns—or approximately $180 billion. Although it appears that returns are slowing in the retail sector, many reports only look at brick-and-mortar retail sales and not e-commerce, which as of mid-2016 accounts for approximately 18.5% of all retail sales.

- Wal-Mart has reported at professional conferences that the value of returns for the company exceeds $6 billion annually. There are companies that would love to have $6 billion in annual sales going forward. The returns for Wal-Mart equate to approximately 17,000 trucks a year going backward with items returned by customers and stores. Simple math shows that this equates to about 46 trucks a day 365 days a year going backward for one company.

- One major cosmetics manufacturer was experiencing over $60 million a year in returned products. Unlike other manufacturers, there is no real after market for used cosmetics. How could there be such a large volume of returned cosmetics? One simple explanation could be allergies to the products; another explanation is tied to formal events. Every format event requires a new dress, shoes, handbag, and matching makeup. When the formal event is over, there is no more need for the matching makeup as formal event etiquette dictates that the outfit cannot be worn again. This helps to drive the cosmetic returns.

- Several years ago, one particular FORTUNE 500 company that I spoke with was $200 million over their $300 million annual returns budget halfway through their fiscal year. This company was experiencing over 40,000 returns a month of which about 55% showed no defects or faults.

- In 1998, the year before they went into bankruptcy, K-Mart established a Vice President of Reverse Logistics. This corporate level position was necessary because of the company's $980 million in returns the previous year. A conversation with this official revealed reverse logistics nightmares for retailers. In the early days of MP3 players, young folks discovered that the value of the players was in the memory chips used to store the songs. As these chips were easily removed, a large number of MP3 players were returned as defective. When the players finally arrived at the returns processing center, it was discovered that the defect was the missing chips. Another reverse nightmare was lawnmowers purchased in the spring and then returned in late summer or early fall as defective since they were still under warranty. When the lawnmowers reached the returns processing center, it was discovered that the reason that the lawnmowers were "defective" was that the lawnmowers had no gas or oil. Thus, the owners got free use of the lawnmowers for the season.

Six Sigma and Reverse Logistics

Can you apply Six Sigma methodologies to reverse logistics? Is it possible to apply the methodology of Six Sigma to managing returns? Would that help prevent such wastes in the system? Absolutely!

- Define—What is our reverse logistics policy and what are the impacts on our operations from the current policies on returns? What is our reverse logistics chain and how many links are there in this chain?
- Measure—What is our actual rate of returns? What are our reverse logistics chain costs?

- Analyze—What are the average industry rates of returns and how do we compare to our industry? What are the average industry costs for processing items through the reverse logistics chain? How do our costs measure up against our competition? Do we have nonvalue-added processes in our reverse chain that add to the costs of processing returns?
- Improve—What best-in-class processes should we add to our reverse chain to make it more profitable and improve the bottom line of the company while improving customer support?
- Control—Once we have identified the new processes and put them in place, how do we institutionalize these processes? That is the real challenge of applying Six Sigma to the reverse logistics processes.

Home Depot has applied similar logic to its returns processes. Although The Home Depot is the fastest company in the United States to reach $50 billion in sales, its returns are only about $10 million a year. When compared with other comparable sized companies, this is very small. The first step was to establish a database of customers bringing products back to the company on a habitual basis—this was actually done to identify potential theft of products and initially was only for customers returning items without a receipt. The next step to reduce returns was to identify which product lines had the highest return rates.

The result of this analysis revealed that the largest volume of returns was for tools. Further analysis into the why of this discovery revealed that once a job was finished, tools were no longer necessary so the "home improver" brought the tool back. Think about it, if you are putting in new tile, you need a wet saw to cut the tile. Once the tile is in place, what is the need for the wet saw?

The Improve and Control steps of Six Sigma resulted in the "Tool Rental Centers" being established in larger Home Depot stores. This proved to be not only a method to reduce returns, but after a few rentals the tools paid for themselves.

OTHER CONSEQUENCES OF REVERSE LOGISTICS ON COMPANIES

As was mentioned earlier, for every item that is going backward and is in a serviceable or resalable condition, there is the potential for a lost sale. Another aspect of the processing of returns was mentioned earlier in the processing times for reverse logistics items. An increase in the volume of items going backward coupled with the increased processing times create impacts on customer order processing times and the flow of products forward. In some supply chains, this creates a constipated supply chain where everything is moving very slow or not at all. This also contributes to customer confidence that leads to inflated orders, which leads to more products going forward and then more products going backward, which constipates the system even more. This also leads to the requirement for larger logistics and supply chain footprints. The increased volume going forward dictates larger distribution centers to include more storage area, more inbound doors, and more outbound doors. This is coupled with the need to have a larger area in the distribution center to process returns.

ELECTRONICS AND REVERSE LOGISTICS

Because of the rapid obsolescence of electronic products, a fear is the growth of electronic waste from the improper disposal of the old electronic products rather than properly recycling them. Worldwide, electronic waste accounts for approximately 20 to 50 million metric tons placed into landfills.

Electronic waste accounts for approximately 3% to 5% of items placed on municipal landfills, but these products account for 70% of the toxins found around landfills in the air, water, and soils. Think about computers and monitors. Annually, over four billion pounds of plastic and approximately four million pounds of lead are put in landfills annually. Both of these items are recyclable, and there are known dangers from lead in the environment. Also remember that lead is a finite metal. Why throw away what can be reused. It is the responsibility of supply chain managers and operations managers to ensure that these products are properly handled in the reverse logistics pipeline.

One company that specializes in processing returned cellular telephones was able to mine 75 lb of gold from approximately 6.5 million handsets in 2012. Another company used the recycled printer cartridges to make sustainable road signs and park benches. The proper handling of electronics and the capturing of value from items going backward are critical aspects of success in the realm of reverse logistics.

SUMMARY

"The truth is, for one reason or another, materials do come back and it is up to those involved in the warehouse to effectively recover as much of the cost for these items as possible."

—Jim Whalen, "In Through the Out Door," *Warehouse Management Magazine*

The Reverse Logistics Executive Council has estimated that the cost to process returned items can exceed 200% to 300% of the actual cost of the item and takes up to 8 to 12 more steps to process the returns.

The reverse logistics operations have become a source of revenue for companies that are intensively managing the reverse logistics chain and continue to be a sore subject for companies that have not yet got a handle on their returns processes. The continued growth worldwide of the Reverse Logistics Association is proof that this not a US-only problem and that more companies are becoming concerned about getting control of these operations.

Reverse logistics impacts other areas of the operations management chain while consuming precious resources and dollars in the company. Reverse logistics operations and activities impact:

- The accuracy of forecasting because of the counting of "sales" that may not actually be sales after all when the product gets returned.
- Carrying costs of inventory by impacting on the number of personnel needed to inventory the items, process the items, and the needed space to "house" the items coming backward.
- Transportation costs for the move back from the retail store or customer to the distribution center or central returns processing center. In addition, it impacts on the costs of transportation by having to ship the same items to a store or customer more than once.
- Marketing costs—this is a result of having to market refurbished or remanufactured items.

Reverse logistics, as a topic of discussion and concern, is relatively new in the study of operations management and may very well be the last great frontier for reaping profits and savings from the total supply chain.

Discussion Questions

1. Check with a local store in your area and ask what their returns policy is and what rate of returns they get as a percentage of sales.

2. What experience do you have with returning an item? Was it a pleasant experience or was the process a hassle? Was the time it took to process the return worth the effort?

3. Visit your local Cabela's (if there is one close to you) and look at the items in their "Bargain Cave." Look carefully at the items that were bought, used, and then returned.

4. Think about the impacts of the reverse logistics operations on your company's operations.

17 Supply Chain Leadership

What is supply chain leadership? What does supply chain leadership have to do with operations management? Every year the Advanced Marketing Research (AMR) prepares a list of the "Top 25 Supply Chains." Is supply chain leadership related to making this list? Or is supply chain leadership about making it to the corporate-level positions as insinuated by a recent magazine article?

This chapter will provide a definition of supply chain leadership as originally put forth by the Supply Chain Leadership Institute in 2001 and will provide a framework for looking at supply chain leadership.

From this very position in City Point, Virginia, General Ulysses Grant learned the value of supply chain leadership as his Army developed the largest supply chain operations in the American Civil War to support the siege of Petersburg and the eventual defeat of the Army of General Robert E. Lee and the Confederate States of America (Figure 17.1).

Supply chain leaders must provide purpose, direction, and motivation to their supply chain employees. As a recent picture of my GPS shows, sometimes even products considered world class do not provide this needed direction—you will note that my GPS has me going two directions at once to get out of the drive-through window (Figure 17.2). The directions from a supply chain leader need to be clearer to the employee!

"Leadership must be demonstrated, not announced."

—Fran Tarkenton

What is supply chain leadership? Is it leading one of the "Top 25 Supply Chains" or leading a supply chain company? Is being on the list of Top Supply Chains truly about leadership? One prominent magazine had an article in 2008 that insinuated that to be a "supply chain leader" one had to be a "C-Level" executive or part of the corporate board of a supply chain company or the chief supply chain officer. Is that really supply chain leadership?

In order to best define and study supply chain leadership, it is first important to set a foundation that includes a definition of leadership. Is leadership the same as management? Most discussions of supply chains would lead one to believe that the two may be the same.

Dictionary.com defines leadership as: "the position or function of a leader."[1] The Webster online dictionary defines leadership as: "the act or an instance of leading."[2] Neither of these definitions really gives us a good foundation to define what leadership really is. The US Army defines leadership as: "Leadership is influencing people—by providing *purpose, direction, and motivation*—while operating to accomplish the mission and improving the organization."[3] This definition gives us a little more to work with in establishing a foundation for studying supply chain leadership.

---

[1] leadership. (n.d.). *Dictionary.com Unabridged.* Retrieved July 09, 2010, from Dictionary.com website: http://dictionary.reference.com/browse/leadership

[2] leadership. (2010). In *Merriam-Webster Online Dictionary.* Retrieved July 9, 2010, from http://www.merriam-webster.com/dictionary/leadership

[3] US Army Field Manual 6-22, Leadership, Department of the Army, Washington, DC, October 2006.

Photograph by Joe Walden

Figure 17.1: City Point, VA; The Location of the Largest Supply Depot for the Union Army During the American Civil War

Photograph by Joe Walden

Figure 17.2: Confusing Directions from GPS

Regardless of where you are in the supply chain, if you can provide your employees with purpose, direction, and motivation you will most likely get the mission of the company accomplished. If the mission is accomplished and the employees are motivated, the chances are good that the company will be improved.

The biggest mistake that people make in regard to leadership is: *believing that they lead a company, department or unit. What they lead are the individuals that make up the enterprise or supply chain.*

Supply chain leadership is about the people in the supply chain and getting those people to do their very best every single day. That is why there is a difference between supply chain management—managing the operations of the supply chain—and supply chain leadership—leading the people that are making supply chains function. The difference between good and great supply chains is leadership. To make the AMR list of Top Supply Chains requires leaders that can and do get the best out of the people that make up the supply chains of the companies on the list. However, there are supply chain leaders in smaller companies that will never see their company on the Top 25 list.

Before we get deep into the look and study of supply chain leadership, as part of our foundation, let's look at management. We have spent a lot of time discussing project management, process management, supply chain management, warehouse management, and inventory management. How does management differ from leadership? Management is defined as: "the act or manner of managing; handling, direction, or control; the person or persons controlling and directing the affairs of a business, institution, etc."[4] This is a very nebulous

---

[4]management. (n.d.). *Dictionary.com Unabridged.* Retrieved June 10, 2010, from Dictionary.com website: http://dictionary.reference.com/browse/management

- • **Loyalty/Respect**
- • **Ethics/Honesty**
- • **Attitude**
- • **D4–devotion, dedication, determination, discipline**
- • **Employee Retention/Recognition**
- • **Responsibility**
- • **Self Confidence/Self Knowledge**
- • **H2–Humor/Humility**
- • **Integrity/Inspiration**
- • **P3–professional pride, passion, people**

Figure 17.3: Attributes of Supply Chain Leaders

definition and does not really distinguish management from leadership. The bottom line difference between leadership and management comes from a discussion with a former military professor that I had in college. LTC Billy Baucomm was the first person to make the difference between leadership and management—"You lead people and you manage things." That being the case, supply chain leadership differs from supply chain management in that supply chain management deals with managing the supply chain activities and affairs as alluded to in the definition of leadership. Supply chain leadership deals with leading the people that make up all of the activities and organizations that are involved in supply chain operations.

Having defined leadership and management, we need one last piece to form the foundation of our study of supply chain leadership. That missing piece is to define what leadership is not. Contrary to popular opinions, leadership is not about telling people what to do. Leadership is not about the leader. Leadership is not about the leader's career. Leadership is not about arrogance, although looking at some people placed in leadership roles, it is hard to realize that. Leadership is certainly not about the leader's ego. Overheard a few years ago from a person in a leadership, "I don't care how you do it as long as you make me look good." That is not leadership; that is arrogance and ego getting in the way of taking care of people and providing the proper motivation.

With this dichotomy between leadership and management established, it is time to look at supply chain leadership and its relationship to the operations management chain. What defines a supply chain leader? What are the qualities of a supply chain leader than enables him or her to lead the employees of his or her supply chain to new levels of excellence?[5] Supply chain excellence is the result of good supply chain leadership. Figure 17.3 looks at the attributes of world class supply chain leaders.

ATTRIBUTES OF SUPPLY CHAIN LEADERS

Loyalty and Respect. Every leader of supply chains has to develop loyalty among his/her employees. In doing so, the leader has to not only show respect but also command respect from his/her employees. Loyalty must be earned by the leader. During certain periods of history, the loyalty of the soldiers could be bought by either side. In today's sporting world also, as demonstrated by recent free agent deals, loyalty can be bought. In today's supply chain, loyalty must be earned and loyalty must be demonstrated. In order to be successful as a leader of the employees in a supply chain, the leader must demonstrate to his/her employees that not only does he/she expect loyalty but must prove daily that he/she is loyal to them. A "leader" that does not demonstrate loyalty cannot achieve supply excellence.

Like loyalty, respect has to be earned. And earned every day. As a leader it is important to remember that respect must be given to be received. As a supply chain leader, it is important to remember that the ultimate reason for having a supply chain is to provide goods to the customer. In order to attract and retain customer loyalty, the supply chain leader has to give respect to the customer and to the employees of the supply chain. There is more than one form of respect. There is respect that goes with being a supply chain manager, a branch

---

[5]*Modeling and Benchmarking Supply Chain Leadership,* Walden, Joseph L., CRC Press, 2009, provides a very detailed look at the qualities and attributes of supply chain leaders. The Supply Chain Leadership Institute first presented the concept of supply chain leadership in 2001 as the next evolution in supply chains as the industry moved from supply chain management to supply chain synthesis to supply chain leadership.

chief, or a division chief—this is positional respect and usually is tied to the job or job position and does not transfer when the employee transfers to a new position. This is also referred to as professional respect.

The more important form of respect is personal respect. Personal respect is given regardless of the position or company. Personal respect follows a leader from position to position and remains even after the job is finished. This form of respect attracts and retains quality employees and also loyal customers.

If the employees do not feel like the leadership is showing respect and loyalty to them, they will not help in developing loyalty and respect for the customer. And without customers the supply chain link is broken and the company goes out of business.

It is important to remember in supply chains that loyalty and respect must go up and down the supply chain, respectively.

Ethics and Honesty. In supply chains there is no more important value or attribute than ethics and honesty. Buck O'Neil, former Negro Leagues Baseball player and manager, said that when he was growing up his father told him, "Always tell the truth and if that is not possible, tell the truth anyway."[6] Not only is this good advice for life but very good advice for the supply chain leader. If the supply chain leader wants to attract and retain quality employees and customers, he/she has to demonstrate honesty and ethics in every action and transaction. We discussed the importance of ethics in Chapter 3. The importance of ethics in decision making is just as important in supply chain leadership. Without ethics, a supply chain manager will never become a supply chain leader. Without honesty there can be no trust; without trust a supply chain cannot be successful.

Without trust, ethics, and honesty that particular link becomes the weakest link in the supply chain and the reaction from supply chain partners will be the same as the response on the British-imported television show, *The Weakest Link*. For those that have not seen that show, the hostess of the show dismissed the contestants voted off the show with the words, "You are the weakest link, Goodbye!" The last thing any supply chain leader wants to hear from their supply chain partners is those words. Honesty, ethics, and trust will prevent the leader from hearing those words.

Every supply chain is built on trust—trust that the proper item will be delivered in the right quantity; trust that the right quantity will be delivered to the right location at the right time and in the right condition. Regardless where you are in the supply chain you are dependent on that trust whether you are a supplier, manufacturer, carrier, or the ultimate customer. Honesty and ethics are critical to establishing and maintaining that trust.

Attitude and Accountability. What does attitude have to do with supply chains and supply chain leadership? Everything! Sam Walton stated in his autobiography, *Made in America*, that it takes about 2 weeks for the attitude that a leader shows toward his/her employees to show up in the attitude that the employees show toward the customers. Former Philadelphia Eagles/St. Louis Rams/Kansas City Chiefs head coach, Dick Vermeil, once stated that a bad attitude is like a cold and easy to catch—the same is true for a good attitude. How many times have you heard someone say "You have an attitude?" Of course you have an attitude. The question is as a leader do you display a good attitude or a bad attitude for your supply chain employees to catch?

As a supply chain leader it is important to display a positive attitude for your employees as well as for your supply chain partners and customers. As a customer who would you rather do business with—the positive attitude supplier or the supplier that has an attitude that reminds you of Eeyore? As a supply chain employee, who would you prefer to work for—a supply chain leader with a negative attitude or the positive, enthusiastic supply chain leader that establishes an atmosphere where everyone wants to do business with the company and all of the employees look forward to coming to work every day? The supply chain leader can and does establish this environment for the entire supply chain and for all of the employees that he/she leads.

What about accountability and supply chain leadership? Supply chain leaders have to be accountable to their supply chain partners. Accountability ties back to the previous discussion about trust. In addition to honesty, accountability helps to develop the trust necessary to be successful.

---

[6]For more information on the Negro Leagues Baseball history and the Negro Leagues Baseball Museum in Kansas City, Missouri, go to http://www.nlbm.com. Buck O'Neil not only played in the Negro Leagues, he also managed the Negro League World Series Champion Kansas City Monarchs and was the first African-American coach in the National League as a coach for the Chicago Cubs.

However, accountability for supply chain leaders also means being accountable for their actions. A recent incident concerning the athletic director of a major university demonstrates a lack of accountability. This particular athletic director was picked up for suspicion of driving under the influence of alcohol—rather than taking accountability for his actions, he kept telling the police who he was as if that should be an excuse or a reason for letting him go. A supply chain leader admits when he makes a mistake by taking accountability for his/her actions.

In addition to taking responsibility and accountability for his/her actions, a good supply chain leader also accepts accountability for the actions of his/her employees. By shouldering the accountability for the actions of the employees, the supply chain leader establishes an atmosphere where employees do not fear making a mistake. When employees do not fear making a mistake they are motivated to take actions that will benefit the company and the customers. This leads to more satisfied customers and more successful supply chains.

Devotion, Dedication, Determination. The job of a supply chain leader never stops. This coupled with the complexity of global supply chains and the desire of customers to have the product NOW places a great deal of stress and demands on the supply chain leader.

These demands on the time of the supply chain leader require a devotion not only to the supply chain and the accomplishment of the missions and goals of the supply chain, but also to the family and friends of the supply chain leader. Everyone in every line of business talks about the need to find a balance between life and work. And everyone that preaches this usually violates what they preach. It is a classic case of "do as I say, not what I do." As a supply chain leader, it is important to set that example for employees and supply chain partners to emulate. Finding the balance between quality time with your family and friends is not an option. The job will be there when you get back, but the family and friends may not be there when you finally find the time to find a balance. I have watched folks go through two, three, or four families before they wake up and realize that being a workaholic is not healthy. Too many supply chain leaders seem to think that they are irreplaceable. Try putting your finger in a cup of coffee, and then pull it out. How big a hole does it leave? Everyone can be replaced. If a leader is doing their job right they will train their employees and then trust the employees to do their jobs even in the absence of the leader.

Dedication is an attribute of supply chain leaders. Supply chain leadership involves dedication to taking care of the customers; dedication to taking care of their links in the supply chain to ensure strength in the links; and dedication to taking care of their employees.

Determination is required of supply chain leaders in order to lead their links in the supply chain to new levels of excellence. Determination is the attribute that enables supply chain leaders to set goals, establish the vision for the future, and then set the conditions for the achievement of the goals and vision. Determination is the attribute that focuses the supply chain leader on not only setting the goals for the supply chain but also the achievement of those goals. Determination is also the supply chain leadership attribute that keeps the supply chain leader focused on making ethical decisions.

Employee Recognition and Retention. Many companies discuss their employee turnover rates, which are really a direct reflection of the leadership of the company in most cases. A more positive spin from a supply chain leadership perspective would be to discuss employee retention. What are you doing as a supply chain leader to keep your quality employees? Employee recognition may be the key to retaining your quality supply chain employees. How much does it cost to catch employees doing something right? Remember the discussion in Chapter 4 about Deming's 14 points? One of those points is to create employee pride. By recognizing your supply chain employees you can develop employee pride.

One method of recognizing supply chain employees and developing employee pride is by "naming the aisle" in the distribution center. This is a very simple process—every aisle has a team that is responsible for the maintenance, housekeeping, and inventory accuracy for the aisle. The team may also be responsible for the picking of the items from customer orders that come from the supplies of that aisle. By placing the team members' names or the supervisor's name or the supervisor's name on the aisle and a board is displayed with all of the metrics that the distribution center is using for inventory accuracy, location accuracy, pick rates, pick accuracy, and so on. Not only will this enhance employee pride (one of Deming's 14 points) but it will also stimulate some internal competition to become the leader in the metrics "game."

Recognizing employees in front of their peers goes a long way in retaining quality employees. The recognition may be as simple as the aisle naming. Some companies that I have visited have passed out dinners for the worker and their significant other, movie tickets or tickets to sporting events for employees that have done something extraordinary. The key is that the recognition has to be timely and should be made in front of the coworkers so that the coworkers see what they can expect if they give the extra effort.

Trying to understand the employee is another technique for enhancing employee retention. What motivates your supply chain employee? There is not a one-size-fits-all motivation technique. One of Steven Covey's *7 Principles of Highly Effective People*[7] is to seek first and then be understood. Applying that principle to the art of supply chain leadership means that the supply chain leader gets to know his/her employee in order to understand the employee and what motivates the employee. Understanding what motivates each employee will enable the supply chain leader to increase employee retention, which will have a collateral benefit of increasing customer loyalty and retention.

Responsibility. A supply chain leader takes responsibility for his/her actions as well as the actions of their supply chain employees and the actions of the boss. Just exactly what does this mean? Let's break it down.

Taking responsibility for your own actions means being able to admit when you are wrong. Taking responsibility for the actions of the boss is necessary to display loyalty. How many times have you heard someone say, "I told the boss that this will not work but he said do it anyway." So what happens? The project or product fails and then the supervisor shifts the blame onto the boss. Not only does this display a lack of respect and loyalty, but it also sets the example and atmosphere that tells the employees that the supervisor will not back the employee if something goes wrong.

Taking responsibility for the actions of the employees tells the employees that the supply chain leader will support the employee even if something does not go according to plan. This sets the atmosphere where the employees realize that they can take some risks without getting chopped off at the knees for taking an action.

Although the supply chain leader takes responsibility for the actions of the supply chain employees, he/she is quick to pass along the praise for the program or product to the employees rather than taking the praise for him/herself.

Self-Confidence and Self-Knowledge. As we mentioned in what leadership is not (and bears repeating here), leadership is not about arrogance or ego. However, supply chain leadership is about self-confidence. Self-confidence comes from knowing your business. This is not an "I know it all" attitude; this is about knowing your job, knowing your profession, and knowing the jobs of your employees. The combination of knowing your profession—possessing technical skills and proficiency—and knowing the jobs of your employees gives the supply chain leader self-confidence. A leader with self-confidence will inspire confidence and self-confidence in the supply chain employees. This enables the leader and the employees to take the company/department/division to new heights of excellence. Self-confidence leads to competent and confident leaders and employees.

Self-knowledge is based on the words of Sun Tzu: "Know yourself and know your enemy and in 100 battles you will be successful." A supply chain leader has to know himself or herself. This includes knowing the leader's strengths and weaknesses. Every leader should conduct a Strengths, Weaknesses, Opportunities, and Threats (SWOT) analysis of his/her strengths and weaknesses in order to "know yourself" and to identify personal opportunities and threats to "know your enemy." Armed with this knowledge, a supply chain leader can establish a program of self-development to improve the leader's weaknesses and strengthen his/her personal strengths.

Humor. *Readers' Digest* has long held the position that "Laughter is the best medicine." Laughter and fun in the workplace is also good medicine for productivity and achieving excellence. In the supply chain world it is important to have fun at work. Let's be honest, one of the most mundane jobs in the supply chain world is driving a forklift. But driving a forklift can be fun if some little competition is put in the workplace. In Kuwait, at the Department of Defense Theater Distribution Center, I would challenge the workers to a "game" of who could properly load the trucks. This made work a little more fun for the full-time forklift drivers—everybody wanted to beat the old man on the forklift. It also provided an extra motivation to the workers.

---

[7]Covey, Steven R., *Seven Habits of Highly Effective People,* Simon and Schuster.

When we talk about humor in the workplace, we are not talking about the kind of humor that offends others. This type of humor has no place in any workplace, especially the supply chain workplace. What we are talking about for the supply chain leader is the ability to laugh at oneself. All of us have done something stupid or not real smart and have been observed doing this in some cases by our employees or fellow workers. The key is, would you prefer to be laughed at or laughed with?

Take your job very seriously. But do not take yourself so seriously that you cannot laugh at yourself!

Integrity. Like honesty and ethics, this may be the most important of the supply chain leader's attributes. Without integrity a leader does not possess the ability to be a successful supply chain leader. Integrity cannot be compromised and without it there is no leadership. You may fool others but the person looking back at you every morning in the mirror knows if you have compromised your integrity and the integrity of your company. Is any deal worth compromising your personal integrity for? All you really own is your word and your integrity—why would you want to give that away?

Professional Pride/Passion/People. One of the most important roles of the supply chain leader is to instill professional pride in his or her employees. Remember one of Deming's points was to instill worker pride. Every product your supply chain delivers has your company's name on it—even if the delivery is made by a third-party logistics provider or contract carrier. Therefore, it is important to instill pride not only in your link in the supply chain but also in all of your supply chain partners. Good or bad, your name is on the product; which do you prefer: having the professional pride to put your name on the product because it is good or be known for bad products or bad customer service? The choice is up to the supply chain leader.

Passion is a critical attribute for any leader but for the supply chain leader it is even more important. We are talking about a passion for getting the job done, a passion for taking care of the customer, a passion for the job itself, and a passion for taking care of people.

The passion for the job is the easiest—as everything in the world is supply chain connected, it is not hard to get excited about supply chain operations. What other profession in the world has direct impact on customers every single day?

Passion for getting the job done is connected to the passion of working in the supply chain. The passion for taking care of people is the cornerstone of leadership at all levels. All too often, leaders lose sight of this purpose and start believing that they are more important than the people that they are leading. Never lose the passion for taking care of employees.

People are the foundation of every organization. Regardless of what business a leader may think that he or she is in, you are in the people business. Supply chains are people oriented or at least they should be. And any business that is people oriented requires a passion for taking care of people. When people are involved, as they are in supply chains, leadership is necessary. In the supply chain world there has been a great emphasis on automation and information systems, but the foundation has to be a passion for taking care of people.

Summary

"A life is not important except in the impact it has on others' lives"

—Jackie Robinson

Leaders have the mission of impacting the lives of others. Supply chains by their very nature impact the lives of the customers. Supply chains are inherently complex and the globalization of supply chains has placed a greater reliance on automated systems. This focus on systems and systems architecture in some companies has put the most important resource of supply chains on the back burner. The most important resource in a supply chain organization is the people. As supply chain leaders we are in the people business. People require leadership and supply chain leaders must possess certain qualities, attributes, and values as discussed in this chapter in order to lead the people of their supply chain organizations to new levels of excellence.

The qualities, values and attributes form what the Supply Chain Leadership Institute calls the "House of Quality." This house takes its inspiration from the quality tool known as the house of quality and looks like the depiction in Figure 17.4.

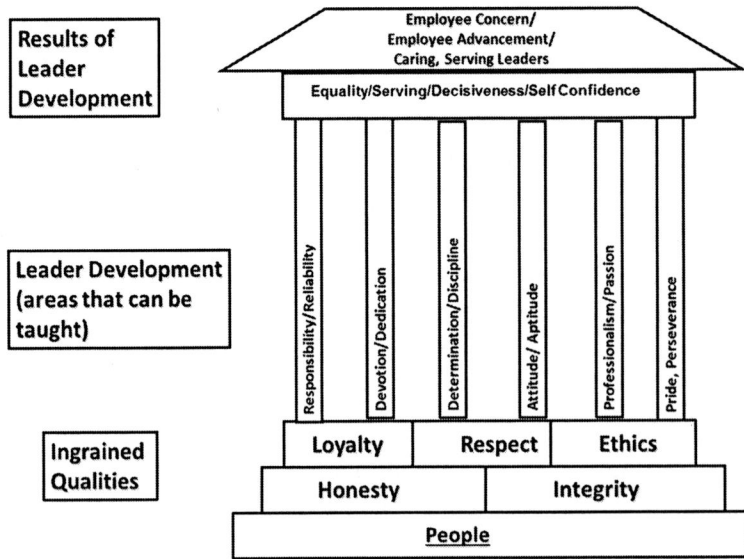

Building the House of Leadership

Figure 17.4: The House of Leadership

Discussion Questions

1. Is there such a thing as situational ethics for a leader?

2. How is professional pride fostered in your organization?

3. Think about a situation at a job that you have worked at that could have benefited from a focus on people rather than a focus on profits.

4. Why is leadership so important to supply chain operations?

5. If you scored yourself on a scale of 1 to 10 on each attribute, how well would you score?

18 Supply Chain Preparedness

Supply chain security has long been a problem for practitioners. As you will see in this chapter, this is not a new problem. The events of September 11, 2001 and the events of the rest of that week emphasized the importance of security and the potential impacts of interruptions to the supply chain. This is not a United States-only problem—supply chain security is an international problem with large implications for everyone involved in supply chain management and operations management. But the time has come to look at other impacts to supply chains that may disrupt the continuous flow of goods and services to the customers.

Why should you care about supply chain security? As long as the items that you order arrive, are you really concerned with how they get there and whether or not the items are secure while in transit? Supply chain risks come in the form of supplier failures, natural disasters as we saw at the Port of New Orleans during and after Katrina in 2005 or the problems at Port-au-Prince after the earthquake in 2010, terrorist attacks, employee theft, or risks from regulatory requirements. The 2016 earthquakes in Japan impacted supply chains as far away as Kansas City, KS. The hurricanes of 2017 devastated the Port of Houston and Puerto Rico.

What is supply chain security and if it is so important how come it is not discussed in most operations management textbooks? The goal of this chapter is to not only familiarize the student of operations management with the topic of supply chain security but also demonstrate to the student the importance of end-to-end supply chain security throughout the entire supply chain and the costs associated with supply chain security. There is not much more in the form of strategy for supply chain security today than there was in the Wu Province of China in 500 B.C. Sun Tzu lived in the Wu Province and wrote in the first chapter of his book *The Art of War* that protecting supply lines was important. The United States published a *National Strategy for Homeland Security* in 2007 that mentions no more about supply chain security than Sun Tzu's work 2,519 years earlier. The National Supply Chain Security Strategy from 2012 has a longer executive summary than the strategy document itself. A lot of energy is going into writing about supply chain security but not a lot of energy is going into actually preparing for interruptions in the supply chain.

Supply chain security is all of the actions taken to ensure the security of items passing through the supply chain. Supply chain security has major impacts on the actions of key players throughout the supply chain and can impact customer responsiveness and supply chain costs. According to several accounts, the impact of an attack on a major port within the United States could cost as much as $20 billion daily to the US economy. According to *FORTUNE* magazine, the costs to the US economy as a result of the terrorist attacks of September 11, 2001 are approximately $50 to $80 billion a year as a result of increased inventory levels, increased security measures, and higher transportation costs. Counterfeit products are the latest threat to supply chains. The fact that supply chains continue to lengthen and become more globalized contributes to the complexity and security implications of supply chains. Although the terrorist activities around the world have put the focus of supply chain security on attacks to the supply chain from terrorists, the fact is that the risks to supply chains requiring attention and impacting security are greater than just terrorist attacks as we will see in this discussion of supply chain security. The threats to supply chains can come internally or externally to the supply chain.

```
  ┌─────────────────────────────────────────────────┐
  │  • Terrorism/Piracy                              │
  │  • Obsolescence                                  │
  │  • Pilferage                                     │
  │  • Information Breach                            │
  │  • Proprietary Data – Camera Phones; Thumb       │
  │    Drives                                        │
  │  • Cyberspace Security                           │
  │  • RFID Data Security                            │
  └─────────────────────────────────────────────────┘
```

Figure 18.1: Threats to Supply Chains

Is supply chain security really a problem? Figure 18.1 lists some of the threats to twenty-first-century supply chains:

Let's take a look at each of these threats to supply chains. The most commonly associated threat to supply chains is terrorism. Another form of terrorism that has received more than cursory attention lately is the threat of piracy. Terrorism threats receive more attention than other potential threats to supply chains.

Obsolescence of materials and products is a threat to supply chains as was discussed in previous chapters. Although this threat to supply chain operations and operations management success is critical, it is not a threat in the sense of supply chain security.

Pilferage and theft within supply chains is a growing problem. This comes in the form of employee pilferage and theft along the entire supply chain. Theft by employees in distribution centers in the United States alone is reported as high as $60 billion annually. According to one investigator specializing in distribution center theft, this figure may be only 10% of the actual losses since some companies do not want to report employee theft.

As we will see in the next section when we look at some recent headlines about security, information breaches are becoming a larger and larger problem as more business is completed on the Internet. A recent article in the *Kansas City Star* newspaper looked at the proliferation of information on the Internet as a result of e-commerce and social networking sites. Everyone read about the 2013 security breach at Target and the trickle-down effects from that debacle—this all started with a supplier's computer system that allowed a back-door into Target's system.

Tied to information breaches and loss of data is the theft of proprietary information by disgruntled employees. Several years ago a secretary at Coke was arrested by Federal Agents for trying to sell the proprietary formula for Coca Cola to Pepsi. Twenty years ago a good computer had a 100 MB hard drive. Today you can buy a 128 GB thumb drive that can hold thousands of pages of proprietary data and information if a disgruntled employee wanted to steal information and sell it to competitors. Cell phones with cameras used to be a science fiction story; today any employee can capture data from work on the phone and pass it to others easily. Some companies do not allow cell phones on tours of the factory—the reason given is to prevent distractions; however, when questioned privately several admit that the ability to take pictures of proprietary operations with the phones is the reason for the rules.

Radiofrequency identification (RFID) security is a grave concern as discussed earlier. If you can read your tag's information, who else can read the information, thus making your data available to many and allowing potential thieves to target shipments? It was not until 2013 that developers started working on an encrypted RFID tag. This after over 20 years of commercial use for RFID tags.

There are other potential problem areas for supply chains that need to be discussed before we move on. As much as 66% of all sealift containers coming into the United States arrive through 20 major ports. Although this sounds significant from a security perspective, it becomes even more significant when drilling down a bit and realizing that more than 58% of the inbound containers to the United States come in through the ports of New York/New Jersey, Los Angeles, and Long Beach. And this becomes even more significant from a supply chain security perspective when one realizes that approximately 44% of the inbound cargo containers arriving in the United States come to the West Coast ports of Los Angeles and Long Beach. From a security perspective, these threats or potential problem areas are a result of the lengthening of supply chains as a result of globalization of supply chains and the continued trend to offshore manufacturing operations to emerging countries.

A Sampling of Supply Chain Security–Related Headlines

- "Maersk Alabama Captain Held by Pirates"
- "Somali piracy is worst in world"—BBC News
- "Russia Sends Warship to Somali Coast to Fight Piracy"—Bloomberg.com
- "UN adopts new Somalia piracy resolution"
- "New Budget includes $10.2 Billion for Border Security"
- "Battling the Bad Guys: 2005 Was a Tough Year"—Dec 2005 Baseline Magazine
- "Major Data Theft Leads to Major Legal Problems"—Baseline Magazine
- "Polo Ralph Lauren—Lost Point of Sale Data"
- "Somali pirates hijack fourth vessel in a week"—January 2, 2010
- "Somali pirates hijack cargo ship near Seychelles"—April 11, 2010, AP News
- "Somali pirates attempt attack on Dutch warship"—March 17, 2010
- "New suite of ISO supply chain management standards to reduce risks of terrorism, piracy and fraud"
- Testimony before Congress on Pharmaceutical Supply Chain Security—July 2006
- "Most companies lag in supply chain risk management"—InfoWorld, September 2008
- "The new reality of supply chain security"—Microsoft.com/uk, May 2010

As more companies start to experience supply chain interruptions, headlines such as the ones listed above continue to increase. As more companies discover the risks to their supply chains, more executives are becoming interested in preventing, mitigating, or eliminating supply chain risks. Even though the focus remains on terrorist threats, supply chain security also includes the risks from natural disasters as has been seen from Hurricane Katrina and the impacts to the shipping into and out of New Orleans and the recent impacts to the food supply chain as a result of the British Petroleum oil catastrophe in the Gulf of Mexico.

> *"We have proved to our management that good security is good business."*
>
> —Ann Lister of Texas Instruments

Examples of Supply Chain Security Problems Not Making Headlines

- Distribution Center, 2014: "A big problem that we are facing now is the printing of shipping labels at home and employees picking shipments for themselves and putting on official looking shipping labels."
- Major Distributor, Dec 2006: A company I was working with during this time had a security problem. This particular company used RFID tags and an Automated Manifesting System to track and process electronics shipments. As a result of this technology and partnerships with certified suppliers, this particular company was in the habit of accepting shipments based on the RFID tags and the Automated Manifesting System.

  This particular truck arrived at the dock of the Third-Party Logistics Provider (3PL) providing distribution center management for the company. This particular truck backed up to the dock at the distribution center to the dock door designated at the entry gate. The driver dropped the trailer at the dock door and left. Thirty minutes later another tractor hooked up to the trailer and departed the yard. No one at the security gate suspected anything as the average time to offload a truck was about 30 minutes.

  Six months later the company, their insurance company, the trucking company, and their insurance company were still in discussions on who was liable for the disappearance of over US $3 million in electronics.
- Locks on trucks: Apparently thieves in the New York area have discovered that getting access to cargo in the back of a semitrailer is not that difficult. All that is needed is a Bic lighter. Holding the lighter under the large locks on the back of the trailer for a set period of time allows the thieves to then hit the lock with a hammer. The lock will split wide open giving access to the thieves to all that is in the trailer. This is why you will see trailers parked back to back in trailer yards when not on the road.
- SAFE Port Act: The full title of this law is the SECURITY AND ACCOUNTABILITY FOR EVERY PORT ACT OF 2006. The act was signed into law on October 13, 2006. This law defines the supply chain as:

"INTERNATIONAL SUPPLY CHAIN.—The term 'international supply chain' means the end-to-end process for shipping goods to or from the United States beginning at the point of origin (including manufacturer, supplier, or vendor) through a point of distribution to the destination."[1]

This law provided for unannounced inspections of cargo containers and added more legitimacy to the Customs-Trade Partnership Against Terrorism (C-T PAT). The law also set forth for the scanning of containers at ports of entry. *"SCANNING CONTAINERS.—Subject to section 1318 of title19, United States Code, not later than December 31, 2007, all containers entering the United States through the 22 ports through which the greatest volume of containers enter the United States by vessel shall be scanned for radiation. To the extent practicable, the Secretary shall deploy next generation radiation detection technology."*[2]

The law also established the requirement for a strategy for improving the "International Supply Chain." Part of this strategy resulted in 2010 of what has become known as the 10 + 2 reporting requirements. According to the Customs and Border Patrol, "The Security Filing, commonly known as the '10 + 2' initiative, is a Customs and Border Protection (CBP) regulation that requires importers and vessel operating carriers to provide additional advance trade data to CBP pursuant to Section 203 of the SAFE Port Act of 2006 and section 343(a) of the Trade Act of 2002, as amended by the Maritime Transportation Security Act of 2002, for non-bulk cargo shipments arriving into the United States by vessel." These reporting requirements must be done electronically via an Automated Manifesting System or an Automated Broker Interface. This reporting is commonly called the 10 + 2 reporting requirements. Figure 18.2 shows the "10" reporting items for shippers/importers:

In addition to the "10" reporting requirements for shippers, the carriers are required to report their vessel stow plan and any container status messages.

■ Scanning of Containers: The goal of the scanning of all containers coming into the United States is to identify any potential dirty bomb coming into the United States in any one of the approximately 12 million

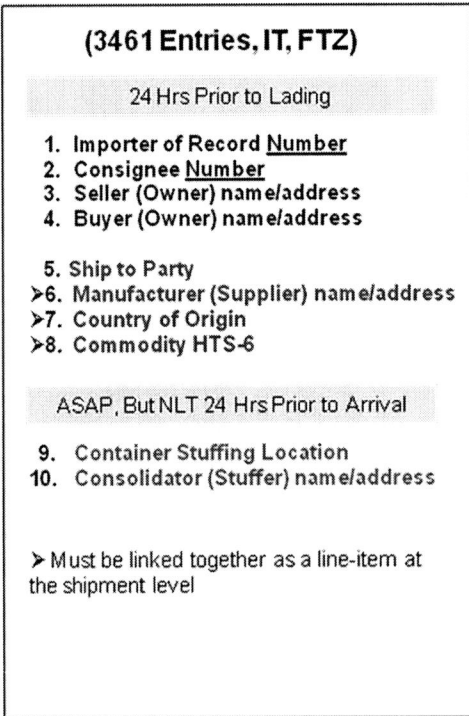

Figure 18.2: Reporting Requirements[3]

---

[1]The SAFE Port Act is Public Law 109–347.

[2]Public Law 109–347—OCT. 13, 2006, **Subtitle C—Port Operations SEC. 121. Domestic Radiation Detection and Imaging.**

[3]http://www.cbp.gov/xp/cgov/trade/cargo_security/carriers/security_filing/, accessed May 30, 2010.

containers coming into the country. The use of X-ray machines and radiation detectors is the plan for this scanning. The concern of the workers at ports is the effect to the workers from the exposure to large X-ray machines. Included in this effort are the Container Security Initiative, the Megaports Initiative, and the Secure Freight Initiative. The National Strategy for Homeland Security explains the process as[4]:

> The **Container Security Initiative** (CSI) creates a security regime to prescreen and evaluate maritime containers—before they are shipped from foreign ports—through automated targeting tools, ensuring that high-risk cargo is examined or scanned.
>
> The **Megaports Initiative** is a Department of Energy program in which the United States collaborates with foreign trade partners to enhance their ability to scan cargo for nuclear and other radiological materials at major international seaports.
>
> The **Secure Freight Initiative** is a comprehensive model for securing the global supply chain that seeks to enhance security while keeping legitimate trade flowing. It leverages shipper information, host country government partnerships, and trade partnerships to scan cargo containers bound for the United States.

The Department of Homeland Security (DHS) initiated the first phase of the Secure Freight Initiative in 2007. This phase included the use of "existing technology and proven nuclear detection devices" at six major ports of embarkation shipping to the United States. According to the DHS, "Containers from the ports will be scanned for radiation and information risk factors before being allowed to depart for the United States." The first six ports in this program are: Port Qasim (Pakistan), Port Cortes (Honduras), Southampton (United Kingdom), Port Salalah (Oman), the Port of Singapore, and Port Busan (South Korea).

There is a link between homeland security for the United States and any country and supply chain security as discussed in *The National Strategy for Homeland Security*. This document was published in October 2007. The strategy starts with:

> America is at war with terrorist enemies who are intent on attacking our Homeland and destroying our way of life. . . . The purpose of our strategy is to guide, organize, and unify our Nation's homeland security efforts. It provides a common framework by which our entire Nation should focus its efforts. . . .
>
> The private and non-profit sectors also must be full partners in homeland security. As the country's principle providers of goods and services, and the owners or operators of approximately 85% of the Nation's critical infrastructure, businesses have both an interest in and a responsibility for ensuring their own security. The private sector plays key roles in areas as diverse as supply chain security. . . .
>
> Our vast land and maritime borders make it difficult to completely deny terrorists and their weapons access to the Homeland.[5]

- Containers in Pakistan: The thieves in Pakistan have figured out that the military containers are weighed when they leave the port of entry and are then weighed again upon entry into Afghanistan. The solution of the thieves is to cut the back of the container off, empty the supplies and materials in the container, fill it back with sand bags until the proper weight is achieved, and then weld the back onto the container. This leaves the security seals intact and gives the illusion of a container that has not been tampered with as it crosses the border.
- C-T PAT: This started after September 11, 2001 as a voluntary partnership between the Customs and Border Patrol and commercial companies. By the time the SAFE Port Act became law, this voluntary organization had over 9,000 participants. The participating companies go through an audit and certification process to demonstrate that they have control of their containers and products from the time the products are loaded into the containers. This then provides the participants a "fast-pass" through the inspection processes established by the SAFE Port Act. "Partners in protection" is the Canadian equivalent of C-T PAT.
- ISO Standards for Supply Chain Security: According to the International Standards Organization, "The **ISO 28000 series of standards** on supply chain security management systems, which have just been upgraded

---

[4]For more on the National Strategy for Homeland Security go to http://www.dhs.gov/xlibrary/assets/nat_strat_homelandsecurity_2007.pdf
[5]National Strategy for Homeland Security, Homeland Security Council, October 2007, pp. 1–6.

The United States and nations around the world depend upon the efficient and secure transit of goods through the global supply chain system. In recent years, advances in communications technology, along with reductions in trade barriers and production costs, have opened new markets and created new jobs and opportunity for workers. The global supply chain system that supports this trade is essential to the United States' economy and security and is a critical global asset.

We have seen that disruptions to supply chains caused by natural disasters – earthquakes, tsunamis, and volcanic eruptions – and from criminal and terrorist networks seeking to exploit the system or use it as a means of attack can adversely impact global economic growth and productivity. As a nation, we must address the challenges posed by these threats and strengthen our national and international policies accordingly.

Figure 18.3: Supply Chain Security Strategy (Government, 2012)

from their status of Publicly Available Specifications to that of fully fledged International Standards, will help to reduce risks to people and cargo within the supply chain. The standards address potential security issues at all stages of the supply process, thus targeting threats such as terrorism, fraud and piracy."

- Terrorism Risk Insurance: The US Terrorism Risk Insurance Act was signed into law by former President George W. Bush in 2002 and renewed in 2007 with an expiration date of 2018. The goal of this law is to supplement commercial insurance companies in the event of terrorist attacks such as 9/11.
- The National Strategy for Global Supply Chain Security was published in 2012.[6] The opening paragraphs for the strategy are shown in Figure 18.3.

RISK ANALYSIS AND SUPPLY CHAIN SECURITY

"If you do things the way you've always done them, you'll get the same things you've always got."

—Darrell Waltrip (Three-time NASCAR Winston Cup Champion)

The goal of supply chain risk analysis is twofold. The first goal is to ensure that you do not do things the way they have always been done in the past. The second goal of risk analysis is to identify the risks to the supply chain and the severity of the impacts if the risks become reality. Supply chains are inherently complex, dynamic, and fluid, characterized by uncertainty, ambiguity, and friction. These characteristics cloud the operating environment. These supply chain characteristics also create risks to the supply chain. The best way to identify risks to your supply chain is to walk the process to completely understand the potential risks to the supply chain.

Once the risks have been identified the next step is to implement a risk management program. The goal of the risk management program is to implement processes that will eliminate, minimize, or mitigate the occurrence and/or impact of any potential risk. The goal is to prevent any catastrophic risk to the supply chain. Just what is a catastrophic risk? Anything that can slow or stop the flow of supplies through the supply chain is potentially a catastrophic risk. It could be a recalled product as Mattel learned in 2008, it could be the inability to meet shipments as Hershey learned in 1999, or as Toys-R-Us learned in the same year. The goal of a good risk management program is to ensure that the problems do not become catastrophic by hitting the front page of *USA Today* or the headlines of CNN.

HISTORICAL PERSPECTIVE OF SUPPLY CHAIN SECURITY

Risks to supply chains are not a twenty-first-century invention. This has been a problem for at least 2,500 years. In *The Art of War*, Sun Tzu wrote that the key to success in any operation depended on protecting and securing supply lines. The Japanese Imperial Navy clearly understood supply chain security as they moved across the northern Pacific Ocean en route to Pearl Harbor.

---

[6]Go to: http://www.whitehouse.gov/sites/default/files/national_strategy_for_global_supply_chain_security.pdf for more information on this strategy.

In his book, *Vietnam Logistics*, General Joseph Heiser wrote, "There were no secure rear areas." He went on to explain that the fuel lost from the pipelines from theft was almost as great as the amount of fuel delivered to the intended recipients.

The pirates of the Caribbean were real and made their fame by interdicting supply lines to the "New World" long before they became part of a ride at Disney World and later a series of movies. Blackbeard based his crew out of the Ocracoke, North Carolina, and made his fortune doing the same off the East Coast of the United States. The goal of the pirates in the 1700s was to stop shipments and take what they wanted from the ships heading west.

In the United States, the Native Americans realized very early that the best way to slow the expansion of the settlers moving west was to attack the wagon trains. Their goal was to stop the supply and resupply of the settlers. The reaction to counter these attacks was the establishment of outposts or military forts throughout the western United States to protect the supply lines.

The German Navy understood the same concept during World War II and did their best to slow the resupply of Allied Forces by attacking the ships at sea. They understood that if the supply lines were severed, the ability to sustain combat operations will be severely diminished.

During the American Civil War, the goal to interdict the supply chains led to the actions that produced the first Congressional Medal of Honor recipients. It also led to a Disney movie, *The Great Locomotive Chase*, in 1956. Understanding that interdicting the supply lines from Atlanta to Chattanooga would cut off resupply of the Confederate States of America soldiers, the Union soldiers infiltrated and attempted to steal a locomotive with the intent of destroying all of the bridges north of Atlanta. Likewise the goal of the Siege of Petersburg, Virginia, was to sever the rail lines heading north from North Carolina to Richmond. Severing the rail lines would cut off the resupply of the soldiers of General Robert E. Lee's Army.

Protecting supply chain operations has been a problem and an issue for most of recorded history. It is just as important today as it has been over time. The difference today is that supply chains are inherently more complex and globalized, thus presenting more potential opportunities to interrupt or interdict and impede supply chain operations. The old Oldsmobile commercial stated, "This is not your Dad's Oldsmobile." Today's supply chain is "Not your Dad's Supply Chain!" The potential risks are greater from inside and outside the supply chain.

FOOD/PHARMACEUTICAL SUPPLY CHAIN SECURITY

One of the areas that has received a lot of attention since the 9/11 attacks is the food supply chain and the pharmaceutical supply chain. The concern about the food supply chain led to the requirement for Country of Origin reporting requirements. These reporting requirements were designed to prevent bioterrorism activities and are now part of the "10 + 2" reporting requirements discussed earlier.

However, let's take a look at some of the most recent "bioterrorism" incidents in the United States. Most of these are not bioterrorism at all but still had great impacts on supply chains and fall under the umbrella of supply chain security.

- Peter Pan Peanut Butter: In 2007, every jar of Peter Pan Peanut Butter was recalled due to *Escherichia coli* contamination.
- Just 1 year earlier, in 2006, all of the fresh spinach was recalled because of *E. coli*. Like the Peter Pan situation, the *E. coli* was not bioterrorism but the impact on the supply chain—both forward and reverse—was dramatic.
- *E. coli* was also responsible for problems experienced by Chi-Chi's in 2003 and Taco Bell in 2005.
- In 2008 there were *Salmonella* and *E. coli* scares in the fresh foods industry. First, all of the fresh lettuce was taken off the shelves; then when that did not fix the problem, all of the peppers were taken off the shelves. Turns out there were problems with the supply chain but not in the bioterrorism area, only in the handling and processing of the foods—all within the United States.
- The largest incident of *Salmonella* poisoning in recent history was another example of supply chain impacts—especially going backward. This like the other examples was not an incident of supply chain

bioterrorism. It was simply a problem of poor control and handling in the supply chain—primarily in the "Make" function of the supply chain.

In this particular incident, the Peanut Corporation of America (PCA) provided products that were contaminated with *Salmonella*. This resulted in over 3,921 separate Stock Keeping Units (SKUs) being recalled and almost 40,000 reported cases of *Salmonella* poisoning. Prior to the use of PCA products, Kellogg hired a consultant company to analyze the operations at PCA. Kellogg used the lowest bidder process for this consultant and was told that there were no problems at the PCA plant. Nestle used a different consultant. This consultant reported potential cross-contamination of products, rat feces in the plant, roaches in the plant, and recommended against the use of the company's products. Kellogg, the parent of Keebler, had multiple products recalled due to contamination while Nestle had no products recalled due to *Salmonella* contamination from the PCA products.

While bioterrorism is definitely a potential international supply chain security problem, the most recent incidents reported have not been terrorism but self-inflicted problems. The security of the pharmaceutical supply chain poses a grave concern for everyone. In the introduction, we mentioned counterfeit items as a risk to supply chains. In the pharmaceutical supply chain this poses a greater risk. One of the counters to this risk is the use of RFID tags to identify products, lot numbers, and expiration dates.

As was seen in the recent Tylenol recall (2010), the use of ingredients that are not pure or controlled can cause problems in the pharmaceutical industry. Because of the potential impacts of contamination of ingredients in pharmaceutical products, supply chain security becomes a larger issue with potentially wider consequences. As more products are sourced globally, this concern increases. According to the Pharmaceutical Security Institute (PSI; http://www.psi-inc.org):

> Counterfeit medicinal products are a threat to the health and safety of patients around the world. They range from drugs with no active ingredients to those with dangerous impurities. They can be copies of branded drugs, generic drugs or over-the-counter drugs.[7]

The link to the supply chain is explained by the PSI:

> Pharmaceutical theft is defined as an illegal taking of medicines. Thefts include burglary, robbery, or an embezzlement of goods. The responsible individuals may be insiders such as employees, or outsiders such as professional thieves. The theft may occur anywhere in the distribution chain such as at the site of manufacture, freight forwarder, distribution centers, warehouses, pharmacies, or hospitals.[8]

Another aspect of pharmaceutical supply chain security being countered by the use of RFID tags is deemed "illegal diversion" by the PSI. Illegal diversion is defined and described as: "Illegal diversion occurs when a genuine pharmaceutical product is approved and intended for sale in one country, but is then illegally intercepted and sold in another country. These schemes are often accomplished through the use of false statements or declarations."[9] The Associate Commissioner for Policy and Planning for the US Food and Drug Administration in testimony before Congress stated: "While the United States drug supply is among the safest in the world, we believe there are increasingly sophisticated threats from drug counterfeiters. Organizations and individuals who peddle fake medicines put unsuspecting patients at risk, by exposing them to unknown contaminants and denying them medicines known to be safe and effective at treating their medical ailments. Counterfeit drug products and illicit drug diversion are major concerns to FDA."[10]

The global impact of counterfeit and diverted products within the pharmaceutical supply chain continues to grow as supply chains become more globalized. Pfizer has taken a plan of attack of buying these counterfeit products and analyzing them to see what components are being used. One of their latest discoveries from counterfeit batch was that there were only 4% active ingredients and 96% concrete dust.

---

[7]http://www.psi-inc.org/index.cfm, accessed May 31, 2010.
[8]http://www.psi-inc.org/counterfeitSituation.cfm, accessed May 31, 2010.
[9]Ibid.
[10]http://www.fda.gov/NewsEvents/Testimony/ucm111840.htm, accessed May 29, 2010.

> - **Rotterdam – 9.287 million Twenty Foot Equivalent Containers (TEUs) in 2005**
> - **Hamburg – 9.088 million TEUs**
> - **Antwerp – 6.488 million TEUs**
> - **Bremen – 3.735 million TEUs**
> - **Giora Tauro – 3.161 million TEUs**
> - **LA/Long Beach – 7.485 mil TEUs**

Figure 18.4: Top European Ports[11]

> - **Singapore – 23.2 million TEUs**
> - **Hong Kong – 22.602 million**
> - **Shanghai – 18.080 million**
> - **Shenzhen – 16.2 million**
> - **Pusan – 11.94 million**

Figure 18.5: International Ports

Other counterfeit items impacting the supply chain include counterfeit condoms, counterfeit cigarettes, and counterfeit liquors and wines. In fact, in 2012 there were more bottles of 1992 Rothschild wine in China than were actually bottled originally. In 2012 there was a court case involving fake 200-year-old wine and later an article online giving the details of how to counterfeit antique wines. The impact of these products in supply chain security and supply chain confidence is great and has ripple effects through the entire supply chain.

A Global Perspective

According to *Logistics Today*, the top European ports are shown in Figure 18.4 and compared to the largest volume port in the United States—Los Angeles/Long Beach.

Figure 18.5 shows the largest international ports:

The Port of Rotterdam Rotterdam is the largest port in Europe with over 9 million 20 ft equivalent containers coming into the port each year. This means over 25,000 containers every day of the year coming into Rotterdam. This drives the over 900 barge moves daily to approximately 72 locations reachable by barge and over 200 rail moves each day from the port to customer locations to the east. The rail and barge movements into and out of Rotterdam provide support to the over 220 million people that live within a 600 mile radius of Rotterdam.

In addition to containers, rail movements, and barge moves, the Netherlands is home to over 9,000 distribution centers with over US $64 billion in logistics operations. These operations help to feed the logistics operations in Belgium where over 13% of the shipments move through the country via rail and into Germany where approximately 15% of the shipments arrive via rail.

Rail security in Europe, like in the United States, is critical for success of supply chain operations. In the United States, there are only four major rail bridges across the Mississippi River. Every rail bridge in the United States and in Europe presents targets of opportunity for supply chain security lapses.

Summary

Supply chain security is not a new issue but one that has the potential to have an enormous impact on the success and profitability of a company's supply chain operations. Sun Tzu warned us 2,500 years ago to protect our supply lines to be successful in any operation. The supply chains of Sun Tzu's day were much less complicated than the supply chains of the twenty-first century. Supply chains were mostly local in Sun Tzu's day; supply chains are mostly globalized and inherently complex in today's world.

---

[11]*Logistics Today*, February 2007, p. 1.

Supply chain security starts with a process walk of the supply chain to identify potential risks and then putting a risk management plan in place to eliminate the risks if possible. If elimination of the risk is not possible, the risk management program should seek to minimize or mitigate the impact of the potential occurrence of the risk. The goal is to protect the items in the supply chain from end to end and ensure that the products reach the intended customer without delay.

There is a link between supply chain security and homeland security—this is not a problem unique to the United States. There is also a link between supply chain security and velocity in a supply chain. The more secure a supply chain is the greater the chance that it may move a little slower. However, it is much better to move a little slower than stop moving at all. A good example of this is the Maersk Lines. They made a decision in 2009 to stop shipping through the Suez Canal and start shipping around the Cape of South Africa to prevent attacks by the Somali pirates. This results in a longer shipping time but a much more secure route. There are trade-offs between security and speed. This is what supply chain managers get paid to do.

In addition, there are natural disasters that have the same impact on the flow of goods and materials that supply chain managers and supply chain leaders need to take into consideration when planning their supply chains. If the security and preparedness of the supply chain are considered as part of the SCOR Model function of Plan the Supply Chain, companies will be postured for success and customers will be assured of an uninterrupted flow of goods and services.

Discussion Questions

1. Discuss the link between supply chain security and homeland security.
2. Pick a retail supply chain and identify potential supply chain risks.
3. Does supply chain security impact profitability?
4. Why is there a trade-off between speed and security?
5. What are the costs of supply chain security?
6. Is supply chain security a problem unique to the United States? Why or why not?
7. What purpose does a process map and process walk have in supply chain security?
8. Why is the Country of Origin a concern from a supply chain security perspective?
9. Would Country of Origin reporting have prevented the problems discussed in this chapter?
10. Why should you be concerned about natural disasters impacting supply chains?

19 Professional Organizations

a. **APICS.** APICS is the largest professional organization for supply chain management and operations management. APICS offers certifications in Production and Inventory Management (CPIM) and a professional certification in supply chain management (Certified Supply Chain Professional). You can read more about APICS at http://www.apics.org. APICS also offers free membership to students.

b. **Institute for Supply Management (ISM).** ISM is more focused on procurement operations but also offers a Certified Professional Supply Manager program. Like APICS, ISM offers free membership for students. For more information go to www.ism.ws.

c. **Council of Supply Chain Management Professionals (CSCMP).** The CSCMP offers scholarships and opportunities for students to attend their annual conference. For more on CSCMP go to www.cscmp.org.

d. **Warehousing Education and Research Council (WERC).** WERC is more of a distribution-focused organization but offers a wide variety of research publications on supply chain and distribution operations. For more information go to www.werc.org.

Answers/Solutions to Select Questions from the Chapters

Chapter 1: Discussion Questions

1. How does the Department of Labor define services and products? http://www.dol.gov

2. What are the differences between the outputs of goods and services? **Goods are tangible and services tend to be labor intensive; services usually decrease in value after the service is rendered.**

3. What are the inputs to the operations management chain?

4. Why does the author introduce the term operations management chain as a concept and what is the operations management chain? **Just as the supply chain is a series of interrelated activities, so is the operations management chain—this chain of management runs from managing the sourcing of raw materials to managing the delivery of products to the ultimate customer.**

5. Discuss the operations management chain from the systems perspective.

6. Is labor a commodity input to the operations management chain? **Labor is an input but should never be considered a commodity. You manage commodities and lead people.**

7. How did the Industrial Revolution impact operations management?

8. Is there a difference between a purely academic approach to operations management and a practitioner's approach? **The practitioner's approach recognizes that the textbook solution does not always work and focuses on real-world solutions to challenges and opportunities.**

9. What is the product design process and why is it important to the study of the operations management chain?

10. Dr. W. Edwards Deming once said "If you cannot describe what you are doing as a system, you do not know what you are doing." Describe operations management as a system. **Inputs–Transformation–Outputs, with feedback loops to ensure the right inputs are received, the right transformation takes place, and the right outputs are produced.**

Chapter 2: Discussion Questions

1. Organizations exist
    a. To provide employment opportunities.
    b. To meet the needs of society that people working alone cannot.
    c. To produce goods in limited quantities.
    d. To access the equipment and technology in order to produce goods and services.
    e. All of the above.
    f. b and d.

2. Operations involves
    a. The distribution of company products.
    b. The production of goods and services.
    c. Obtaining people, capital, and materials.

    d. Accounting, marketing, finance, and engineering.

    e. All of the above.

    f. a, b, and c.

3. Production and operations management is

    a. Managing a company's level of inventory.

    b. Managing the inputs to a production process.

    c. Managing the people who work in manufacturing companies.

    d. Managing the transformation process that produces goods and services.

    e. All of the above.

    f. a and d only.

4. Operations managers apply ideas and knowledge in order to

    a. Cut production time to speed new products to market.

    b. Improve flexibility to meet rapidly changing customer needs.

    c. Enhance product quality and customer services.

    d. All of the above.

    e. None of the above.

    f. Only a and b.

5. Inputs to the transformation process of operations include

    a. Goods and services.

    b. Accounting, finance, engineering, and marketing.

    c. Production planning, inventory control, and quality management.

    d. People, capital, and material.

    e. All of the above

6. The outputs of the transformation process of operations are

    a. Accounting, finance, engineering, and marketing.

    b. Production planning, inventory control, and quality management.

    c. Goods and services.

    d. People, capital, and material.

    e. All of the above.

7. An important difference between goods and services is

    a. Only goods are tangible.

    b. Only goods are produced using materials and equipment.

    c. Only services are produced according to customer needs.

    d. All of the above.

    e. None of the above.

8. Ethics is a set of standards that are generally

    a. Lower than what is legal.

    b. Higher than what is legal.

    c. Equal to what is legal.

    d. Not considered in product safety.

    e. a and d.

    f. None of the above.

9. Productivity is the ratio of inputs consumed divided by the outputs achieved.

    a. True

    b. False

10. An important step in developing a strategic plan is

    a. Short-range forecasting.

    b. Measuring productivity.

c. Working with suppliers on product design.

d. **Assessing the organization's strengths and weaknesses**.

Chapter 3: Discussion Questions

1. Why is ethics important in decision making?

2. What company's actions prompted the passing of the Sarbanes-Oxley Act? **Enron**

3. What is the goal of the Sarbanes-Oxley Act?

4. Making a decision includes what variables? **Knowing if a decision is necessary, if necessary when to decide, and understanding that there are impacts/consequences from decision making.**

5. What is ethics?

6. Is there such a thing as situational ethics? **No, what is right or wrong does not change with situations.**

7. What is the maximax decision-making criteria?

8. Think about maximax as an optimistic decision criteria; is it possible to be disappointed if this criterion is the basis for a decision from a payoff table? Why? **Absolutely, if maximax is used and the expected state of nature does not occur, the payoff could be considerably less.**

9. What is the significance of the point of indifference?

10. What is the purpose of the Expected Value of Perfect Information? **This calculation tells the customer how much more they could make with the better or perfect information.**

11. How do you calculate the Value of Perfect Information?

12. Using Decision Making Under Uncertainty solve the following:
    The profit level for a furniture manufacturer using four different plants 1, 2, 3, and 4 and the demand level A, B, and C is shown. What decision would be made using **maximax** criterion?

Plant/Demand	A	B	C
1	200	350	600
2	250	350	540
3	300	375	490
4	225	275	603

Using maximax, look for the largest payoff in the table. In this case, the maximax decision would be Plant 4.

13. If the following weights are added to the above table, what are the expected maximum values for each alternative and the Value of Perfect Information for this decision?
    State of Nature A. 5
    State of Nature B. 35
    State of Nature C. 15

Chapter 4: Discussion Questions

1. Why is quality important from an operations management perspective? **Quality impacts corporate reputation and profitability, as well as customer satisfaction with your product.**

2. Think a situation that you have been in that would have benefited from the use of a process map.

3. Use your current job or a recent job and prepare a process map of the operations.

4. How could you use an Ishikawa diagram to improve your operations? **In any operation the goal of the Ishikawa diagram is to identify the root cause of issues and fix them, not just treat the symptom.**

5. Look at an annual report for a company and review the report to see if the company is ISO 9001:2015 compliant for their quality programs.

6. Why is it important to be ISO 9000 compliant? Who cares? **In order to do business with European Union partners, this is a requirement. Also the process of achieving ISO 9000 may help the company improve their operations.**

7. Is ISO 9000 series compliance/certification an order winner or an order qualifier? Explain your answer.

Chapter 5: Discussion Questions

1. What is the difference between warehouses and distribution centers? Or, are the two terms interrelated?

2. Many discussions of supply chains use the terms logistics and supply chains interchangeably. Is this accurate or are the two different? If they are different, how do they differ? **Logistics is the function of moving items/people from one location to another, it is a subset of the overarching supply chain management concept. They are not the same.**

3. What are the advantages of the different modes of transportation?

4. Logistics was derived from the military as a concept. In today's supply chain, what function is closely associated with the military logistics concept of moving supplies and personnel? **Distribution**

5. What is intermodal transportation?

6. How has the distribution center been impacted by the increase in customers ordering direct from the manufacturer via the Internet? **Distribution centers have had to add an individual item picking area as well as returns processing areas.**

7. What is the mode of transportation most common for international shipping? What impact does this have on the supply chain?

8. What are the functions of the Supply Chain Council's "Supply Chain Operations Reference" Model? **Plan, Source, Make, Deliver, Return, and Enable.**

9. Describe the supply chain.

10. What does cash to cash have to do with supply chain operations? **Getting cash from customers quickly impacts the ability to pay suppliers and keep the supply chain functioning.**

11. What is a Warehouse Management System and how does a WMS impact supply chain operations?

12. What is the difference between single sourcing and sole sourcing? Define each of the concepts. **Single sourcing is a concept where there are multiple suppliers but a company chooses to do business with only one supplier. Sole sourcing literally implies that there is only one company or one person that can provide that particular support.**

13. What part does information have in the operation of supply chains?

14. Is security a concern with information systems? **Absolutely. Every week someone reports a security breach of their data. The most prominent one was the 2013 breach of data at Target resulting in millions of customers' data being stolen.**

15. What is the role of bar codes in today's supply chains?

16. What does an RFID tag provide supply chains that a bar code does not? If no improvement or advantage, why would you use an RFID tag? **RFID tags provide the ability to be read from greater distances and can provide more data than the bar code and help companies' ability to track and trace items in the supply chain.**

Chapter 6: Discussion Questions

1. How does the PERT chart differ from the CPM chart?

2. What does the Gantt chart do for a project manager? **Provides a useful and visual tool for managing projects and keeping the projects on time.**

3. What purpose does the statement of work provide?

4. What is the "troop to task" analysis for project management? **How many people are needed for the project based on the statement of work.**

5. What is the difference between projects and programs?

6. What are the goals of project management? **To be completed on time and within budget.**

Chapter 7: Discussion Questions

1. Why is designing for the environment becoming more important? Is this a recent occurrence? Provide examples of designing for the environment.

2. If a product has fixed costs of $1,000,000 with variable costs of $200 per item with a sales price of $1,500, what is the break-even point? Why is this important? **770; everyone wants to know when they will start making a profit.**

3. Using the data from above, what are the total costs at the break-even point?

4. What are the goals of the product design process? **Design a product that meets the needs of the customer.**

5. Should the product and production plan be developed consecutively or concurrently?

6. What is the difference between traditional and concurrent product design? **Lockstep approach vs. a project team approach.**

7. What is Design for Six Sigma and how does it differ from the Six Sigma process discussed in Chapter 4?

8. Can the design process provide the company with a competitive advantage?

9. What is the difference between availability and maintainability? **Availability is the percentage of time that a product can be used by the customer; maintainability is the time to repair the product if it fails.**

10. What is mean time between failure?

11. What is mean time to repair?

12. If Product A has a MTBF of 175 hours and a MTTR of 25 hours; Product B has a MTBF of 250 hours and a MTTR of 60 hours; and Product C has a MTBF of 150 hours with an MTTR of 20 hours, what is the systems availability of the products and which one should the company select for production?

Chapter 8: Discussion Questions

1. Why is process development important to the Operations Management Chain?

2. What is the goal of process design? **Get the product to the customers as quickly as possible.**

3. What is the importance of the point of indifference?

4. If a company has the option of choosing between two processes for the production of their product, calculate the point of indifference with the following data:
   Product A: Fixed Costs = $500,000; Variable Costs = $125 per item produced
   Product B: Fixed Costs = $750,000; Variable Costs = $75 per item produced

5. If the forecasted production for the above data is 9,000 units, what process should the company select?

6. Research RFID tags and explain the size and capability differences between active and passive tags.

7. What aspects should a company consider if making a make or buy decision? **Some of the considerations include: quality, cost, capacity, speed, and perhaps proprietary information.**

8. What is ERP and why is it important?

9. What documents comprise the recipe card for a product? **The Bill of Materials, the Assembly Chart, and the Routing Sheet.**

10. Create a process map of a process.

11. What is the purpose of a process map? **The process map is good for diagramming a process and determining nonvalue-adding activities.**

12. What is the difference between Six Sigma as discussed in this chapter and the Design for Six Sigma as discussed in Chapter 4?

Chapter 9: Discussion Questions

1. A company has a machine that produces 6,000 nails per hour. An upgrade is available that will allow the machine to produce 6,600 nails. What would be the increase in productivity with this upgrade?

2. The AEB Company spent $25,000 on materials last month. From these materials they produced 35,000 surf boards. What is their materials' productivity?

3. The AMB Company wants to look at total productivity (multifactor) and compiled the following information for last year:

	Kansas City	Raleigh	Melbourne
Output/month	15,000	14,500	15,500
Labor cost $	3,000	4,500	2,500
Materials cost $	10,000	10,000	10,500
Overhead $	2,500	3,500	2,000
Total inputs	15,500	18,000	15,000
productivity	0.97	0.81	1.03

4. If AEB compiled the following data for this year, what is their change in productivity?

Output this year	285,000
Labor cost $	325,000
Materials cost $	120,000
Overhead $	40,000
Total inputs	485,000
Productivity	0.59

5. What is the relationship between nonvalue-adding processes and productivity?

6. Why are some intended improvements in technology not necessarily a cause for increased productivity?

Chapter 10: Discussion Questions

1. Go to a retail activity and look at their layout. What is the store trying to do with their layout? Is there an obvious pattern to their layout?

2. Based on your visit to a retail facility is there a better way to layout the facility to maximize exposure to products?

3. Visit a Home Depot or Lowes and look at the warehouse layout that they have. Is there a pattern to their layout?

4. Create a Murther's grid to improve the layout of the Home Depot that you visit.

5. What is the difference between a product, process, and fixed facility layout?

6. What is a hybrid layout and what advantages does it provide?

7. When should you not choose to use a cellular layout?

8. Can the layout of the facility become the bottleneck for the company?

9. Why is site selection so important to the success of the company?

Chapter 11: Discussion Questions

1. Why or why not is 100% utilization important? **If utilization at 100% means making more product than the company can sell it is not a good measure.**

2. What are some of the reasons for not working at 100% utilization?

3. What are the remedies for having more capacity than demand?

4. What are the remedies for having more demand than capacity?

5. What is the difference between utilization and efficiency? **Utilization measures time worked against time available, whereas efficiency measures production against a set standard output.**

6. From your perspective, what is one example of the Theory of Constraints?

Chapter 12: Discussion Questions

1. Why do companies have inventory?

2. Is inventory an asset or a liability? Can it be both? Explain your answer.

3. Can an inventory item that is an asset become a liability? Give an example.

4. A company has an average inventory value of $450,000,000 and their cost of goods sold for the year is $4,500,000,000. What is their inventory turns? Is this good or bad?

5. A company decides to add safety stock to its distribution centers. The company has 15 distribution centers throughout the United States. Would the company be better served to have safety stock at each location or should they consolidate the safety stock at one location? Justify your answer.

6. If SGB, Inc. has a fixed lead time for replenishment of its Widget B of 10 days and an average demand of 12 Widgets per day. Where should SGB, Inc. set their reorder point? **ROP = demand during lead time $\times$ lead time: therefore, the ROP should be set at 10 $\times$ 12 = 120. When they reach 120 on the shelf it is time to reorder.**

7. KW Industries has analyzed their inventory and come up with the following data:
   Inventory carrying costs = 15%
   The cost of placing an order = $45/order
   Annual sales of Product X = 3,000,000
   Calculate KW's EOQ for Product X

8. Using the information from question 7, how many orders will KW place in the next year?

9. Using the data from question 7, what happens to the EOQ if the ordering costs increase to $65/order?

10. What are the types of inventory a company may have?

11. What is safety stock and why would a company have safety stock? **Safety stock is an additional level of inventory to cover variations in demand or variations in lead times.**

12. When is the EOQ not necessary?

13. Is the EOQ calculation still valid in today's business environment when applying the assumptions of the EOQ? Explain your answer.

Chapter 13: Discussion Questions

1. Why is perfect order fulfillment so critical to successful operations?

2. If a company is at 95% across the board for the entities of perfect order fulfillment, what is their perfect order fulfillment rate? Is this good? **Their perfect order fulfillment rate = 73.5%. This company is not meeting the needs of their customers.**

3. What are the attributes of world class distribution systems?

4. Why is cross-docking important to reducing customer response times? **The product never goes on the shelf but moves from inbound to staging to outbound within 24 to 48 hours.**

5. A company has calculated their inventory turns at 12. Is this good or bad? Explain your answer.

6. A company has calculated their cost of goods sold at $25,000,000 and their average inventory as $12,500,000. What is their inventory turns rate? Is this good or bad? **The number of turns is 2. Such a low number is never good as this means that the company is only replenishing their entire inventory two times a year. This may indicate a large number of nonselling inventory items.**

7. A company has 14 inventory turns a year. The average turns calculation for their industry is 28. What should the company do to improve their turns?

8. Why is a flow important to the success of a facility?

9. What is time-definite delivery? Why is it important from the customer perspective?

10. From what perspective should on-time delivery be measured? **This should always be measured from the perspective of the customer.**

Chapter 14: Discussion Questions

1. Is Just-in-Time an inventory management technique or a continuous process improvement program? Justify your answer.

2. Does every system have a constraint? If so, describe the methodology to improve the constraint or eliminate the constraint.

3. How do JIT, Six Sigma, and the Theory of Constraints compare and contrast?

4. Are JIT, Six Sigma, and TOC the same?

5. What is the goal of Six Sigma?

6. What are the seven wastes of the Toyota Production System? Give examples of each.

7. If a company increases the capacity of their system at a nonbottleneck process, what is the impact on the system? **There is no impact to the system because the capacity of the system is the capacity at the bottleneck or constraint.**

8. Does nonconstraint also mean nonimportant? Explain.

9. What is "zero inventory" and how does it relate to JIT?

10. Describe the concept of the Drum-Buffer-Rope.

11. Can Six Sigma be applied to services?

12. What is Kaizen? How does it apply to JIT? **Kaizen is continuous process improvement. The goal is to eliminate nonvalue-adding processes, thus eliminating waste.**

13. The JY Company wants to move to Kanbans to move its supplies forward in the supply chain. If the lead time is 2 days, the demand during the lead time is 400, and the company is using a container that holds 50 items, how many Kanbans will the company need?

14. The JY Company wants to improve the efficiency of the company and its Kanbans, what will that do to the calculation in question 14?

15. How can quick set-ups improve operations?

Chapter 15: Discussion Questions

1. A _____ is an up-and-down repetitive movement over a long period of time. **Cycle**

2. _____ methods of forecasting are based on best guesses, past experience, and other subjective methods. **Qualitative**

3. What impacts does forecasting have on the operations management chain?

4. Look at the newspaper or an online article or an annual report for a company and see if forecasting is a problem for that particular company.

5. Calculate the 3- and 5-month simple moving average for the following data:

	Actual Demand	3-Month Moving Average Forecasted Demand	5-Month Moving Average Forecasted Demand	Forecast Error
2002	275			
2003	195			
2004	250			
2005	275			
2006	325			
2007	400			
2008	225			
2009	275			

6. Using the data above calculate the mean absolute deviation for the forecast error for both the 3- and 5-month calculations.

7. Using the table below and the following weights, calculate the weighted moving average starting in 2005. Most recent data $=.45$; next previous data $-.35$; next previous data $=.2$

	Actual Demand	Weighted Moving Average
2002	275	
2003	195	
2004	250	
2005	275	
2006	325	
2007	400	
2008	225	
2009	275	

8. Using a smoothing factor of α = .75, calculate the forecast for the following sales data:

	Actual Demand	Forecast
January	1,100	
February	1,125	
March	1,125	
April	1,300	
May	950	
June	2,000	
July	2,100	
August	2,500	
September		
Smoothing Factor = .75		

9. Using the data above, calculate the forecast through September using a smoothing factor of .45.

10. Which of these forecasting calculations provides the company with the most accurate forecast?

11. Think of a situation, politically or otherwise, where the actions may have impacted the forecast. **The 2008 election impacted the forecasts for the sales of weapons and ammunition because of a fear of regulation changes with the new administration.**

Chapter 16: Discussion Questions

1. Check with a local store in your area and ask what their returns policy is and what rate of returns they get as a percentage of sales.

2. What experience do you have with returning an item? Was it a pleasant experience or was the process a hassle? Was the time it took to process the return worth the effort?

3. Visit your local Cabela's (if there is one close to you) and look at the items in their "Bargain Cave." Look carefully at the items that were bought, used, and then returned.

4. Think about the impacts of the reverse logistics operations on your company's operations

Chapter 17: Discussion Questions

1. Is there such a thing as situational ethics for a leader? **Ethics do not change from situation to situation.**

2. How is professional pride fostered in your organization?

3. Think about a situation at a job that you have worked at that could have benefited from a focus on people rather than a focus on profits.

4. Why is leadership so important to supply chain operations?

Chapter 18: Discussion Questions

1. Discuss the link between supply chain security and homeland security. **If you cannot secure the supply chain and the ports of entry, you cannot secure the country.**

2. Pick a retail supply chain and identify potential supply chain risks.

3. Does supply chain security impact profitability?

4. Why is there a trade-off between speed and security? **Extra security measures may mean a slowdown in the supply chain but not near as impactful as an interruption would be.**

5. What are the costs of supply chain security?

6. Is supply chain security a problem unique to the United States? Why or why not?

7. What purpose does a process map and process walk have in supply chain security?

8. Why is the Country of Origin a concern from a supply chain security perspective? **Think about food security and bioterrorism. This helps identify which country a contaminated food product came from.**

9. Would Country of Origin reporting have prevented the problems discussed in this chapter?

10. Why should you be concerned about natural disasters impacting supply chains?

CPSIA information can be obtained
at www.ICGtesting.com
Printed in the USA
FFOW01n1023020618
47042678-49349FF

9 781524 938659